Paris and the Art of Transposition

Paris and the Art of Transposition

EARLY TWENTIETH CENTURY SINO-FRENCH ENCOUNTERS

Angie Chau

University of Michigan Press
Ann Arbor

Published in the United States of America by the
University of Michigan Press
Manufactured in the United States of America
Printed on acid-free paper
First published December 2023

A CIP catalog record for this book is available from the British Library.

Library of Congress Cataloging-in-Publication data has been applied for.

ISBN 978-0-472-07651-2 (hardcover: alk. paper)
ISBN 978-0-472-05651-4 (paper: alk. paper)
ISBN 978-0-472-90392-4 (open access ebook)

DOI: https://doi.org/10.3998/mpub.12256143

Library of Congress Control Number: 2023942256

Publication was made possible with a book subvention fund granted by the University of Victoria.

Open access funding for this publication was provided by the Lieberthal-Rogel Center for Chinese Studies (LRCCS).

The University of Michigan Press's open access publishing program is made possible thanks to additional funding from the University of Michigan Office of the Provost and the generous support of contributing libraries.

Contents

Digital materials related to this title can be found on the Fulcrum platform via the following citable URL: https://doi.org/10.3998/mpub.12256143

Figures

Timeline of Historical Periods

10,000–2000 BC	Neolithic cultures
c. 2100–1600 BC	Xia dynasty
c. 1600–1050 BC	Shang dynasty
c. 1046–256 BC	Zhou dynasty
221–206 BC	Qin dynasty
206 BC–220 CE	Han dynasty
220–589	Six dynasties
581–618	Sui dynasty
618–906	Tang dynasty
907–960	Five dynasties
960–1279	Song dynasty
1279–1368	Yuan dynasty
1368–1644	Ming dynasty
1644–1912	Qing dynasty
1912–1949	Republican period
1949–present day	People's Republic of China (PRC)

Acknowledgments

This project started over a decade ago when I was a graduate student in comparative literature at UC San Diego planning to continue my studies in English and French literature. In the literature department, I was fortunate to take classes with Rosemary George, Lisa Lowe, Wai-lim Yip, Yingjin Zhang and Nina Zhiri, among others. Paul Pickowicz and Joe Esherick enthusiastically welcomed me into their research seminar sequence for graduate students in their modern Chinese history program, and from there, my dissertation advisor Yingjin Zhang and committee members Paul Pickowicz, Wai-lim Yip, Winnie Woodhull, Meg Wesling, and Ari Heinrich encouraged me to pursue a topic that linked my interests in visual art, literature, and language. During my time at UCSD, I enjoyed and learned from my friendships with Alvin Wong, Joo Ok Kim, David Cheng Chang, Judd Kinzley, Benny Cohen, Gabrielle Mar, Kedar Kulkarni, Yin Wang, Ling Han, Kimberly Chung, Jun Lei, Michael Lundell, Ryan Heryford, and Chien-ting Lin.

In 2010, an NEH summer seminar on interwar Shanghai and Germany at Stanford organized by Ban Wang and Russell Berman provided contextualization for my project during its earliest stages, and Frederik Green introduced me to Xu Xu's travel writings. With funding from UCSD's Dean of Arts and Humanities and the literature department's dissertation fellowship, I was able to spend time in Paris and Lyon, working in the archives at the Bibliothèque nationale de France, with the assistance of Muriel Détie and Li Xiaohong, and with Valentina de Monte at the Fonds chinois de la Bibliothèque municipale de Lyon. Over the years, I have also appreciated the assistance and support of Eric Lefebvre, Jiayan Mi, Jennifer Epstein, Paul Bevan, Carrie Waara, Paul Manfredi, Claire Roberts, Mabel Lee, and Antonia Finnane.

The organizers of the Worst Chinese Poetry workshop at UC Santa Barbara and fellow workshop participants provided valuable feedback on my poetry chapter in Spring 2021. I am also grateful to the organizers and participants of the "Literary Transversals: Modern East Asian and Diasporic Literature" conference held in April 2022 at the University of Chicago's Center for East Asian Studies, who gave me the space to share a version of my chapter on Pan Yuliang.

Since graduate school I have been lucky to be surrounded by a generous intellectual community. At Arizona State University, I greatly benefitted from the warmth of colleagues in the School of International Letters and Cultures, especially Stephen West, Xiaoqiao Ling, Young Oh, Will Hedberg, Ana Hedberg Olenina, Joanne Cao, Jiwon Shin, Stephen Bokenkamp, Mark Cruse, Dan Gilfillan, Jianling Liao, Hoyt Tillman, Zhaokun Xin, and Joe Cutter, as well as Qian Liu and Ralph Gabbard at the ASU library. I am also grateful for the hospitality of Tansen Sen, Adrian Thieret, Joanna Waley-Cohen, Leksa Lee, Maya Kramer, Brad Weslake, Celina Hung, Eric Hundman, and Valerie Deacon during my brief stay at NYU-Shanghai.

At the University of Victoria, my current and former colleagues in the Department of Pacific and Asian Studies and at the Centre for Asia-Pacific Initiatives have shared their time and space with kindness and good humor: Sujin Lee, Ben Wang, Mamoru Hatakeyama, ann-elise lewallen, Richard Fox, Andrew Marton, Cody Poulton, Richard King, Hiroko Noro, Mika Kimura, Michael Bodden, Martin Adam, Tim Iles, Jun Tian, T.C. Lin, Helena Watling, Hoa Nguyen, Tri Nguyen, Thiti Jamkajornkeiat, Qian Liu, Helen Lansdowne, Victor Ramraj, and Ralph Croizier. I am thankful for Alex D'Arcy's mentorship and the chance to present my project in the Division of Continuing Studies' Deans' Lecture Series in 2020, as well as for the Centre for Global Studies' Faculty Research Completion fellowship for providing support during the pandemic.

The University of Michigan Press has been incredibly supportive of my project, in particular Emily Wilcox, Mary Gallagher, and Sara Cohen. In addition, Nicolai Volland, Michelle Bloom, and Lihong Liu provided feedback in the manuscript workshop organized by the Lieberthal-Rogel Center for Chinese Studies, motivating me to complete the last chapter on Pan Yuliang, which I first considered (but did not have the courage to do) back in 2008. My gratitude also to the two manuscript reviewers for their endorsement of my project, production editor Mary Hashman, copyeditor John Raymond, and Lisa Regan's awesome indexing team at TextFormations. Thank you to Chen Zishan for his permission to reproduce Guo Jianying's cartoon, the Chen Cheng-po Cultural Foundation, the Asia Society Hong Kong Center, and the Anhui Museum for providing digital images of Pan Yuliang's works. My research could not have happened without the staff at the Li-Ching Foundation in Taipei, especially Rita Wong and Horatio Hsieh, for their prompt assistance throughout the years with handling permissions for reproducing Pan Yuliang and Chang Yu's work. I am thankful for Ying Liu at the University of Victoria Library, who tirelessly replied to my requests, as well as to Jing Liu and her staff at the UBC Library.

Over the years, I could not have persevered without the humor and wisdom of good friends especially Alvin Wong, Karlis Rokpelnis, Suzanne Buffam, and Chicu Reddy. A special thank you to piano instructor extraordinaire Allison Star for her insights on the concept of transposition and to Chicu Reddy for his feedback on my book proposal.

The greatest thank you goes to my family, from my relatives in Shanghai, Sunny and Peiwen Wang, who helped me pursue images in Anhui, to my writer-translator-artist sister Bonnie, and my parents Nelson and Grace who fostered my interest in all things artistic—especially those related to France and China. Much gratitude to my in-laws Anne and Conor for their sustained love and energy in Reno, Paris, and Shanghai. To Neil, who put up with moving heavy boxes of books and papers to and from what feels like infinite homes in three countries, and to my daughters Sophie and Ella, who went from babies to nearly-full-grown humans in the time it took for this project to get done: thank you for your endless love and patience.

Finally, deep gratitude that is difficult to express in words here goes to my longtime mentor Yingjin Zhang. Without his persistent encouragement to continue exploring and expanding the vast categories of Chinese cultural and media practices, and his dedication to building connections between the sinosphere and the rest of the world, this project could not have taken shape.

An early version of a portion of this book was published in 2017 in *Modern Chinese Literature and Culture*, and sections of the book have also appeared as "Paris and the Art of Transposition, 1920s–1940s" in *A World History of Chinese Literature* (Routledge, 2023).

CHAPTER 1

Introduction

I conceived of two-way mirrors as a metaphor for the kind of study that, in focusing on the other, reveals as much about the self, and where object becomes self and self becomes object. This ironic act of exploration—going away to discover home—is, of course, familiar to any traveller.

—EUGENE EOYANG, TWO-WAY MIRRORS

THE MODERN ARTIST IN PARIS

In Guo Jianying's (郭建英 1907–79) 1930s cartoon *Introduction* (Jieshao 介紹), a Chinese man in a Western-style suit stands stunned as a male artist holding a painter's palette presents him with a nude, curly haired female model, who dangles a cigarette holder in her hand and poses suggestively on a loose pile of drapery (Guo 2001, 21). The caption, "Old Huang, please allow me to present to you Miss Chen," implies that Mr. Huang's shocked expression is the result of being confronted with the model's full-frontal nudity. The cartoon's humor relies on the ironic contrast between formality, indicated by the physical appearance of Huang and the artist's speech in respectfully presenting the model as "Miss Chen," and the shock produced by the viewing of a naked female body. The familiar greeting "Old Huang" invoked by the artist only emphasizes the awkwardness of the encounter, as he mocks both parties by addressing the nude model with the proper title Miss (Xiaojie 小姐).

The three figures depicted in the cartoon represent being "modern" in their own ways, but the artist is of particular interest: with his short-sleeved collared shirt and belted pants, dress shoes and cravat, he serves as a mediator between the controversial practice of using nude models for life drawing (Western scientific method in art pedagogy) and Old Huang, who appears

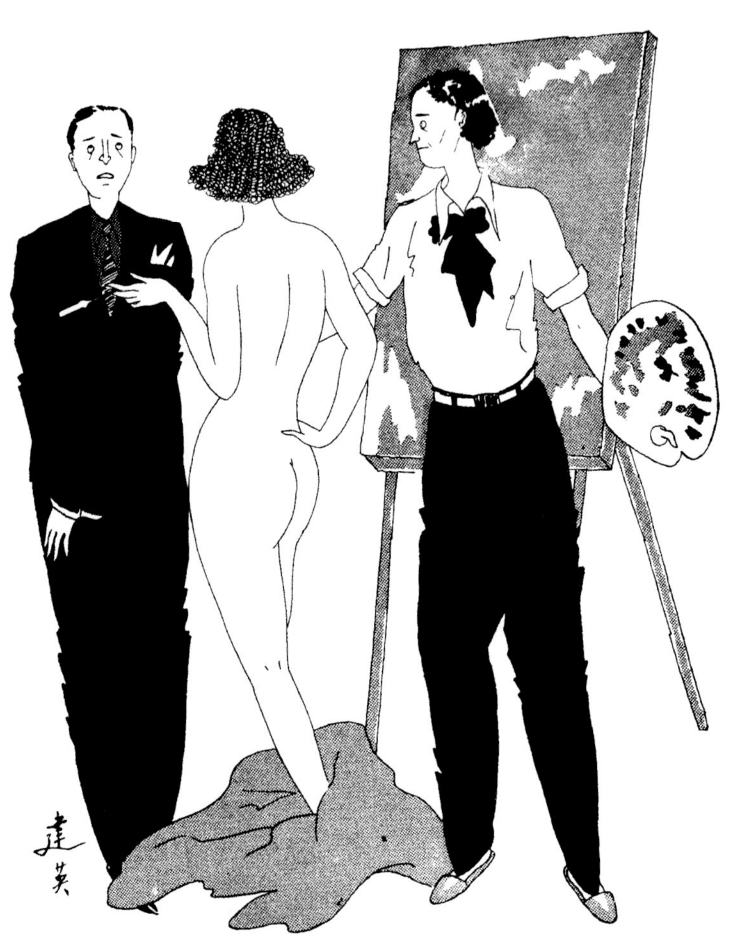

Figure 1. *Introduction* (Jieshao 介紹), cartoon illustration by Guo Jianying 郭建英. Reproduced with permission from Chen Zishan 陳子善.

modern in dress but has yet to change his conservative Chinese mindset. The question of *what* the artist has depicted is not really important here, as the canvas surface is mostly obstructed by the artist, and the visual center of the cartoon is squarely focused on the blank expanse of Miss Chen's nude backside, inviting us to imagine Mr. Huang's titillating view. The dilemma, then, is not with aesthetic style or the content of the artist's work, but rather the uncomfortable position in which the everyday modern Chinese citizen may find himself when presented with a woman's naked body under the pretext of scientific accuracy or artistic enlightenment.

The trope of the bohemian Chinese artist with his nude model as a source of anxiety and allure is a recurring image especially prominent in creative work from the 1920s to 1940s by Chinese artists and writers in connection with travel to France during this period. Imagining the art studio as a potentially transformative site of negotiation, Guo Jianying's illustration relies on the interplay between text and image: the caption implies a conventional ritual of polite introduction among friends and acquaintances, while its corresponding image overturns the viewer's expectations by boldly centering the nude female body in a public formal setting. How much power the nude female model has in this interaction is debatable, but the artist is clearly the one determining the message being conveyed, and he provides the physical space for provocation. The encounter captures the moment of *transposition*, a fluid and strategic artistic process that depends on the tension between foreign and familiar, new and old—one that celebrates simultaneously both novelty and recognition when a text gets placed into a fresh context. After all, there is nothing inherently strange in the viewing of a woman's naked body—it is the context in which she appears that elicits conflict. Introducing new ideas may cause initial shock and discomfort, but the artist also asserts creative agency by maintaining certain social conventions and aesthetic practices while breaking from others.

Scholarly studies of Republican-era cultural production have conventionally focused on Shanghai, where a flourishing publishing industry and growing consumer culture contributed to a hybridized and transcultural semicolonial urban space (Lee 1999; Lu 1999; Zhang 1999; Shih 2001; Pickowicz, Shen, and Zhang 2013; Schaefer 2017). Shifting the discussion of Chinese aesthetic modernism from Shanghai to the setting of Paris, this book reveals the impact of cultural displacement on artistic production, by asking, What was the role of modern art in promoting intercultural understanding—and misunderstanding—among Chinese intellectuals and the West in the early twentieth century? More specifically, what kinds of expectations did Chinese writers and artists face in Paris, the city described as "the capital of the literary world, the city endowed with the greatest prestige on earth" (Casanova 2007, 24)? And what images of the modern Chinese artist circulated in China and France as a result of these encounters? Rethinking these cross-cultural encounters through the lens of transposition permits us to assign value to forms of artistic engagement that have slipped through the cracks.

My book bridges the fields of Chinese and French literary and art histories, by revealing how, through the circulation of diverse images of the artist, Paris served as a site of negotiation where Chinese artists and writers were motivated to emphasize recognizable aspects of Chinese culture and identity, or "Chineseness"—an imaginary concept whose contours became at once more pressing as a way to represent China to the rest of the world, and also more flexible and susceptible to experimentation outside of China. This book aims to shed light on the experiences of Chinese writers and artists in Paris by tracing the multitude of representations of the modern Chinese artist, produced both by themselves for an increasingly global audience and also in dialogue with images of the artist that circulated in literature and other forms of popular media. The five modern literary and artistic figures of my project were chosen on the basis of how they positioned themselves to varying degrees as being politically detached from the larger revolutionary project of national salvation. At the same time, they were deeply invested in their respective roles as cultural middlemen between the West and their place of origin in China, an honorary status bestowed upon them due to their overseas experience. But in some ways they were venturing down a path that had been paved earlier by late Qing *wenren* (scholar) travelers to France in the late nineteenth century, such as the translator Wang Tao (王韜 1828–97) and the diplomat Chen Jitong (陳季同 1851–1907).

Travel literature written by Wang Tao, the Shanghai-based translator who worked for the London Missionary Society Press and served as assistant to the missionary, sinologist, and translator James Legge, featured the exotic description of a Parisian cabaret, for instance, in which he praised the dancers: "The actresses were all beautiful and lovely. When they went onstage, they bared their bosoms and shoulders. Their jade-like flesh and the lamplight reflected off one another like arrows" (Teng 2006, 113). Chen Jitong, Chinese diplomat to France under the Qing government, arrived in Europe in 1875 with the first official delegation, and took a markedly different approach to conveying the allure of overseas travel. Chen lived in Paris for fifteen years before returning to Shanghai and the title of his 1883 book *Les chinois peints par eux-mêmes* coincidentally picks up on the metaphor of Chinese people "painted by themselves," to give voice and agency to individuals rather than being passively described by outsiders. Ironically, his position of supreme confidence depended on essentializing both cultures, as Chen's goal of smoothing out the incommensurability between gender roles in Chinese and French cultures required that he adopt a position of fully understanding the two. Like Lin Yutang (林語堂 1895–1976), who would follow in his footsteps a half century later with *My Country and My People* (1935), an instruction manual of Chinese culture for American readers, Chen used his position as an outsider in France to give French readers an insider peek at Chinese culture. In his introduction he wrote, "I propose in this book to represent China as it is—to depict Chinese manners and customs by means of my actual acquaintance with them, but in a European spirit and style. I desire to place my native experience at the service of my acquired experience; in a word, I think as a European would who had learned all that I know concerning China, and who wished to draw those parallels and contrasts between Occidental and extreme Oriental civilizations which his studies might justify" (original French in Tcheng 1884, vii–viii; English translation in Yeh 1997, 438).

In contrast to Wang Tao and Chen Jitong, the young Chinese students in this book belonged to the next generation of travelers who considered themselves members of an intellectual class whose relevance in modern Chinese society was being called into question in the 1920s. During a period of significant cultural transformations and political upheaval until the 1940s, as the boundaries between the binaries of race and ethnicity (white vs. Asian, Chinese vs. French), gender roles (male vs. female), and temporal modalities (modern vs. traditional) grew increasingly blurred, France became a site for Chinese intellectuals to experiment with new and creative forms of self-expression. Craig Clunas's observation about the emphasis on the performative aspects of the artist in twentieth century China is especially helpful as a point of departure: "It is images of the artist, disseminated as they are through a broad range of media, and not images of the viewer, that come to stand for 'painting'" (Clunas 2017, 181). Compared to the images found in traditional painting, which often depicted wenren appreciating completed works of art on display, Clunas identifies a shift beginning from the 1910s that emphasizes the act of painting, particularly "the performance of the role of the Chinese artist for foreign audiences" (Clunas 2017, 181). Chen Jitong's book title, dating from decades earlier, already gestured toward this tendency, by alluding to the possibility of the Chinese civilization as an artistic agent in charge of painting its own self-portrait for the consumption of the French reading-viewing public. While Clunas is more interested in the concept of painting, his observation nonetheless pertains to the case of Chinese artists in Paris, which reveals that the boundaries demarcating the "Chinese artist" and "foreign audiences" were not as consistent or as distinct as Clunas suggests.

As part of the New Culture Movement's national salvation project in the face of encroaching western and Japanese imperialism, leading intellectuals like Chen Duxiu (陳獨秀 1879–1942) and Hu Shih (胡適 1891–1962) called for sweeping reforms in Chinese language, literature, and art in the late 1910s. In the field of visual art, two modes of painting—*xihua*, referring to imported Western-style painting, and *guohua* or "national painting," the use of traditional literati characteristics in the modern period, especially traditional ink painting—were often pitted against each other in intellectual debates. And just as the movement for new literature triggered the outraged reaction of many conservative thinkers, Kang Youwei's (康有為 1858–1927) rant lamenting the decline of Chinese painting and blaming the literati spirit of painting as a leisure activity for preventing national artistic development, followed by Chen Duxiu's call for Western science-based art for national salvation in *New Youth* (*Xin qingnian* 新青年), became sore points of contention for traditionalists (Wu 1990, 47–48). In 1917, Cai Yuanpei (蔡元培 1868–1940) published the text of a lecture he gave in Beijing in *New Youth*, arguing that "art should be disengaged from the individualism and intimacy of the traditional literati art, which emphasizes personal cultivation, 'apprenticeship', and is subordinated to the other humanities" (Jin 2009, 95). As literati art was increasingly attacked for being irrelevant and outdated, just as classical *wenyan*, the literary language, was criticized for being an untenable impediment to progress, *xihua* was viewed as a potential remedy and began to be taught in art institutions, in some places even replacing *guohua* curriculum. The elitism of literati art was viewed as harmful for China's uncertain future, but the promise of Western art was no less contentious. When Chen Duxiu blasted Ming dynasty Dong Qichang's (董其昌 1555–1636) literati school of expressionist painting that same year in the hopes of destroying the orthodoxy of the Four Wangs tradition, he insisted upon the tenets of Western realism, not the whole of the Western modernist art movement, to take its place.[1] If there was any point of agreement among intellectuals, it was that a synthesis of Western and Chinese art would be most likely to rescue Chinese painting from extinction.

Chinese writers and artists were faced with the daunting prospect of creating "modern" art forms markedly distinct from those of their predecessors, but ironically, their primary role models for learning were the same sources of semicolonial oppression. By the 1920s, many young Chinese were traveling abroad to Japan or Europe to study in the aftermath of the May Fourth Movement, the cultural and political push to modernize China after World War I. From 1919 to 1921, the work-study movement alone sent more than 1,600 Chinese students to France to work in factories in exchange for a Western college education (Levine 1993, 7). Historically, France has been recognized as a key stepping stone in the formation of future Chinese Communist Party leaders, including Zhou Enlai (周恩來 1898–1976) and Deng Xiaoping (鄧小平 1904–97). In *The Found Generation*, Marilyn A. Levine confirms, "Although feelings of displacement were engendered by traveling to a new world, travel during this period was an important politicizer. New sights and experiences, particularly for those who traveled to Europe, gave rise to new abilities and new knowledge" (Levine 1993, 204–5). However, the effects of travel were not always political in the sense of contributing to the Communist revolution, nor did everyone agree on the value of "new abilities and new knowledge."

In the aftermath of the abolition of the civil service examination system in 1905, some intellectuals responded to the rapidly changing social and political environment by reinventing themselves with a modern literati sensibility that involved a "mastery of foreign languages and knowledges" (Louie 2009, 123). Leo Ou-fan Lee lists nine qualifications for how to succeed on the literary scene of the 1920s, including, most notably, temperament: "A modern wen-jen should be bohemian, amorous, boastful, lazy but tricky, complaining all the time, and emotional rather than rational"; lifestyle: "He should like modern, fashionable clothes, have gourmet tastes, indispensable habits of drinking and smoking, peripatetic residences, gamble and patronize brothels, have debts, an illness (especially tuberculosis and syphilis), and the ability to chat and meditate"; and social intercourse: "He should have up-to-date knowledge of major trends and configurations on the literary scene, visit literary celebrities, form societies, engage in factional fighting, be able to retain friendly links and make new friends—both national and international" (Lee 1973, 38). Although the tone of Lee's checklist is decidedly facetious, it insists on the modern and cosmopolitan citizen being at the core of the ideal scholarly persona.

For those who could afford to travel abroad, Paris, the birthplace of Western modernism, was seen as the most desirable destination for aspiring writers and artists not only from China but also from other parts of Asia and Europe. The archives of the Institut franco-chinois in Lyon confirm that it was not good enough to study in the West, or for that matter to study in France: it had to be Paris. Letters written to school administrations from art and literature students like Lü Sibai (呂斯白 1905–73), Pan Yuliang (潘玉良 1899–1977), and Luo Dagang (羅大岡 1909–98) express the necessity to be in Paris. For instance, in the winter of 1930, Lü Sibai (Lu spa) and his classmate, sculptor Oin Lin-y, wrote to their professor in Lyon, "Do we really need to remind you that Paris, the capital of France, whose famous museums attract visitors from all over the world, where masters from the entire world take meetings, whose salons, exhibits, and all other artistic manifestations have always taken place, that Paris is the ultimate place for those who study the fine arts? Moreover, in all of France, is there even one professor at the École des Beaux Arts who did not study in Paris? We came to France especially to study European art; would it not be a great loss for us to not be able to study in Paris, the fine arts capital?"[2]

The international coterie belonging to the informal School of Paris (École de Paris) became associated with the neighborhood of Montparnasse, which was established during the interwar period as an artistic community for non-French artists working in Paris, including artists such as Pablo Picasso, Marc Chagall, and Amedeo Modigliani, who all migrated to France in the first decade of the twentieth century. While considerable anti-Semitic and anti-immigrant sentiment was directed toward some of these artists, the foreign community helped foster national pride, affirming the cultural prestige of Paris. The art critic André Warnod coined the phrase "School of Paris" in 1925, declaring, "It's undeniable our museums are famous, but even more than our artistic riches, these artists want to know the country where our great painters lived, breathe the air they breathed, be moved by our perspectives . . . to finally know the joy of living and to enjoy this liberty without which art cannot blossom" (Warnod 1925, 8). Warnod's vision of faithful foreign artists on pilgrimage in Paris certainly aligns with Pascale Casanova's depiction of "an idealized city where artistic freedom could be proclaimed and lived" (Casanova 1999, 24), but not all of its visitors were able to translate their so-called creative freedom into artistic influence and critical success.

Lin Fengmian (林風眠 1900–1991), a pioneer of modern Chinese art who studied in Paris and eventually founded the Hangzhou National College of Art upon his return in China, published an essay in 1926 on "The Promise of Oriental and Western Culture" in the Shanghai-based journal *Oriental Miscellany* (*Dongfang zazhi* 東方雜誌) that stressed the importance of Chinese artists learning from Western artists in order to achieve a "Chinese art renaissance." He recommended two key objectives for modern artists: "We should import basic western art methods, by introducing historical concepts and specific ways of implementation, and also re-organize traditional Chinese art in order to contribute to the world" (Shi 2014, 88–89). The prescription for national success and cultural rejuvenation was conceived as inextricable from the circulation of Chinese art on an international stage.

China's participation in April-October 1925 at the Exposition internationale des arts décoratifs et industriels modernes was an early attempt at fostering intercultural Sino-French dialogue through art diplomacy. For the occasion, prominent education reformer Cai Yuanpei penned a preface for the exhibition catalogue. Bemoaning the poor state of philosophy and scientific development in China, Cai wrote, "There has been some progress in our strongest area, the decorative arts, but we still cannot compete with more scientifically advanced countries" (Jin 2009, 215). Cai's essay, written in August 1925, tried to reconcile his admiration for the French artistic legacy with his encouragement to Chinese artists to not be complacent: "The French people's disposition is friendly and open, similar to ours. Their fine arts are graceful and magnificent in nature; its function to influence outweighs any mysterious function, and is close to our fine arts" (Jin 2009, 215). While Cai Yuanpei's preface emphasized the importance of the fine arts (meishu 美術), the exhibit itself was a venue to display applied and decorative arts such as furniture, carving, and textiles—not the fine arts—and the modestly sized Chinese section featured no contemporary styles. Noting the ironic "invisibility" of China at the 1925 Exposition, Clunas points out that "exotic" Chinese inspiration was omnipresent in European art and design in forms such as chinoiserie, yet "the lack of receptivity to the contemporary art of China was paralleled by an intense urge to speak for China, to appropriate it, absorb and neutralize it in the classic orientalist manner" (Clunas 1989, 105). Clunas concludes, "Ancient China was a real presence in the cultural life of Europe, but a China striving to speak for itself was nowhere" (Clunas 1989, 105). But how to determine what constitutes a "real presence" and the distinction between a "real presence" and "nowhere"? What indicators qualify as the signs of a nation "striving to speak for itself"? This book offers a closer look at instances when Chinese artists and writers spoke for themselves, not so much invisible as overlooked or misunderstood by previous audiences.

Eric Hayot's observation about Chinese culture and identity being represented by its association with classical China, and therefore perceived to be uncontaminated by Western influence, can provide one possible way to think about these questions: "In comparison to its classical version, contemporary China (the only China the West has ever really known, in this century or any other) is contaminated, shifting, and impure. The irony of all this is that classical China's mythical stability makes it an incredibly reproducible object. Classical China exists always as object of knowledge rather than an object of experience. It is thus available for thought—transportable to new contexts—in a way that is not as readily present for notions of contemporary China, which can always be countered with the 'facts'" (Hayot 2003, 178). According to Hayot, both Chinese and Western observers of China rely on this stability to know China in a way that is allegedly untouched by change. Many modern artists shared in their reluctance to give up their attachment to a literati sensibility—in many cases, an imagined or learned attachment that manifested itself in their creative work.[3] Drawing from recognizable attributes of the intellectual elite or traditional wenren as cultural capital, these travelers cultivated a distinctly new wenren sensibility that encompassed a range of malleable identities in the face of encroaching challenges such as Western imperialism. As the literati's social status declined and their culture waned in the early twentieth century, wenren affiliates—modern intellectuals who, in most cases, despite not having received formal training in the Confucian classics, calligraphy, and painting, were specifically influenced by classical art and literature—nonetheless continued to find ways to represent literati culture and its aesthetics in their work.

Hayot's analysis sheds light on why certain elements of classical Chinese literature and art were seen as more amenable or desirable to transport or transpose to the context of Paris, and it accounts for the ambivalent tone of Cai Yuanpei's 1925 Exposition essay, which attempts to recognize the rich legacy of traditional Chinese art while voicing an urgent call for its transformation. The myth of classical China's "stability," and its perceived reproducibility and transmissibility, further point to the limitations of Clunas's analysis, which insists on the "West's unwillingness to hear what Chinese art is trying to say," as modern Chinese artists experimented with how best to represent Chinese art on the world stage (Clunas 1989, 106).

Another attempt to promote Chinese art on a global level took place in 1933, when the painter Xu Beihong (徐悲鸿 1895–1953) helped organize an exhibit of nearly 200 Chinese works of art at the Musée du Jeu de Paume in Paris. The exhibition catalogue featured a piece by Académie française cultural celebrity Paul Valéry (1871–1945), who commended the "noble and very brave" young Chinese painters like Xu. Valéry likened the wave of Chinese art students studying in Paris at the time, finally exposed to European artwork, to an artist from the Middle Ages who suddenly becomes enlightened through the discovery of ancient Greek art: "But the gap here is infinitely greater. . . . Physiology intervenes, even vision is at stake. Two ways of seeing, wonderfully different, are presented to the artist. What will he do? What lesson will he take from our museums? What work will he be able to carry out with our brushes and our oil colors? What interpretation will he give to the Titian he copies?" (Valéry 1933). Valéry urged his compatriots to elevate the prestige of Chinese art, beyond the conventional western European view of it as mere "curiosities, bizarre inventions, monstrosities," to the level that had previously been accorded only to classical Chinese poetry. His depiction of the hypothetical modern Chinese artist was limited to a paternalistic imagining of a nation in crisis mode, perhaps a projection of his own anxiety over the perceived decline of France in the interwar period: "In China, as elsewhere, periods of marvelous creation are not infinite. There are times, almost empty, when talent sleeps, more or less long silences: there are centuries during which one is 'at a standstill' [on n'est past en train]." Similar to Lin Fengmian's proposed recipe for a rebirth of Chinese art through Western learning, Valéry hoped that Chinese art learning in Paris could be a mutually beneficial transaction used to rejuvenate Western art.

But the language used by both men in their futuristic speculations about the potential outcome of new ways of seeing and the creative possibilities that French art provided to Chinese artists were still constrained to perpetuating or even preserving existing forms of national art. And unlike linguistic differences, which could presumably be smoothed over by translation or transliteration, how could cultural practices situated at the heart of artistic creation and expression be best reinterpreted and reimagined? The majority of contemporary works showcased in the Musée du Jeu de Paume exhibit were those inspired by traditional Chinese ink paintings by artists like Zhang Daqian (张大千 1899–1983) and Qi Baishi (齐白石 1864–1957), not those more obviously influenced by Western masters. Still, the Exposition de la peinture chinoise was a resounding success; it attracted 30,000 visitors over two extended runs, and the catalogue was reprinted twice and sold out each time, indicating the public's interest in viewing Chinese art (Hearn and Smith 2001, 137).

In the last decade, the period of 1920s-1930s Sino-French cultural exchange has been increasingly commemorated by artistic institutions in China and France. The Musée Cernuschi in Paris held an exhibition in 2011, featuring the works of Chinese artists in Paris from 1920 to 1958, marking this as a formative period responsible for the artistic rupture from Chinese tradition. In 2014, the China Art Museum in Shanghai held an exhibit titled "Shanghai/Paris: Modern Art of China" to celebrate the influence of Shanghai-based artists who traveled to Paris from the 1920s through the beginning of the twenty-first century, affirming Shanghai's development as "a portal of China for receiving and interacting with western cultures" (Shi 2014, 3). An introductory essay in the exhibition catalogue by French curator Philippe Cinquini is titled "Shanghai Asked, Paris Replied" (Shi 2014, 22), reflecting how the exchange between these two symbolic cultural centers has been narrativized in art historiography. Cinquini explains in his introduction, "The Chinese phenomenon at the École des Beaux-arts in Paris became a stake between different tendencies and resulted in feeding those who sought realism and naturalism in France, the factors that modernized Chinese art" (Cinquini 2018, n.p.). Outside of museum institutions, which have their own stakes and motivations to consider in their presentation of the movement, the same story, as my book demonstrates, may sound different.

While Chinese artists and writers were understandably excited about opportunities to study and learn in France, these intercultural exchanges did not guarantee critical or even popular success in China or France as suggested by historical accounts. Some intellectuals like Xu Beihong were deeply invested in their respective roles as cultural intermediaries between the West and their place of origin in China, an honorary status bestowed upon them due to their overseas experience, but not all became politically or directly attached to the larger revolutionary project of national salvation. Instead, Nan Z. Da's conceptualization of the "intransitive encounter" provides a reconsideration of conventional narratives about intercultural exchange, urging us to pay attention to "the expressive potential in the works of distant others" (Da 2018, 11). As a caution against the circular argument underlying assumptions in East-West transnational studies that "an exchange—indeed any exchange—simultaneously forges ties and shows that ties have been forged" (Da 2018, 10), Da argues that thinking about transcultural exchange in terms of intransitive encounter promotes "a mode of apprehending the lightness of contact in a very close world" (Da 2018, 11). This "lightness of contact" in cross-cultural Sino-French encounters is well documented in literature from this period, although it has received understandably less attention in historical accounts that are invested in the visible forms of political repercussions of studying abroad, such as Zhou Enlai's involvement in the founding of the European branch of the Chinese Community Youth Corps in Paris in 1922 (Levine 1993, 3). Unlike students who assumed active roles in political activism abroad and could return to China with discernible skills and a renewed revolutionary commitment to the Chinese Communist Party, Chinese artists traveling to Paris were aware that their overseas experiences could be more difficult to articulate in concrete terms.

Reminiscing about the impact of his brief time in Paris in the 1920s, the poet Xu Zhimo (徐志摩 1897–1931) described the liminal state of being an engaged observer: "Most of the time, I only watched the excitement from the banks of the Seine, but I can't really say that I never went into the water either—even in those cases, I stayed in the shallows, never daring to go deeper. This thin whorl of influence and the force of having swam far outweighed anything I would have gained from standing far away onshore" (Xu 1927, 4). The image of the returned Chinese student from overseas circulated widely in fiction and nonfiction narratives during the Republican period, perhaps most famously in Qian Zhongshu's (錢鐘書 1910–88) novel *Fortress Besieged* (*Wei cheng* 圍城, 1947). Qian, who studied in England and France right before the outbreak of the Second Sino-Japanese War, satirized the experience of studying abroad through the story's protagonist, the antihero Fang Hongjian, whose time in Europe is described as unproductive at best: "He took a few courses here and there, and though his interests were fairly broad, he gained nothing at all in the way of knowledge, mostly dissipating his life away in idleness" (Qian 2004, 12). Returning to his hometown with a fake foreign degree as war breaks out, Fang is nonetheless regarded as a local celebrity. Yet internally, he is beset with disappointment: "After he had been home for a week, Fang Hung-chien felt as if he had not left home at all; his four years abroad were like water running over a lotus leaf leaving no trace behind" (Qian 2004, 40). Although the passage emphasizes Fang's disdain for the lack of transformation in his village, it also implies his failed expectation that as a returned traveler, his experiences overseas would result in discernible transformation.

In France, humorous versions of the returned student figure circulated as well. For instance, the writer Marc Chadourne, who traveled to China in the 1930s, profiled "Les returned students" in one chapter of his 1931 book *Chine*: "The least changed, and I think the most innocuous, are those that come back from the Boul'Mich' or the Place Bellecour. A little scruffy, very 'franco-chinois,' with their fluttering cravats and corkscrew pants, lazily dancing the Charleston, their sense for scams, their sly skepticism, their taste for hollow sayings and pompous speeches, and rosy opinions borrowed from famous but outdated authors they haven't actually read like Proudhon, Auguste Comte, Émile Zola"[4] (Chadourne 1931, 163). Chadourne's condescending portrait of the Chinese returned student moves from the outward signs of fashionable dress to speech mannerisms that belie an unsubstantiated familiarity with French culture that is deemed no longer intellectually relevant by those in the know. His critique of "borrowing" from renowned French writers certainly rings true in the case of Li Jinfa's poetry, most notably in "Chat with Verlaine," which will be discussed in chapter 4, and it highlights an inherent tension at the crux of discussions about Chinese modernism and the modernist insistence on innovation. Ezra Pound's slogan "Make It New" was, after all, a reworking of neo-Confucian scholar Zhu Xi's (朱熹 1130–1200) *Great Learning* (*Da xue* 大學), which extolled the virtues of daily self-renewal during the Song dynasty. For Chinese artists and writers, the dilemma remained, how could art ever manage to appear truly innovative through "historical recycling" without being viewed as derivative by critics (North 2013, 168)?

Furthermore, the literary accounts by Marc Chadourne, Qian Zhongshu, and Xu Zhimo attest to the cultural capital based less on "authentic credentials" granted by formal academic or artistic institutions than what Nicolai Volland calls "the intangible aura" of one's association with Paris (Volland 2019, 193). Shu-mei Shih, writing on the relationship between the writer Shi Zhecun's (施蟄存 1905–2003) lack of opportunity to go to Paris and his unshakeable security in Chinese language as constitutive of Chinese identity, surmises in *The Lure of the Modern*: "This privileging of France, much as one may call it cosmopolitan openness, was born of an absence of actual lived experience in France as the racial Other. The cosmopolitan fantasy of coevalness with the West, then, would only have been possible within the imaginary, textually mediated relationship with the metropolitan West"

(Shih 2001, 346). Even in the cases of actual lived experience in France, as shown in the work of the literary and artistic figures at the heart of this book, the potential impact of traveling abroad remained elusive and difficult to define. One possible outcome can be seen in the more "successful" trajectory of Xu Beihong, who stood out initially upon his return to China after studying abroad in Paris in 1927, presumably in preparation for his 1928 move to Nanjing: "It was easy to see where had been. The long hair, velvet coat and flowing tie and his detached languid manners, as well as his excellent French, suggested the Latin Quarter" (Huang 1988, 40). Xu Beihong quickly followed in the footsteps of his colleague, Liu Haisu (劉海粟 1896–1994), in changing tune, and art historian David Clarke suggests that newly returned artists "faced the difficult task of adapting what they had learnt there [abroad] to the Chinese context, of producing works with specifically Chinese meanings" (Clarke 2000, 23). Clarke reads the "return" of artists like Xu and Liu as an indication of their "lack of willingness to commit completely to the Western-inspired artistic languages they had made so much effort to develop" (Clarke 2000, 25), but their motivations may have been more pragmatic in the hope to survive, find jobs, and continue their artistic careers in mainland China.

As Xu Zhimo admits self-consciously in *Fragments of Paris*, just because a traveler's experience in Paris did not live up to his own expectations of how submerged or immersed one should be in a foreign environment, this did not mean that the experience was entirely inconsequential. And like Chadourne's flippant assessment suggests, some travelers returned, not necessarily having undergone dramatic changes beyond superficial appearance. These lackluster depictions also explain why many people today are surprised to hear that a significant number of Chinese people even traveled to Paris during this earlier period. Those same people, however, are probably familiar with the handful of famous French intellectuals remembered for their incorporation of "a 'China tributary' into French narrative and poetry," such as André Malraux and Victor Segalen (Thornber 2009, 224). My research introduces a range of responses to the demand of "knowing" China through its art, even if these works failed to achieve commercial and critical acclaim. As Da points out: "Literary exchanges often exaggerate their own qualities of being read, impactful, well traveled" (Da 2018, 17). To further develop Da's conceptualization of "lightness of contact," I contend that the following case studies offer a reconsideration of French and Chinese national histories that overstate the impact of overseas studies while also marginalizing the cultural production and lived experiences of these five artists and writers. By thinking about cultural exchange in terms of "lightness" rather than impact (as indicated by critical acclaim or sales figures, for instance), we can better recognize which literary and visual elements of Chinese culture were perceived as inscrutable, impenetrable, or incommensurate; and on the other hand, which elements were seen as desirable and worth transposing to a new context.

My book builds on William Schaefer's research on the instability of photographic images in Shanghai in the 1920s and 1930s in *Shadow Modernism: Photography, Writing, and Space in Shanghai, 1925–1937* (2017). Schaefer's study proposes that instead of viewing Chinese modernism in terms of essentialist binary oppositions and polarities (universal vs. individual; national vs. international; global vs. local; past vs. present; East vs. West; traditional vs. modern), we should investigate how aesthetic practices in Shanghai constantly attempted to question, cross, or dismantle those binaries. The concept of transposition therefore helps address the critical questions Schaefer poses about the tensions and conflicts "used to clarify or obscure" these perceived differences: "What differences were being suppressed? What differences were being reified? What differences do such differences make?" (Schaefer 2017, 13). In these cases of intransitive encounters, artists made deliberate aesthetic decisions to retain, discard, replicate, or re-create markers of Chinese cultural identity. The debate over realism and expressionism played a crucial role in these decisions, and my book further builds on Shengqing Wu's research on lyricism and art photography in *Photo Poetics: Chinese Lyricism and Modern Media Culture* (2020). Wu points out that in the face of competitive pressure from advocates of Western realism, Chinese artists and intellectuals developed the binary between *xieyi* (寫意, literally translated as "writing the intention," and often referred to as free sketch or sketch conceptualism) and *xieshi* (寫實 realism) to act as a stand-in for what was framed as the fundamental aesthetic polarity between East and West: "The encompassing, particularly shifty trope of *xieyi*, characterized by its transmediality as well as its intertextual relationship to the literary past, asserted new significance in early twentieth-century historical conditions and cultural politics" (Wu 2020, 218). The expressive mode of *xieyi*, transmedial in nature from its conception, and never conceived as the polar opposite to realism at its origins, now became used in various ways to scapegoat traditional Chinese aesthetics, at the same time that its potential was recognized as protomodernist.

Finally, this book's comparative framework intervenes in current studies in French literature, particularly in the ongoing effort to render French literature more inclusive (read: relevant) beyond the controversial category of *francophonie*. Subha Xavier's theorization of the migrant text as a mode for "studying literary texts that derives from and capitalizes on the experience of immigration" (Xavier 2016, 12) informs my approach to the literary and artistic works at the heart of this book, and provides a reminder that migrant texts "always carry with them the traces of exoticism and otherness that allow for their creation and dissemination in the national, and later global literary marketplace" (Xavier 2016, 19). While the individuals discussed here do not fall neatly into the category of migrants, Xavier observes that travel writing and migrant textuality share a common ground: "Indeed, many works may fall within both realms, thereby increasing their potential for academic scrutiny" (Xavier 2016, 20). For various personal and political reasons, some Chinese travelers, such as Fu Lei, returned to China permanently, while others, like Chang Yu and Pan Yuliang, became migrants in France or elsewhere.

Rosalind Silvester and Guillaume Thouroude's 2012 edited volume *Traits chinois/lignes francophones* traces the lineage of Chinese francophone writing to Chen Jitong, but picks up in the 1990s, conveniently overlooking the political instability of mainland China in the early- to mid-twentieth century, a historical gap that my book addresses. Silvester and Thouroude observe that, as time passes, "French has disappeared from the world economy and international politics. If it still retains any power in the twenty-first century, it may be due to its status as a language that is at once increasingly rare and relatively still prestigious" (Silvester and Thouroude 2021, 15). While it's certainly worthwhile for the insular field of French studies to think beyond national and linguistic borders for the sake of survival, the myth of the French language as guarantor of global recognition and cultural prestige also demands dismantling. Ileana D. Chirila argues that French cultural institutions have legitimized Sino-French literature—French-language literature written by writers originating in China—due to a significant increase in the numbers of Chinese migrants in France and diasporic Chinese in the rest of the world in the twenty-first century, which "signifies the imminent death of Francophonie as the paradigm of a *peripheral* literature" (Chirila 2017, 43). According to Chirila, Sino-French literature can destabilize the myth of French literature and language as universal: "Classical, rigorous, and temperate, French is henceforth considered the most harmonious and the most universal language. By transposition, the cult of style becomes indispensable to the creation of harmony in literature" (Chirila 2017, 41). In other words, Chinese diasporic literature appropriates French literature in order to legitimize transcultural literature, but ideally, recognition of the former should extend beyond a nationalistic space.

Most recently, Shuangyi Li's 2022 monograph *Travel, Translation, and Intermedial Aesthetics: Franco-Chinese Media and Visual Arts in a Global Age* provides four case studies of contemporary diasporic writer-artists, namely François Cheng, Dai Sijie, Gao Xingjian, and Shan Sa. Adopting a transmedial approach, Li identifies defining characteristics of Franco-Chinese literature and art, outside of the frameworks of francophone and sinophone studies, to "inspire multilayered reading, seeing, and even hearing of Franco-Chinese literature and visual arts" and also to "open up the notion of world literature towards multiple medial, modal, and translational forms of travelling, encountering, and understanding" (Li 2022, 244). While *Paris and the Art of Transposition* addresses an earlier historical period prior to the "global age" of Li's study, my book nevertheless shares the conviction that a comparative perspective "not only enables us to stay vigilant about forms of France- or China-centrism, but also encourages us to discover and explore other areas of investigation" (Li 2022, 244). The subsequent chapters demonstrate a range of attitudes toward the French language in relationship to Chinese literary and visual practices, and its perceived suitability for expressing artistic identities.

TRANSPOSITION AS ALTERNATIVE TO TRANSLATION

Dedicating *Les poèmes de T'ao Ts'ien*, a collection of French translations of classical Chinese poetry by Tao Qian (陶潛 365–427), to his contemporary the writer Jean Prévost, the poet Liang Zongdai (梁宗岱 1903–83) recounted having the long-completed translations dormant in his desk, not daring to share them with his colleagues, until one night, "alongside the night glow of the Seine," Prévost enthusiastically approved his translations. Liang credited Prévost with giving him the initial support and encouragement for the volume, which was published in 1930 by Éditions Lemarget in Paris, and concluded, "These poems, which we read together gradually as they were transposed into French, have since undergone many minor changes. But I am sure that you will recognize them" (Liang 1930). Liang Zongdai's use of the verb "transpose" describes the collaborative, if mysteriously inexact, process of reading and translating Tao Qian's poetry, from literary Chinese to French, the latter a language relatively new to Liang. For Liang, revisions may be numerous and even desirable, but ultimately the French reader must still recognize the translations as renditions of classical Chinese poetry.

For Chinese writers experimenting with translation in freshly acquired Western languages, transposition offered a liberating approach that defied the conventional requirement of a translator's linguistic fluency in the target language. As Walter Benjamin claimed in 1923 in "The Task of the Translator," a translation, "instead of resembling the meaning of the original, must lovingly and in detail incorporate the original's mode of signification, thus making both the original and the translation recognizable as fragments of a greater language" (Venuti 2004, 81). Around the same time, Charles Baudelaire's poetry and prose appeared in China, translated by leading literary figures such as Zhou Zuoren (周作人 1885–1967) and Xu Zhimo. Liang Zongdai himself subsequently published four translations of Baudelaire in 1934, including "Correspondances" from *Les fleurs du mal*, and he was likely familiar with the creative implications of transposition versus linguistic translation as he wrote his dedication to Prévost (Bien 2013, 51). The artist Chang Yu (常玉 1901–66) was commissioned to create a series of three copperplate etchings for *Les poèmes de T'ao Ts'ien* to accompany three of the most famous poems. As an example of collaborative intercultural dialogue between Chinese and French cultural players, this book reflects the flexibility of transposition as an open concept in the Baudelairean sense of moving across artistic media, geographic place, and historical time.

Les poèmes de T'ao Ts'ien also boasted a preface by Paul Valéry, which attributed Liang's literary skill to his Chinese identity: "Although Chinese . . . but no! . . . Because he was Chinese, Liang was necessarily better able than the average European, better than the average Frenchman even" to transform language, extracting the most important bits to create "a rare stone out of one word" (Liang 1930, 17). The logic expressed in Valéry's intuitive confession that one's ethnic background could be a linguistic setback, followed by its ensuing reversal, attests to a broader cultural ambivalence toward perceptions of Chinese and French literary prestige. Liang Zongdai's French translations, together with Chang Yu's visual renderings, serve as affirmation of Valéry's claim that "the Chinese race is, or was, the most literary of races," by paying homage to one of the most venerated literary figures in classical Chinese poetry (Liang 1930, 17). Viewing these works as transpositions provides insight about the kinds of artistic agency that Liang Zongdai and Chang Yu had in France as Chinese intellectuals. In these uneven relationships with their French "mentors," Liang Zongdai and Chang Yu, perceived as inheritors of Tao Qian's legacy, could hope to reclaim discursive control over French perceptions of Chinese identity through literature and art, a tangible way through which they could conceivably insert themselves and their work, along with Chinese art and literature at large, into a global art movement and literary history.

The issue of language, framed usually in terms of the process of translation, is widely accepted as a crucial piece in the puzzle of intercultural encounter and exchange. Emily Apter's *The Translation Zone* identifies the field of translation as bookended by opposite theoretical poles, best expressed through two generalizations, both of which are somehow convincing yet misleading: "Nothing is translatable" and "Everything is translatable" (Apter 2006, xi–xii). The question of how to determine whether a translation is "good" or not (if this is even a task that can be accomplished) continues to entice and frustrate scholars, writers, and critics. In her book on national culture and translated modernity in China from 1900 to 1937, for instance, Lydia Liu defines translingual practice as "the process by which new words, meanings, discourses and modes of representation arise, circulate, and acquire legitimacy within the host language due to, or in spite of, the latter's contact/collision with the guest language" (Liu 1995, 26). While Liu's recognition of translation as a site of struggle—by no means a neutral event—is important, I propose that thinking about this historical period through the alternative lens of transposition helps to move away from the linguistic guest-host model of translation and offers a more expansive way to account for creative adaptations that defy conventional national, linguistic, and media boundaries. This lens helps us understand, for example, why a poet like Li Jinfa (李金髮 1900–1976), the subject of chapter 4, would use non-Chinese language in his experimental poems, which are not quite bilingual, nor do they fit under the labels of francophone or sinophone writing.

Transposition, used most frequently in music, refers to transposing music from one key or clef to another, or to transposing a song originally composed for one instrument to another. As such, this "deliberate misreading," to borrow from David Kelley, relies on two seemingly conflicting goals: recognition of an original source of inspiration, and celebration of creative transformation (Collier and Lethbridge 1994, 183). While translation relies on verisimilitude and emphasizing tropes of equivalence, transposition highlights the transposed work's recontextualization, including into new media. This alternative mode allows us to think more openly and flexibly about cross-cultural intermedia encounters, instead of assuming that translation is inextricable from loss, in the vein of W. J. F. Jenner's complaint about modern Chinese literature in English translation: "For translation is, alas, always destruction and betrayal, and only inferior originals can be translated well. All we can do is to limit the losses and compensate for them as best we can. But we always fail to some extent" (Goldblatt 1990, 194). Transposition, like translation, is based on transformation, but unlike translation, it does not rely on the implicit evaluation of a "good" or "bad" translation, and instead celebrates what has been changed in the new iteration.

On a practical level, the motivation to transpose may be as straightforward as accommodating a singer's vocal range or an instrument's chromatic range, or allowing a clarinet to play music composed for the piano, at the same pitch alongside a pianist. Doing so requires theoretical knowledge of the natural scale, the interval system of sharps and flats, full and half-tones, that enables conversion from one musical key to another. As the author of a short handbook instructed readers in 1780, musical transposition requires "no more than to preserve the distance of tone between one note and another, the same as in the natural scales of C and A, according to which it belongs" (*A Treatise on the Transposition of Music*, 22). Beyond its characterization as simply a "polite and fashionable accomplishment," the skill of transposition has deeper implications for musical learning and appreciation (*A Treatise on the Transposition of Music*, 22). Transposition can increase "physical, in addition to visual, sense of key at the piano," reducing the "gap between readable and performable music" (Burger 2022, 37), which means that the more a musician is comfortable with sight-reading and transposing music, the more music they have access to play. By potentially opening up the world of what is playable through the discovery of new material, musicians can therefore be inspired to continue playing.

Extending the musical concept from its algorithmic origins, French literary studies have used the metaphorical concept of *transposition d'art* to discuss the relationship between visual art, music, and literature, primarily in the work of nineteenth-century poets and art critics like Théophile Gautier and Baudelaire (Lloyd 2002; Stephens 2017), as Baudelaire famously claimed in his "Salon de 1846" that "the best account of a picture may well be a sonnet or an elegy" (Baudelaire and Kelley 1975, 82). The symbolist poetry of Stéphane Mallarmé (1842–98) inspired numerous musical compositions, including Claude Débussy's (1862–1918) orchestral symphony *Prélude à l'après-midi d'un faune* (1894), and French composer Maurice Ravel's (1875–1935) *Trois poèmes de Stéphane Mallarmé*, a series of three songs, were also based on Mallarmé's poetry. Although music scholar Emily Kilpatrick notes that the composer used the verb "transposer" twice in the 1920s to describe the relationship between his music and Mallarmé's poetry, she offers no clear conclusion, other than calling Ravel's repeated decision to use the word a "fascinating" one (Kilpatrick 2020, 514). In a 1927 interview, Ravel proclaimed Mallarmé "not merely the greatest French poet, but the *only* French poet, since he made the French language, not designed for poetry, poetical" (Kilpatrick 2015, 76). Ravel's praise, based on perceptions of national identity and literary prestige, offers a clue as to why the composer would choose Mallarmé's notoriously "difficult" poetry to transpose into music: "The inextricability of form and content is a defining characteristic of Mallarmé's poetry: his chosen forms are not simply containers for the sentiment, but often themselves make it manifest" (Kilpatrick 2020, 514). In other words, through the transposition of Mallarmé's language into music, Ravel's compositions help evoke the poet's lyrical sensations and images.

The aesthetic philosophy of intermediality in nineteenth-century literature and art must have been immediately seen by Chinese intellectuals as a cross-cultural (if belated) parallel to Su Shi's (蘇軾 1037–1101) famous praise of Tang dynasty literatus Wang Wei (王維 699–759), whose work led Su Shi to proclaim, "Savoring Mojie's [Wang Wei] poetry, there is painting in his poetry; viewing Mojie's paintings, there is poetry in his painting" (味摩詰之詩，詩中有畫；觀摩詰之畫，畫中有詩) (Wu 2020, 273). Historically, the shared practice of transposing from one medium to another as a way to evoke and arouse a wide range of senses also serves as a reminder of the relative difficulty with which images, texts, and sounds circulated in the nineteenth and early twentieth centuries, compared to the present day when readers and audiences have quicker and easier access to the same materials as the writer or artist. Rosemary Lloyd points out in *Baudelaire's World* that critics faced the challenge "of summoning into the reader's imagination the colors and tones and shapes of a work they may never have seen" (Lloyd 2002, 191). Chinese travelers faced this same problem when they were abroad, in that many of their compatriots would not be able to visit museums in Paris or view even reproductions of the art masterpieces in question, just as most French readers could not read classical Chinese poetry or necessarily know what Chinese calligraphy looked like. But this challenge also presented unique advantages in freeing up limitations shaped by long-held beliefs about style or language, potentially opening up the horizon of reader expectations.

I theorize transposition as a fluid and strategic artistic process that depends on the tension between foreign and familiar, new and old—one that celebrates simultaneously both novelty and recognition when a text gets placed into a fresh context. Transposition is a flexible and deliberate mode of creative engagement that relies on displacement of medium and cultural context; in the early twentieth-century Chinese context, the practice became especially useful for artists to experiment with conveying abstract conceptions of "poetic flavor" (shiyi 詩意) and "sentiment" (qing-diao 情調) to a newly imagined global audience. After viewing an exhibit of Pan Yuliang's paintings in 1938, the writer Su Xuelin (蘇雪林 1897–1999) complained, "I never understood the paintings of poets from the past. As for the paintings of today's poets, they make me even more confused. I can't find half a line of poetry in their paintings, but all I see are messy lines in bright red and green" (Su 1938, 208). Su concluded her essay by advising young Chinese artists to heed Yuan Zicai's (袁子才 1716–97) poetic theory: "When you become skilled at writing poetry, once in a while, just be decadent and weird—compose poetry that is not Zen, it will be naturally lovable. But this is not for beginner poets, otherwise they will never amount to anything" (Su 1938, 213). In Su Xuelin's opinion, to seek artistic inspiration from poetry was a given; to produce truly innovative art, however, one had to break from well-established conventions, but only after having first mastered a particular skillset.

Building on semiotician Julia Kristeva's work on intertextuality, literary theorist Gérard Genette defines transposition very broadly as any kind of "serious" transformation among the broader category of "hypertextual practices," referring to the meaning that is produced through studying the network of relationships among literary texts. Inclusive of, and extending beyond the literary sphere, my book highlights the interconnected networks of relations among texts, images, and ideas. Genette argues for the potential of transposition to create new works "whose textual amplitude and aesthetic and/or ideological ambition may mask or even completely obfuscate their hypertextual character" (Genette 1997, 213). In the context of Ravel's relationship to poetry, this "masking" or obfuscation results in creative flexibility of interpretation, and he described his philosophy to the poet Jules Renard (1864–1910), whose work Ravel set to music in *Histoires naturelles*

(1906): "I think and I feel in music, and I would like to think and feel the same things as you" (Kilpatrick 2015, 78). For artists such as Ravel, subjective interpretations of emotion and fantasy constitute major sources of expressive potential in the creation of new works.

The degree of flexibility articulated in Ravel's account is absent from Genette's designation of transposition as a "neutral and extensive term" (Genette 1997, 28). Although Genette concedes that "there is no such thing as an innocent transposition" (Genette 1997, 294), linguistic transposition for him designates "transpositions that are in principle (and in intention) purely *formal*, which affect meaning only by accident or by a perverse and unintended consequence," compared to thematic transposition, which refers to the deliberate transformation of meaning (Genette 1997, 214). The belief that transformation of meaning is either "perverse and unintended" or "deliberate" is another version of the good versus bad translation dichotomy. As my book demonstrates, the process of transposition can be related to linguistic translation, but it extends beyond the limitations of language to acknowledge a wider repertoire of creative possibilities, ranging from the act of placing familiar material in an unfamiliar setting, to making something strange more approachable, and even to producing misreadings—intentional or not. Rather than tracing a historical chronology of China world-making in Paris, my book aims to reveal the connections and range of creative expression through which Chinese writers and artists experimented with cultural notions of new and old, foreign and domestic, Chinese and French identities. Transposition generated innovative ways of questioning these imagined binaries and polarities, and can account for some of the resistance that artists and writers encountered when they created "deliberate misreadings" of Chinese and French art and literature, by experimenting with familiar images and narratives from classical Chinese poetry in new languages and media. Compared to translation, which Casanova states is "a process of establishing value" (Casanova 1999, 23), transposition is therefore precarious with no guaranteed results. If *littérisation* refers to the transformation that a text undergoes to be recognized as proper literature, to acquire literariness (Casanova 1999, 136), then transposition is a much riskier undertaking that defies aesthetic constraints and conventions. Viewing Sino-French encounters through the alternative lens of transposition shifts from the linguistic guest-host model of translation and offers a much-needed way to account for creative adaptations that defy conventional national, linguistic, and media boundaries.

FIVE CASE STUDIES

A closer look at some "failed" experiments in Chinese literary and art histo-riography suggests that the myth of Paris is not as universal as is commonly assumed. Each subsequent chapter focuses on a particular writer or artist, and is structured around a key conceptual term to reflect the myriad ways in which each traveler's work illuminates an aspect of his or her relationship to the development of modern Chinese art.

Chapter 2 focuses on the artist Chang Yu, whose work complicates con-ventional binaries of traditional vs. modern and East vs. West. Although art historiography celebrates him for achieving a "harmonious synthesis," his visual art and writing demonstrate a self-conscious engagement with notions of nationality and ethnicity in making Chinese culture legible for a global (French) audience. The concept of transposition highlights both the artist's physical movement of place, as well as the figurative imagining of a wider context of reception of Chinese culture outside of China during the Republican period. While Chang Yu drew on easily recognizable elements of literati sensibility in poetry and calligraphy to negotiate French expectations of Chinese aesthetics, efforts to transpose Chineseness ended up emphasiz-ing instead the incommensurability of time and place between the two cul-tures. His art now sells for millions of dollars at auction, and museums in Taiwan have organized solo retrospective shows of his paintings in recent years, such as the exhibit of forty-nine oil paintings held at the National Museum of History in 2017, titled *Parisian Nostalgia: The National Museum of History's Sanyu Collection*. The concept of "pose"—referring to both the art-ist's self-reflexive literati identity and the contorted bodies in his paintings—provides a nuanced view of what being called "mistimed" and "misplaced" implies, uncovering the layers of negotiation that a Chinese artist in Paris encountered, as a cultural mediator, marketer, and translator, revealing the reasons why his work took so long to be rediscovered.

Chapter 3 builds on Chang Yu's cultivation of a literati persona and traces the critic Fu Lei's (傅雷 1908 66) claim that his love for Chinese painting was initially sparked by studying Western art at the Louvre. Rather than focusing on Fu Lei's celebrated translation theory, the chapter ana-lyzes his letters to readers back in Shanghai alongside his essays on art criti-cism, reflecting on how Fu Lei voices his ambivalent attitude toward deep cultural contradictions between China and the West. In 1934, Fu Lei com-pleted an edited volume of twenty lectures he gave on world art masterpieces, but the project was published posthumously only in 1985. The role of the critic, considered by Baudelaire as instrumental to artistic expression, and the perception of its importance in the promotion and advancement of Chinese art, are reflected in Fu Lei's travel letters to Chinese readers collected in *Letters on the Way to France*, which were composed on his journey from Shanghai to Marseille and Paris in 1928. The transpositions related to everyday intercultural practices, such as musical performance, ship games, and restaurant food, inform Fu Lei's marginalized position as a modern Chinese art critic, whose success depends on his ability to transpose elements from one artistic tradition to another, even when these encounters result in moments of conflict and tension.

Chapter 4 turns from the work of Fu Lei, who strove for clarity and hoped that art could play an active role in the nation's future, to Li Jinfa, the "eccentric of poetry" who proudly declared, "I just cannot be like others and use poetry to write about revolutionary thought, or stir people to strike out or shed blood" (Denton 1996, 390). Literary critics have often pointed to his lack of mastery in both Chinese and French languages, his poor timing, and his ignorance of classical Chinese poetry, among other reasons, as explanations for why his ambitious project to revolutionize modern Chinese poetry went awry, and why he was subsequently relegated to the periphery of the modern Chinese literary canon. In his experimental poetry, Li Jinfa subverted the aesthetics of classical poetry by appropriating only the specific elements he found effectively evocative, without claiming legitimacy for its sacred heritage. The chapter surveys the mixed reception of his poetry since its publication in the late 1920s and 1930s to more recent evaluations, suggesting that his greatest literary crime was promoting the potentially liberatory but also offensive idea of artistic inspiration—the idea that anyone without proper literary or language training can compose poetry. I read Li Jinfa's experimental poems written about his time in Paris as transpositions that foreground the inspirational figure of the artistic muse, opening the role of poet to those with no linguistic expertise or special training.

Chapter 5 focuses on another well-established source of artistic inspiration—the artist's studio—in the writer Xu Xu's (徐訏 1908–80) semifictional travel stories from his 1941 *Sentiments from Abroad (Haiwai de qingdiao)*. Xu Xu traveled to Paris in the fall of 1936, where he earned his doctorate in philosophy then returned to Shanghai in 1938 after the outbreak of the World War II. Despite publishing fiction prolifically in the period from the 1930s to the 1950s, and having his work adapted into movie screenplays, Xu Xu has never been considered a major figure in modern Chinese literature. In the 1930s and 1940s, his works were harshly criticized for being escapist romances and having no political relevance, potentially causing harm to its readers and society, to the point that Xu Xu went into self-exile in Hong Kong in 1950, like many Chinese intellectuals at the juncture of the Communist Party's takeover of mainland China in 1949. In the PRC, his work was not "rediscovered" by Chinese literary critics until after the Cultural Revolution, in the 1980s (not exceptional in this sense). But unlike writers like Eileen Chang (張愛玲 1920–95) and Shen Congwen (沈從文 1902–88), whose literary legacies in mainland China were restored after the socialist period, with the exception of two recent English-language publications (Rosenmeier 2019; Xu 2020), scholarly attention on Xu Xu's work continues to be limited in both Chinese and English scholarship on modern Chinese literature.

In two stories from the collection, "Montparnasse Studio" and "The Duel," which both take place in Paris, Xu Xu transposes perceived traits of oriental culture—referred to loosely as mood or sentiment (qingdiao 情調, which, coincidentally, has musical connotations that refer to melody or tone *diao*)—that are usually criticized for being passive, backward or out-dated. Fantastic expressions of "oriental sentiment" recast in Paris, for instance, as the narrator's classical-style poetry and a more reserved mode of courtship, are proven to be desirable and superior in these stories. Transposition serves as a way for Xu Xu's narrator-protagonists to achieve romantic-sexual victory in the form of Chinese aesthetic expertise, which is imagined as being desired and appreciated in Paris. Thinking about Xu Xu's stories and his contemporary readers in the early 1940s, we can turn back to Guo Jianying's cartoon *Introduction*, which appears in comparison as reductive in its simplicity. Xu Xu's protagonists occupy a far more ambiguous role by being projected as embodying traditional aesthetics against the cosmopolitan setting of Paris and a cast of beautiful Chinese and French love interests.

Chapter 6 responds in yet another way to Guo Jianying's *Introduction*, by highlighting the life and work of the artist Pan Yuliang, who traveled to France in 1921 and graduated from the School of Fine Arts in Paris in 1925, then studied in Rome before returning to China for a decade to teach at the Shanghai Academy of Art. In 1937, Pan Yuliang returned to Paris to participate in the Exposition international de Paris, and stayed there until her death in 1977. Known in France as Pan Yu Lin, her reputation has attained a legendary status, and Pan's biography has been peppered with unsubstantiated facts and speculation, among which include the literary and filmic representations stemming from a brief period of Pan Yuliang fever (re 熱) in the 1980s after the 1983 publication of Shi Nan's biography *Soul of a Painter: Zhang Yuliang, a Biography*, including *A Soul Haunted by Painting* (*Hua hun* 畫魂), Huang Shuqin's 1994 biopic film; the 2003 TV series, *Painting Soul* (*Hua hun* 畫魂) by Stanley Kwan; and *The Painter from Shanghai*, a 2008 English-language historical fiction novel by Jennifer Cody Epstein.

There are two underlying myths about her identity associated with these creative reimaginings of Pan's life: one is the well-told origins story of her being sold to a brothel at fourteen when her parents died (even though this element of her biography has never been confirmed), before she was "rescued" by Pan Zanhua (潘贊化 1885–1959), who married her as his concubine. The second is Pan's nickname of "The Woman of Three No's" (San bu nüshi 三不女士), which attests to her ability to survive and work in Paris as a woman artist for decades: "No foreign citizenship, no love affairs, and no contracts with art dealers" (Bu ru wai guoji, bu lian'ai, bu he renhe huashang qianding hetong 不入外國籍，不戀愛，不和任何畫商簽定合同, Wang 1988, 98). So why has Pan Yuliang's life inspired so many forms of imaginative speculation, while her artistic work has led to relatively scant scholarship? Viewing Pan Yuliang's self-portraits as transpositions can be a starting point to addressing this question, as the self-portraits occupy the in-between space of visual images of the modern Chinese woman artist that circulated in popular media in China and France, and Pan's nude paintings, which are viewed as the ultimate evidence of a successful liberal French art training and the educated sexually progressive Chinese woman.

Together these chapters complicate our understanding of modern Chinese cultural identity and reshape our recognition of the ways in which both Shanghai and Paris have been mythologized by national histories that privilege particular artistic modes and categories over others. While *Paris and the Art of Transposition* tries to destabilize assumptions about circulation and transmission of the cultural power of Paris, I am cognizant that my book contributes to the further perpetuation of this Francophile tendency to some degree. As my sister writer and translator Bonnie Chau has been described, so too, was I "born to a Francophile family of Chinese descent in California" (Ramakrishnan 2021), which is why Eugene Eoyang's metaphor of travel as a "two-way mirror" resonates with my early experiences in Paris as a youth. My discussion is therefore attentive to balancing these opposing pulls, the first being how to render more visible the invisible contours of overlooked voices and "failed" experiments.

Simultaneously, this book unsettles the trajectory of nationalistic cultural hegemonies in both China and France, challenging national historical narratives such as the heroic account commemorated in the 1988 *China-Paris, Seven Chinese Painters Who Studied in France* exhibit at the Taipei Fine Arts Museum: "Their greatest achievement was to blend elements of Chinese and Western art, in order to pave a new path for modern Chinese painting" (他們的成就，是中西合璧的開端，為中國現代畫，打開一條新的道路 Huang 1988, 9). Instead, my book reveals a more complicated and nuanced perspective on the artistically formative period of the 1920s through the 1940s. The following case studies also illustrate how five artists and writers experimented with the concept of transposition in very different ways to articulate creative visions of the modern Chinese artist to the global art community. Conversely, as the five cases tease out the various contours of transposition, transposition as a way of thinking about artistic agency aims to recuperate the stories and creative work of these overlooked figures.

To return to the question of art diplomacy between China and the West, cultural exchanges are shaped by social, political, and economic conditions, but they also have the potential to shape those very conditions. In 1984, Taiwan artist Xie Lifa (謝里法 b. 1938) wrote an essay about Pan Yuliang's career for the magazine *Lion Art* (*Xiongshi meishu* 雄獅美術) and reminisced about 1960s Paris: "Back then, there were only two artists who had lived in Paris for a long time: one was Pan Yuliang, the other was Chang Yu, and they were known as the two old 'Yu's.' Outsiders always used the word 'dejected' [liaodao 潦倒] to describe them, meaning they lived in poverty having failed to carve out a prestigious position in the art world" (Xie 1984, 35). Xie considers, however, the difficulty of defining "dejected": "As long as an artist produces art to survive, in the end, we can only determine its value by evaluating the works of art. They were labeled 'dejected' because art made them 'dejected,' just as art would have been their means to success" (Xie 1984, 35). Transposition argues for the possibility of recognizing artistic value based on criteria beyond the number of works produced or prestige (canonization, artistic prizes, or translation), centering instead active creative engagement with time and place.

While paying attention to previously marginalized archives is important, my book recognizes the tension between these intellectuals as privileged minor celebrities in Chinese cultural history yet having relatively little impact in national history and international cultural histories. In doing so, we can better understand the artistic strategies employed by Chinese artists and writers in the early twentieth century, and the reasons that Paris became the site for experimenting with the circulation of Chinese cultural identity. These reasons may not fit with what national histories in China and France have asked us to imagine, that the nurturing atmosphere in Paris fostered creative freedom previously inaccessible in China, or that either nation's artistic legacy was unshakeable. Instead, viewing literature and art through the lens of transposition uncovers what remained recognizable overseas and what was transformed in this context, showing how cultural difference was circulated and promoted to challenge existing notions about modern Chinese art to an international audience.

CHAPTER 2

Chang Yu and the Pose

Who says a painting must look like life?
He sees only with children's eyes.
Who says a poem must stick to the theme?
Poetry is certainly lost on him.

—SU SHI, "WHO SAYS A PAINTING MUST LOOK LIKE LIFE?"

In a poem dated November 1 from an unknown year, the artist Chang Yu wrote in oil,

> Autumn chrysanthemums are for poets to praise
> At the literati's drinking parties
> These poor chrysanthemums here
> Are only for decorating graves

> 秋菊詩人賞
> 文人對酒杯
> 可憐此間菊
> 只供作人墳

The unusual piece, composed in oil on a mirror, commemorates the Double Ninth Festival (Zhong yang jie 重陽節), a traditional holiday on the ninth day of the ninth lunar month that emphasizes long life and remembering one's ancestors, commonly celebrated by going climbing in the mountains and represented symbolically by the chrysanthemum flower. The melancholy poem consists of one unrhymed quatrain, with each five-character line appearing in the customary form, and written in thick brushstrokes of black painted over a white oil background. Chang Yu's brushstrokes appear

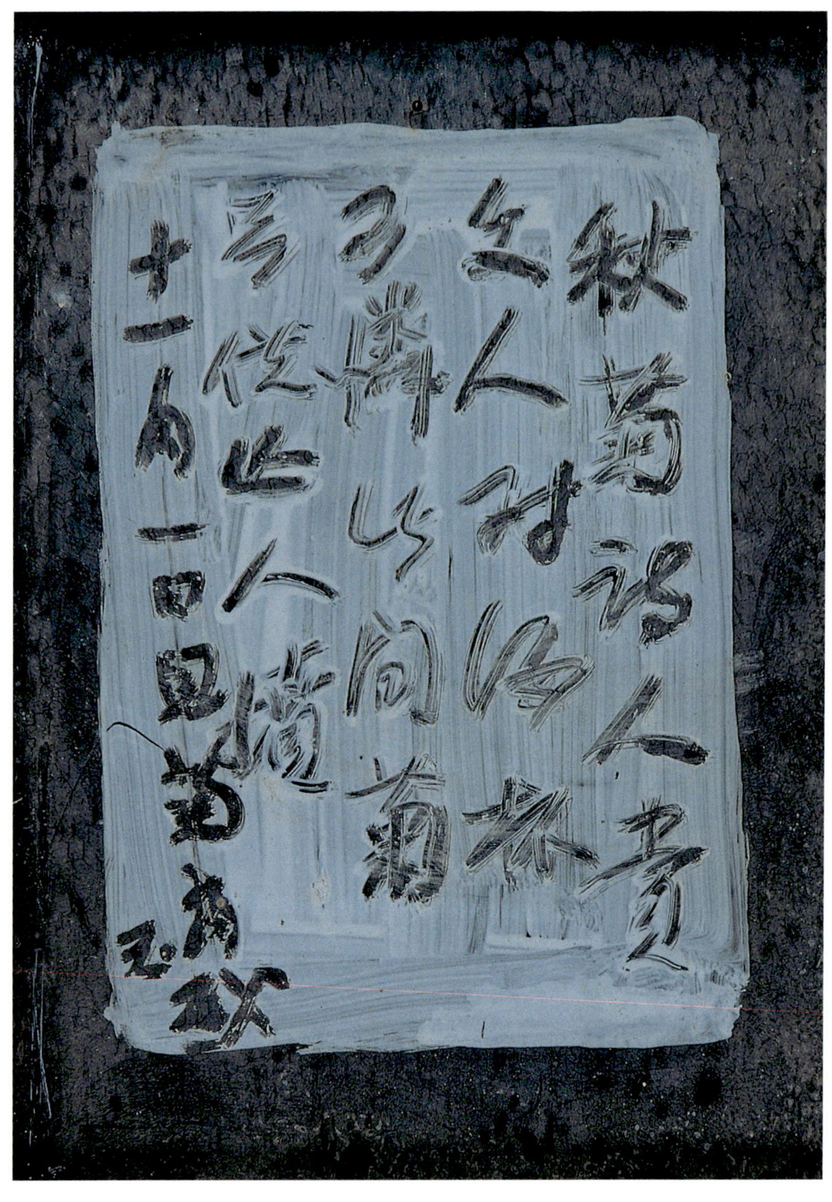

Figure 2. *An Autumn Poem* (Qiu zhi shi 秋之詩), undated oil painting on mirror by Chang Yu 常玉, 17.5 x 12.5 cm. Courtesy of the Li Ching Cultural and Educational Foundation.

hurried and spirited, and the composition of the characters makes the poem seem spontaneous, with an improvisational quality. But the subject matter was a familiar one to the artist; not only do many of Chang Yu's oil paintings feature chrysanthemum flowers, usually potted in a vase, but the image of the chrysanthemum is ubiquitous in classical Chinese poetry, particularly in association with Tao Qian, the poet whose work Liang Zongdai translated and for which Chang Yu was commissioned to produce etchings in Paris. Chang Yu's work juxtaposes the relatively new Western medium of oil painting with Chinese brush calligraphy; and while aspects of the poem's outward form, structure, and theme recall classical poetry, its tone and topic is decidedly modern. A playful rejoinder to Hu Shih's appeal to "use the living words of the twentieth century than the dead words of three millennia past" (Denton 1996, 138), the piece also commemorates the artist's subjective experience of cross-cultural encounter.

This chapter shows how Chang Yu continually overturned both French and Chinese expectations of the modern Chinese artist in his life and creative work. As such, his artistic oeuvre and career reflect a creative resistance to perceptions of what being "modern" and "Chinese" should look like in Paris, a projection constituted by what William Schaefer describes as the "mythic identity of image and writing," an "essential civilization marker of Chinese cultural identity" (Schaefer 2017, 8). By transposing markers of literati culture such as the chrysanthemum and Tao Qian's poetry, Chang Yu replanted these seeming relics of the past to twentieth-century Paris as a response to what French audiences expected and demanded yet presented the global audience a weird subversive version. At the same time, his fixation and experimentation with the nude female body, a seemingly obvious symbol of progressive art education and modernity, resulted in distorted "deliberate misreadings" of the nude body's purported potential as a site of objective realism, instead being perceived as evidence of Chang Yu's connection to a calligraphic legacy.

In the untitled poem-painting, Chang Yu calls attention to the theme of cultural incommensurability, contrasting the jovial and refined social drinking practices of Chinese literati associated with their admiration for the chrysanthemum with its greatly diminished role in French social practice, relegated to the status of funereal décor. The poem's references to the artistic practices of the poet (shiren 詩人) and scholar (wenren 文人) raise the self-referential question of where Chang Yu perceives his own position. As the artist technically composing the poem and creating the painting, does

Chang Yu situate himself as the poetic speaker, yearning nostalgically for the past and an imagined life back in China? Or is he a detached third-person observer, objectively documenting the distance between two cultures? The poem laments both temporal and spatial distance, as the literati ritual of drinking and composing poetry in the manner of Li Bai (李白 701–62) and Tao Qian is an outdated relic of traditional Chinese culture. Yet in his transposition of the chrysanthemum flower to the new context of French mourning culture (also in relation to the fall season), Chang Yu highlights the artist's unique ability to appreciate difference. The "poor chrysanthemums" are poor in status, at least partly due to their physical location ("here," ci jian 此間), pointing out a connection of place between the flowers and the figure of the artist, whose value is determined by cultural context, not entirely arbitrarily but over which he has limited control.

Known in France as "Sanyu," and often referred to as the "Chinese Matisse," Chang Yu was born on October 14, 1901 in Nanchong, Sichuan to a relatively prosperous family that owned a large silk mill. As a youth, he studied painting from his father and calligraphy with the Sichuan master Zhao Xi (趙熙 1867–1948). After studying in Japan and a brief period in Berlin, he traveled to Paris as an art student in 1921, most likely sponsored by the Chinese government and also funded by his family. Chang Yu's decision to study at the Académie de la Grande Chaumière in Montparnasse, the avant-garde hub of Paris, rather than the École des Beaux-Arts, the more typical choice of students seeking a proper academic setting—combined with his untimely death in France in 1966—set Chang Yu apart from other modern Chinese artists like Xu Beihong, Lin Fengmian, and Pang Xunqin (龐薰琹 1906–85), all of whom also studied in Paris during this time.

In 1946, the Parisian journalist Pierre Joffroy published an article about the "inventor of essentialism" in the French daily paper *Parisien libéré*: "The curious could ask if San-Yu is a Chinese who is an artist or an artist who is Chinese. There is no answer to this question. The particular gift of this artist is to unite East and West in his painting, not in a confused sacrilegious hotchpotch, but in a sublime form where one loses usual points of reference" (Joffroy 1946). Chang Yu's persona as a Chinese artist in Paris was the product of careful cultivation and at times intersecting or conflicting motivations by the Chinese and French press, editors, art dealers, other artists, and Chang Yu himself. The concept of the pose aptly captures the artist's experimentation with the postures of the human form, and also his positionality as a Chinese painter in Paris to French and Chinese media. Chang Yu's three copperplate etchings of Tao Qian's classical poetry, along with the deliberate allusions to Chinese literature and philosophy found in his paintings and interviews, represent not so much a "harmonious synthesis" of East and West, as has been argued by art historians, but rather the transposition of classical aesthetics. While his minimalist language has been interpreted by critics as the defining feature of Chang Yu's literati persona to French audiences, and Chinese colleagues celebrated his bohemian lifestyle, his greatest contribution in transposing Chinese literati culture was creating a visual language that accentuated cultural difference.

"MISPLACED AND MISTIMED": THE LONELY ARTIST

In 1948, an article in *Arts and Entertainment* referring to Chang Yu was titled "A Chinese Artist Who Has Lived in Paris a Long Time" and described him as "a second-rate artist following artists like Picasso and Matisse" (Wong 2014, 39). The article continued, "None of the Western-style artists in China can compare to him in artistry, but he has vowed never to come home. It has been said that he said, 'I would starve to death if I returned to China because nobody would understand my paintings.'" Contrasting Chang Yu's alleged success in the French art market with his lack of fame in China, the article concluded, "In China, however, aside from a few people who studied in France, few people know of this artist who is claiming glory for China in the international circles."[1] The image of an artist underappreciated in his home country yet "claiming glory for China" on a global scale is frequently invoked in the stories of artists' lives and careers impacted by time spent abroad, especially in Paris, and Fu Lei addresses this artistic trend in his essays on Liu Haisu and Pang Xunqin in the next chapter. These stories confirm the status of Paris as an international artistic capital superior to other cities, and its inhabitants as more sophisticated and receptive audiences to "foreign" art practices, at the time that they discount domestic readers in China for being close-minded and short-sighted.

Mixed assessments of Chang Yu raise the question of what it means for an artist to be understood, and a reexamination of his work provides clues as to why he was "almost eradicated" from Chinese art history (Desroches and Chioetta 2004, 77). Rita Wong, the foremost curator of Chang Yu's work, has likened Chang Yu's promotion of "ping-tennis," the mashup game combining ping pong and tennis that he invented, to his artwork, concluding, "Like his art, also a hybrid, it was recognized and appreciated for its originality and creativity, but being misplaced and mistimed, it did not have a lasting impact and could not be sustained" (Wong 2011, 63). Art historian Eugene Wang calls Chang Yu's entire career "a story of missed opportunities":

> He was in the right place, Paris, and at the right time, the 1920s and 1930s. His sensitivity in adapting traditional Chinese art to new possibilities and idioms could well have made him a great modernist when European modernism was drawing inspiration from Asian art. Yet his lack of enterprise, his self-absorption and carefree hedonism—all traits associated with traditional Chinese literati—left him insensitive to the pulse and pressures of the art market. (Hearn and Smith 2001, 151)

Wang's ad hominem assessment points out the role of poor timing, suggesting that Chang Yu could have capitalized on the popular French demand for classical art, for example, to sell more of his work. The obsession with up to date timing can be traced to the nineteenth-century realist edict *"il faut être de son temps,"* which has been attributed to French artists like Honoré Daumier (1808–79) and Édouard Manet (1832–83). In her study of European realism, art historian Linda Nochlin identifies three possible ways for an artist to express contemporaneity: (1) use symbolism or allegory to express the social ideals of one's time, (2) confront the actual, concrete events and experiences of one's time, or (3) imply being in advance of one's time, as in the case of avant-garde art (Nochlin 1971, 105–6). Even though his art has been interpreted in this last category, the elements of literati art that Chang Yu did transpose did not translate to financial or critical success during his lifetime.

Chang Yu's commercial and critical failure has been explained by way of his unusual personality and his bohemian lifestyle, especially his consorting with Parisian locals and contemporary Western artists, implying his isolation from Chinese contemporaries. Since the 1920s, the critical reception of Chang Yu has been inextricable from the ebbs and flows of the art market, and Julia Andrews suggests that a related reason why Chang Yu's work was neglected for much of the twentieth century is that "many paintings and documents that survived the perils of the 1930s, '40s, and '50s were destroyed during the Cultural Revolution, and anyone tainted by foreign experiences marked as a traitor," resulting in "China's cosmopolitan artistic period, the era of Sanyu's greatest success" being "ripped out of the record" (Desroches and Chioetta 2004, 77).[2] To read Chang Yu's lack of financial success (and therefore career) as one of "missed opportunities" loses sight of the key role that his wenren sensibility played in his artistic choices, and overlooks the collaborative projects and intercultural conversations he actively participated in, such as Liang Zongdai's French translation of Tao Qian.

Art historian Gu Yue's 2009 study *Avant-Garde Decadent: Sanyu and the Study of Alternative Perspectives in Modern Chinese Art* is the earliest published monograph on Chang Yu from mainland China, as most previous publications originated in Taiwan. Gu Yue's title picks up on the theme of the misunderstood artist by reference to "alternative perspectives" (linglei shijiao 另類視角) as a new way of viewing, and, echoing Eugene Wang, attributes Chang Yu's "complete lack of interest in material gain" to the "desirable self-control of a Chinese literatus" and the "integrity and independence of a Chinese artist" (Gu 2009, 39). In his foreword to the volume, Du Dakai identifies the "poetic quality" (shixing 詩性) of Chang Yu's work as key to defining the modernness of Chinese art: "Chang Yu tells us that poetics, although it does not define all of modern Chinese art, at the very least it does constitute one very important part of it, because this part is the element that links together the history, present and future existences of Chinese art" (Gu 2009, i). Transposition in this sense is central to the poetic-literary quality of his visual art, which can be seen as a continuation of classical Chinese art practice that links calligraphy with painting in the form of poetic inscription that accompanies visual representation on the same surface. As Wen C. Fong explains, the shared function of calligraphy and painting is both representational and presentational, because the "signifying practice of an image as a sign originates in the body and mind of the image maker" (Fong 2003, 259). As such, "the key to Chinese painting lies in its calligraphic line, which bears the presence, or physical 'trace' (*ji*), of its maker" (Fong 2003, 259). Du Dakai's analysis therefore shows the persistence of that connection to the circulation of Chang Yu's work and the promotion of his artistic persona during his lifetime, as well as the relationship between his posthumous prominence on the auction circuit and how his eclectic artistic legacy is interpreted by Chinese art historians.

Following Andrews's line of argument, Du Dakai carefully writes, "In the early 20th century, of the artists who studied abroad in Europe, although there were many whose fates were not fair, most by now have been treated equitably and justly received, except for Chang Yu, who remains exceptional in that he remains nearly forgotten" (Du 2012, 137). Explaining why he was forgotten (yiwang 遺忘) Du suggests that it may be too difficult today to determine the reasons or whom is to blame for the oversight: "The reasons may be irrelevant, what's important is that we remember Chang Yu now" (Du 2012, 137). This chapter contends that the reasons are not irrelevant, as understanding the reasons beyond the blame-the-Maoist-period reduction-ist narrative sheds light on why Chang Yu's works are only now making profit on the auction circuit, and it also shows how monetary valuation of his work influences academic scholarship. Nearly a decade after Du's plea, Chang Yu remains largely "forgotten," except for the posthumous profitabil-ity of his work.

Given the relative silence surrounding Chang Yu since his death in 1966, Chang Yu's name has appeared with surprising frequency in recent media headlines due to the extraordinarily high prices his paintings have sold for on the auction markets, especially in Taiwan and Hong Kong (Kamp 2020; Villa 2021). In the last decade, the dramatic growth of aca-demic interest in his work in mainland China, Taiwan, and Hong Kong has been a direct result of the increase in profitability tied to valuation of his work on the auction circuit. In "The Solitary Chang Yu: The Unusual Expe-rience and Market of an Oil Master," Hu Yixun locates Chang Yu's legacy as anomalous on two levels: in art historiography and also on the contempo-rary art market. While Hu admits there is no way to change Chang Yu's place in art history, he offers a way to reread or understand Chang Yu's paintings from the present moment through providing historical context of "a Chinese painter living his European life during a specific period" (Hu 2013, 108). A closer look at Chang Yu's career in the first half of the twenti-eth century pushes against the assumption that his painting seamlessly integrated Chinese and Western art and forces us to rethink the notion of artistic exchange as always generating concrete material results. For instance, Justin Kamp writes for *Artsy* that "the artist's most recent market surge can again be traced to institutional shows rooted in international exchange" (Kamp 2020). These earlier forms of Sino-French exchange were tied to questions of national and ethnic identity, and Chang Yu's transpo-sition of identifiably Chinese cultural markers reflect shifts in social prac-tices of art viewing and consumption.

DECONSTRUCTING AND RECONSTRUCTING TAO QIAN

For Liang Zongdai's translated volume *Les poèmes de T'ao Ts'ien*, Chang Yu produced three copperplate print images: the first accompanies Liang's translation of "Biography of the Gentleman of Five Willows" (Wu liu xiansheng zhuan 五柳先生傳), the second illustrates "Begging for Food" (Qi shi 乞食), and the last is an illustration of Tao Qian's most famous poem, "Peach Blossom Spring" (Taohua yuan ji 桃花源記). Thematically, these poems are representative of Tao Qian's career and subsequent rejection of official life; the poems also resonate with Chang Yu's personal experiences as a traveler and foreigner. In both accounts of the male intellectual's life, the act of displacement allows for creative flowering, as the remoteness of physical setting fosters poetic inspiration.

The first of Chang Yu's etchings for the volume is a depiction of "Biography of the Gentleman of Five Willows," which is conventionally read as a thinly veiled autobiographical account by Tao Qian. The narrative describes a recluse's quiet life, one that disavows fame and fortune. In Chang Yu's visual rendition of the poem, the bulk of the composition consists of a strikingly empty expanse of water that runs through the center of the etching, which is offset by the equally blank sky and desolate mountainscape in the background. The viewer's focus is drawn to the dark, bending outlines of the willow trees in the right side of the foreground, and there is no sign of the gentleman in question, except for the simple outline of a hut, nearly hidden by the willows. Chang Yu's visual rendition echoes Tao Qian's poetic sentiment, as translated by Liang, "Tranquille et taciturne, il n'aimait ni la gloire ni la richesse. Il se délectait dans les livres, mais répugnait à toutes explications minutieuses" (閑靜少言，不幕榮利。好讀書，不求甚解/ Liang 1930, 29–30). The scene's minimalist aesthetic resonates with the tranquility and simplicity of the "biography" and its subject, a recluse defined not by his identity (origins, name) but by the natural markers of his hermetic existence (the willow trees).

Art historian Eugene Wang traces the inspirational sources of these etchings to a number of literati landscapes (Hearn and Smith 2001, 125–26). The composition of the *Five Willows* etching, for example, closely resembles fourteenth-century Yuan dynasty master Ni Zan's (倪瓚 1301–74) characteristically monochromatic and sparse landscapes, often dominated by bodies of water. However, Chang Yu's etching departs noticeably from the original

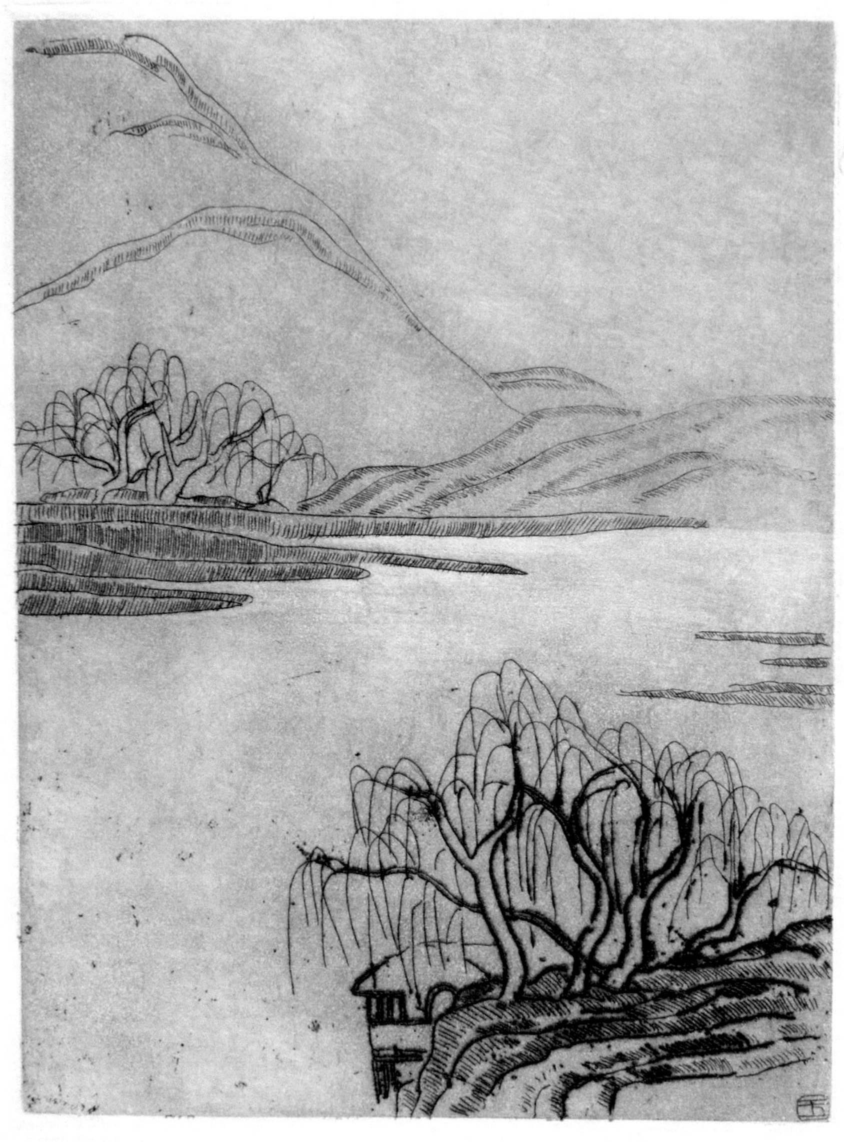

Figure 3. Etching accompanying "Biography of the Gentleman of Five Willows" (Wu liu xiansheng zhuan 五柳先生傳), copperplate print by Chang Yu 常玉 for *Les poèmes de T'ao Ts'ien*, 1930, 15 x 9.2 cm. Courtesy of the Li Ching Cultural and Educational Foundation.

poem and Liang Zongdai's translation by foregoing any mention of the "let-tré" male subject of the biography in Tao Qian's original text. Liang's translation of the poem's title to "Le lettré des cinq saules" removes the mention of the biographical literary genre (zhuan 傳), but Chang Yu's creative retelling goes one step further by omitting all traces of the poet, focusing instead on the idyllic natural setting surrounding the simple outline of a hut. In this intermedial transposition, Chang Yu reinterprets Tao Qian's thinly veiled autobiographical account of a hermit's retreat from society by retaining only the key identifier to his identity: the bending branches of the willow trees that serve the basis for the enigmatic figure's assigned nickname. Instead of following Liang Zongdai's steps by taking literary liberties in rendering Tao Qian's sparse verse into more accessible colloquial French, Chang Yu takes advantage of the etched medium to show the dark, short, shaded lines in the river bank, offset by blank white space of the mountains and water, and the curvy sinews of the willows. The intaglio technique was an unknown print-making medium in China at the time, so Chang Yu was not constrained to follow any conventional visual depictions of the gentleman, and could freely choose how to convey the spirit of the hermit's insular life, without giving any hint of his love for wine, the source of his poetic inspiration, or his ascetic lifestyle (Wong 2017b, 28–31).

In these etchings, Chang Yu revisits elements of classical Chinese land-scape painting by reducing them to their most basic lines, strokes, and curves. Among the three works, only the second depicts a human figure, the traveler and speaker of the poem, whose form is represented by a simple out-line and no facial or bodily detailing. Like the hut in "Five Willows," signs of human life barely register on the meandering landscape of "Begging for Food," even though the human subjects they represent are the focus of the poems. Eugene Wang states that the piece accompanying "Begging for Food" is "reminiscent of the fantastic topography of Shitao ([石濤] 1642–1707)," an early Qing landscape painter (Hearn and Smith 2001, 126), and the art histo-rian's project of tracing the artistic lineage of the etchings is a fruitful endeavor. However, for the purposes of this project, my analysis focuses on the visual-textual connection, or what can be categorized as Chang Yu's "deliberate misreading" of Tao Qian's poetry. The speaker of "Begging for Food" recognizes the limitations of verbal language outside of its creative purposes of singing and composing poetry, as he accepts the impossibility of expressing gratitude through thankful words: "Comment pourrais-je vous rendre grâce" (銜戢知何謝/ Liang 1930, 48). Originally composed in a series

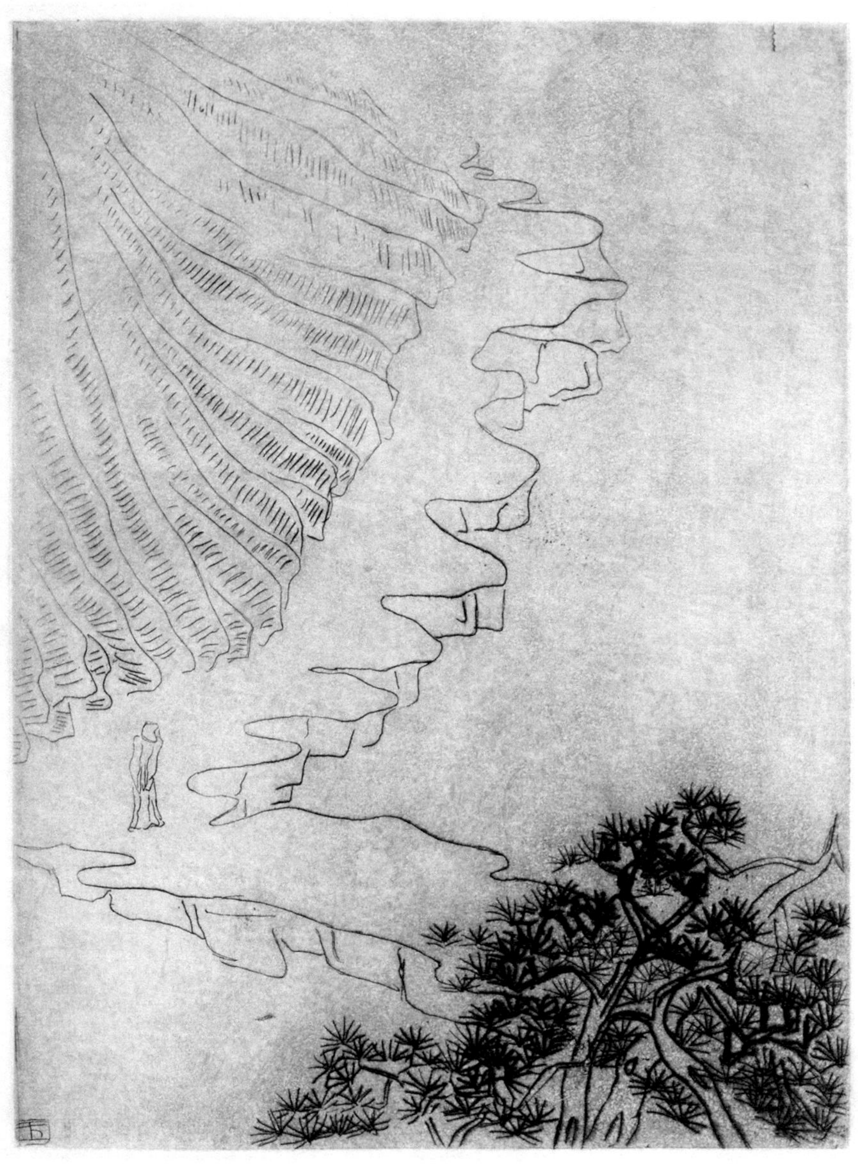

Figure 4. Etching accompanying "Begging for Food" (Qi shi乞食), copperplate print by Chang Yu 常玉 for *Les poèmes de T'ao Ts'ien*, 1930, 15 x 9.2 cm. Courtesy of the Li Ching Cultural and Educational Foundation.

of standard length five-character-long lines, Liang Zongdai's French translation adopts free verse to convey a tone of collegial intimacy.

Chang Yu's illustration captures the sense of human solitude and the traveler's initial trepidation and uncertainty, but not the unexpected outcome of eventual camaraderie depicted in the poem. Just as his transposition of "Five Willows" rejects the biographical genre form as one in which the artistic subject occupies the narrative center, Chang Yu's depiction of "Begging for Food" rejects Tao Qian's message of communal artistic practice, and focuses instead on Liang's repeated "Cheminant, cheminant" at the beginning of line 3, used to describe the initially wandering mindset of the first-person poetic speaker in the poem's opening lines. The figure's slightly stooped posture, with arms together, legs splayed outward, and head in a tilted, beseeching manner, is positioned strategically in the bottom left corner of the plane, allowing the viewer to see both the serpentine mountain path from which he has traveled and the forward trajectory of his meandering, fortuitous journey. In both of these works, Chang Yu's etchings carefully retain the human subject's relationship with the landscape environment detailed in Tao Qian's poems and Liang Zongdai's French translations, while subverting the poetic narrative of artistic creation as socially constructed.

In the last etching for the book, Chang Yu's illustration of "Peach Blossom Spring" accompanies Liang's translation of one of Tao Qian's most famous works, a prose poem about a lost fisherman who stumbles upon an otherworldly haven covered with peach trees in blossom. Chang Yu's work departs from earlier paintings by such Ming artists as Qiu Ying (仇英 1494–1552) and Wen Zhengming (文徵明 1470–1559), and Qing masters Shitao and Wang Hui (王翬 1632–1717), by depicting the mythical village without showing any sign of its inhabitants or the fisherman. The unspeakability of the utopian village's existence is exhorted by the villagers, who insist to the fisherman upon his departure, "Inutile de parler de nous aux gens du dehors" (不足為外人道也/ Liang 1930, 75). While the intersection of the mountain, river, and peach blossom spring at the center of the etching marks the location of the fabled grotto, the composition's overwhelmingly blank expanse emphasizes the remoteness of the village, without showing the actual village itself. Chang Yu's illustration reduces Tao Qian's fable to both its beginning and conclusion, as the travelers are lost and unable to retrace their path to the "région inconnue" (Liang 1930, 76). The fable's last lines remind the reader of the limitations of learning and virtue, and Chang Yu's etching visu-

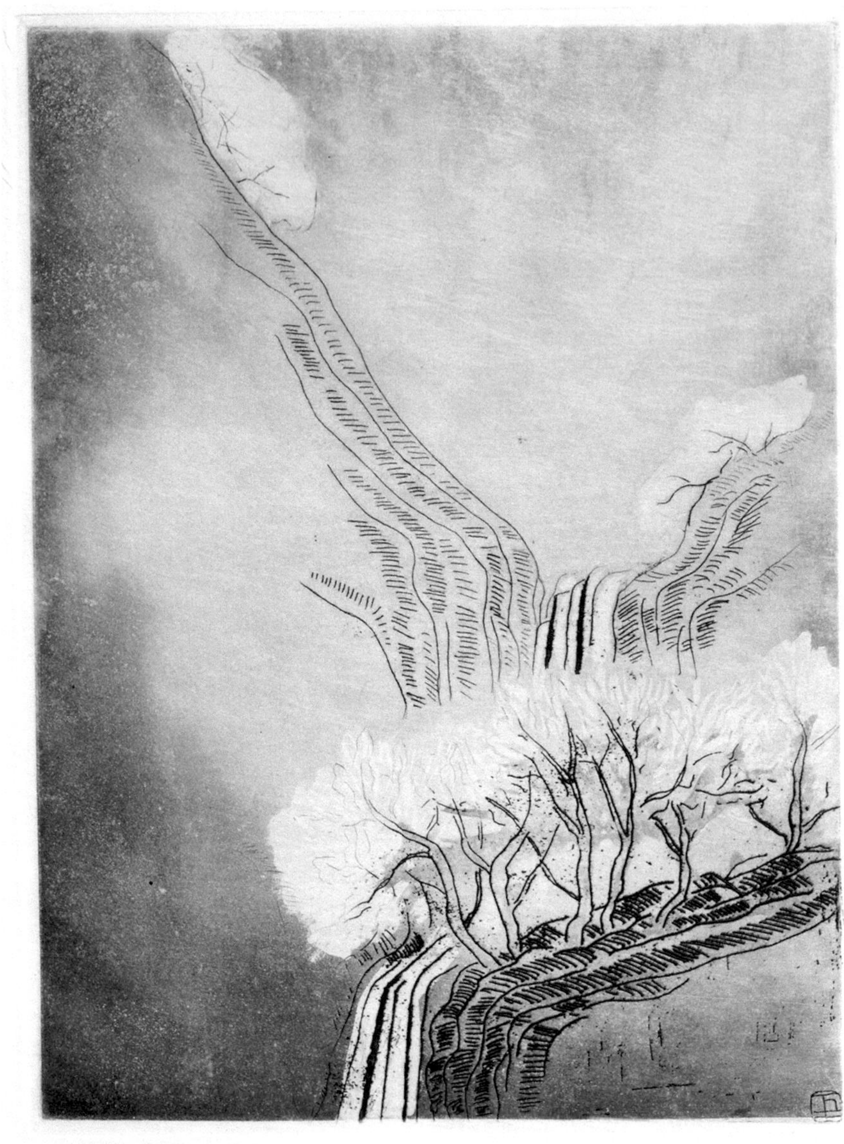

Figure 5. Etching accompanying "Peach Blossom Spring" (Taohua yuan ji 桃花源記), copperplate print by Chang Yu 常玉 for *Les poèmes de T'ao Ts'ien*, 1930, 15 x 9.2 cm. Courtesy of the Li Ching Cultural and Educational Foundation.

ally depicts only the most essential aspect of the story—the impossibility of rediscovering the utopian village's existence.

In all three of the illustrations, Chang Yu relies on the vertical composition of the etched plate to highlight intersecting planes of land and water, taking advantage of the unique medium's constraints—fine lines, perspectival depth indicated through repetitive shading, black and white color—to convey a mood of tranquility and solitude. The narrative detail provided by Liang Zongdai, inspired by Tao Qian's poems, are eschewed by Chang Yu, perhaps most simply because they cannot be technically expressed in etching form. But no matter the reason behind Chang Yu's deliberate artistic choices to leave out the focal moments of artistic community in the original poems and their French translations, the impact of these images is inarguably that they challenge the viewer's expectations of a landscape ink painting. The series of images reveals the capaciousness of transposition on multiple levels. First, Liang Zongdai's translations of Tao Qian's poetry into French should be read, as instructed by Valéry in his preface to readers, as a cultural bridge that brings together the "immense difference in languages" (Liang 1930). Valéry's confirmation of the quality of Liang's translation departs then from Liang's interpretation of the translations as transpositions, as his basic assumption is that poetry in translation is generally aesthetically inferior, diluted of almost all its original "substance." The last line of Valéry's preface also reveals an inherent weakness when it comes to the question of translation quality: Valéry can only vouch for Liang's translation by trusting the very subjective experience or what describes as the "literary sensation" of being "surprised and delighted" at reading Liang Zongdai's French translations.

Chang Yu's images, which play a crucial contribution in conveying the aesthetic sensibility of Tao Qian's poems (and Liang's translations) visually to French readers, by virtue of their visual medium, may not be perceived to suffer from the same consequences in translation as poetry. The concept of transposition warrants recognizing Chang Yu's dramatic decision to de-emphasize the human subjects at the center of Tao Qian's poems, which may have as much to do with material factors as philosophical or aesthetic concerns. Pang Xunqin, an artist who will be discussed in greater detail next in chapter 3, recounted Chang Yu's choice of medium for the project in his memoir: "A publisher once asked him to make four illustrations for the French version of a book of poems by Tao Yuanming, and he accepted. The project was delayed for quite some time until the publisher understood that

Sanyu could not afford the supplies to make the illustrations. The publisher sent him the copper plates, but he still did not have the tools. Finally, he came up with the idea of using his nail clip to make the copper plates" (translated in Wong 2011, 51; originally in Pang 1988, 85). The "chosen" medium of etching undermines both Liang and Valéry's claims of a seemingly spontaneous art process, instead emphasizing the painstaking intricacy required to produce the series of prints. Yet as transpositions, the visual images effectively present both elements of traditional Chinese landscape painting and poetry as well as the expressive freedom afforded by the change of artistic medium and geographical and historical context.

The etchings, read in the vein of Chang Yu's minimalist aesthetic, are situated in dialogue with the ink portrait of Tao Qian, which appears before the title page and is attributed to Qing dynasty painter Huang Shen (黃慎 1687–1772). If the ink portrait of the poet appears to fall in line with a more conventional expectation of a visual rendering of classical Chinese poetic identity, Chang Yu's etchings, particularly the illustration for "Begging for Food," make starkly obvious how much flexibility the artist has taken with the poetic flavor of Tao Qian's poetry to adopt an expressionist approach that draws on a pared-down interpretation of the awkwardness of being in an unknown environment and finding companionship unexpectedly. The collaborative act of poetic creation between friends that constitutes the narrative climax in the poems does not exist in the accompanying images, leaving the solitary individual who has been "driven out from hunger, I go / without knowing where my steps lead," on a meandering path approaching the unknown with no end in sight. This image of the poet-artist recluse as a starving wanderer resonates literally with Chang Yu's life story, and the visual starkness highlighted in the etchings is representative of Chang Yu's aesthetic philosophy, which in turn builds on Tao Qian's poetic style. The latter's minimalist approach is highlighted by Liang Zongdai in "Notes sur T'ao Ts'ien," his translator's note on Tao Qian's trademark poetic verse: "It is remarkable that, living in an era predominated by literary abundance and rich imagery, Tao Qian distinguished himself through simplicity and naturalness" (Liang 1930, 25). Valéry confirms Tao Qian's status as a literary "classic": "He does not think to exhaust his sensations. The classics do not describe what can only be viewed by the painter's specialized eyes, or what requires an entire dictionary to understand" (Liang 1930, 21).

These same traits are also associated with Chang Yu, who was referred to in one *Parisien libéré* headline as the "inventor of essentialism" for his limited use of color and "bare" aesthetic (Joffroy 1946). Comparing his style to western European painting, Chang Yu explained to *Parisien libéré* in 1946: "European painting is like a rich feast resplendent with roasts, fried foods, all sorts of meats of different shapes and colors. My paintings are, if you like, vegetables and fruits, and salads too, which can give you a break from your usual tastes in painting" (Joffroy 1946). Chang Yu highlights the hallowed legacy of European art, but not to glorify it but rather to propose something new and different. Describing his artistic process, Chang Yu explained, "I paint, then I simplify, and simplify again" (我先畫，然後再化簡它 . . . 再化簡它 Chen 1995, 41), and his approach to the human body also reflects this constant process of deconstruction and simplification.

REDEFINING BEAUTY THROUGH DISTORTION

Considering how Chang Yu moves away from the depiction of human subjects in his illustrations of Tao Qian's poetry, it may be surprising to learn that the bulk of his oil paintings are centered around the human body, specifically the nude female subject. As if directly rebuking the demand for objective realism, Chang Yu's nude paintings defy any attempt at scientific realism and instead defiantly invoke a new beauty standard based on distortion and the reimagining of human beauty. This kind of deliberate misreading of the human female body, by treating it as a site of distortion, openly challenges aesthetic discourse in the 1920s about realism, and here Chang Yu transposes the new healthy woman's body for health and science to bringing together the conflicting philosophies of *xieyi* versus the "life sketch" (xiesheng 寫生) and "realism" (xieshi 寫實), terminology that came to dominate art discourse at the beginning of the twentieth century. Calling the subjective mode of *xieyi* the "scapegoat for the decline of traditional painting" according to leading intellectuals such as Kang Youwei and Chen Duxiu, Shenqing Wu writes, "The expressionist approach of *xieyi* contrasts sharply with a newly introduced model of 'drawing from nature' (xiesheng 寫生), a visual principle that emphasized careful observation to obtain realistic effect, as well as an ascending modern cultural ideology associated with 'advanced' Western values" (Wu 2020, 217). The ultimate example of drawing from nature was the practice of nude painting from live models, which became a huge source of controversy among male artists, politicians, and intellectuals in the 1920s and 1930s, on two different but related levels. First, conservatives objected to it morally. In the fall of 1925, Shanghai city coun-cilor Jiang Huaisu wrote a letter of complaint to Minister of Education Duan Qirui: "Art school is not medical school. What importance is the structure of the human body and the process of life to art? Why does the appearance of the spirit have to be represented by a naked girl? Men and women all have human bodies. The students of the art academy are all male. Why can't you use male models?"[3] Published on September 26, 1925, Jiang Huaisu's letter was written in response to Liu Haisu's proud radio broadcast and print proc-lamation that he was the first educator to adopt the use of nude models in art instruction in China. Jiang demanded that Liu Haisu, who was the director of the Shanghai Academy of Art, be punished and that the practice of using female nude models be abolished. Jiang Huaisu's conservative position was eventually supported by Jiangsu warlord Sun Chuanfang, resulting in a tem-porary ban on nude models a year later.

As Jiang Huaisu's letter reveals, the debate over nude models was cen-tered particularly on the female body. He likened the female models to pros-titutes who "use their bodies as a living specimen," describing them as "shameless women" who "work naked in front of the crowd, reclining or lying down, bending into all sorts of positions." His letter also points out how realism played into the debate. Although some intellectuals were quick to embrace Western painting technique for its scientific depiction of the human body and new modes of representation, such as photography, for their ability to capture the real, Jiang Huaisu did not see the appeal of mixing art and science: "In recent years, pictures of nudes were sold on the street, in photographic or in painted form, and all look just as though they were real." By 1932, Fu Lei was affirming that "the use of nude models for research pur-poses in art studios has been formally and officially acknowledged" (Roberts 2010, 41), suggesting that the use of nude models needed some sort of scien-tific justification to overcome the moral objections.

Leo Ou-fan Lee traces the lineage between Western realism in Chinese art and the proliferation of images of "healthy" young women in pictorials such as *Liangyou*:

> To move from the portrait of a fashionable woman to that of a female nude generated a further anxiety for readers living in that still transitional age, because drawings of naked female bodies in traditional Chinese culture were found largely in pornographic books. The invention of photography and its adoption by the modern newspaper and magazine added a mimetic dimen-sion: the nude figure now looked like a real person. (Lee 1999, 73)

In this sense, the realist depiction of the female nude could be justified with the lofty goal of biological research. More recent scholarship on the bilingual monthly pictorial *Liangyou* has further elaborated on the representational figure of the healthy modern girl during the Republican era, including its relevance in women's athletics and in the popular scientific discourse surrounding the promotion of norms of modern femininity (Pickowicz et al. 2013). Images of the beautiful female body also frequently appeared in commercial art, such as advertisements and calendar posters (yuefenpai 月份牌), especially in 1930s Shanghai. Ellen Johnston Laing explains: "Where once Western models of feminine beauty in décolleté dress as advertising images were rejected as 'meaningless' or even scandalous to the Chinese eye, now seminudity and bare breasts are approved, despite the fact that seminudity and bare breasts had long been sanctioned in certain genres of Chinese traditional art" (Laing 2004, 219). By the time that Chang Yu was producing his nude oil paintings in the 1930s, the nude body was acceptable so long as it remained in the context of advocating a healthy standard of feminine beauty.

Throughout his career, Chang Yu produced more than 2,000 nude drawings and paintings. Moving from early pencil and ink illustrations to oil paintings, Chang Yu's work became increasingly sparse as he moved closer toward his trademark minimalist aesthetic, away from realist detail, similar to the way that the intaglio eau-forte medium of etching in *Les poèmes de T'ao Ts'ien* inevitably shaped Chang Yu's transposition of classical poetry into landscape images. In 1932, Johan Franco, Chang Yu's close friend and patron, summarized to viewers at his exhibition in Holland at J. H. de Bois in Haarlem the "essentialist" mode or what he called *le simplicisme* in his preface to Chang Yu's exhibition brochure: "At first, his work gives most viewers a feeling of artlessness and only after long and repeated viewing makes a sincere and serious impression. He knows how to depict the essence and often the humour of things with astonishingly little means" (Sotheby's Taiwan 1995, n.p.). Chang Yu's deliberate choice of the oil medium over ink baffled some art critics, such as the Dutch critic Jan D. Voskuil whose review of Chang Yu's 1933 exhibition at the Galérie van Lier in Amsterdam is cited by Eugene Wang: "Sanyu . . . attempts to create a certain effect in the oil medium . . . which would probably have been achieved more immediately with pencil or brush and ink. With the quick and sensitive hand of a Chinese calligrapher, he etches lines of flower baskets and horses out of the thick layer of oil. . . . It is hard to figure out though why he needs to resort to oil to accomplish his creative purpose" (Hearn and Smith 2001, 140). In critiques of Chang Yu's work, his classical training as a calligrapher repeatedly comes up as the primary way to interpret his paintings. As Voskuil's assessment demonstrates, Chang Yu's decision to use the oil medium was a perplexing one for viewers who saw it as incompatible with their preconceptions of his "creative purpose," the imagined spirit of spontaneity conveyed by his "Chinese" technique of sketch conceptualism.

The insistence on reading Chang Yu's oil paintings in the context of his calligraphy background was not limited to foreign critics but appeared equally in Chinese-language responses to his work. When Shanghai-based poet Shao Xunmei (邵洵美 1906–68) returned from a trip to Paris in the 1920s, he published an essay titled "A Treasure in the World of Modern Art" in the *Golden Chamber Monthly*, a pictorial journal run by his family's publishing company. The essay, which refers to Chang Yu as the "treasure," describes the allure of the artist's nude drawings: "All the lines of his nudes can speak, and they cry out the anguish of sex! . . . Look at the composition! The lines! . . . Simplicity affirmed by complexity! Complexity embraced by simplicity!" (Wong 2014, 13). The shared tendency to understand Chang Yu's nude oil paintings in terms of a traditional, minimalist Chinese aesthetic indicates a curious phenomenon; despite the artist's choice of a blatantly modern Western subject matter, critics persistently returned to the "mythic identity of image and writing" (Schaefer 2017, 8) that was believed to be the underpinning of literati culture, which largely overshadowed Chang Yu's contribution of depicting a decidedly distorted nonrealist body.

For Chinese colleagues like Shao Xunmei, recognizing Chang Yu's artistic lineage as Chinese was absolutely crucial, and Shao placed the entire burden of modern Chinese art on Chang Yu as the "artist who is claiming glory for China in the international art circles" (Shao 2006, 343). Shao even cited Chang Yu's wife, Marcelle Charlotte Guyot de la Hardrouyère, as added legitimacy: "Thankfully at this time we still have Chang Yu, who is staying in Paris. His wife is a Frenchwoman, also an artist, and every day she holds a brush and paints on her own canvas" (Shao 2006, 343). Chang Yu, whose reputation as a bohemian artist in the eyes of his Chinese compatriots was solidified by his marriage to a white Frenchwoman, was equally of interest to French audiences. In 1946, a headline in the newspaper *Parisien libéré* referred to Chang Yu by his French name, "Sanyu: Peintre chinois de Montparnasse, ne peint ni en francais ni en chinois" (Chang Yu: Chinese painter of Montparnasse who paints neither in French nor in Chinese) (Joffroy 1946), indicating that his identity as a Chinese artist was especially peculiar and appreciated in Montparnasse, in turn adding to Montparnasse's international cachet.

Back in Shanghai, Chang Yu's status as a French artist was promoted in the September 9, 1929 issue of *Pictorial Shanghai* (*Shanghai huabao* 上海畫報), which published a photograph of his painting *Nude on Tapestry*. Attributing the work to "French painter" (faguo huajia 法國畫家) Chang Yu, the accompanying caption in the journal, written by the journalist Ge Gongzhen (戈公振 1890–1935), lauded the recent painting for having appeared in a Paris art exhibit, and located the appeal of Chang Yu's paintings in the West in its distinctly "elements of oriental color" (dongfang secai yuansu 東方色彩元素) (*Shanghai huabao*, no. 9, September 9, 1929). Viewing Chang Yu's work and the reception of his art through the lens of transposition reveals why critics had trouble categorizing the painting as either Chinese or French, as the caption's appeal rests in the apparent tension between the label of the artist's purported nationality and his work's cultural characteristics.

Nude on Tapestry depicts a black-haired nude model with a stylish bob haircut, and is a representative example of Chang Yu's nude paintings from the 1930s. The artist's use of color is simple, and the focus of the composition is on the model's expansive white flesh, outlined in a black, calligraphic curve. The woman subject lies on top of a taupe colored, intricately illustrated textile that depicts various animals and nature scenes, and her short, cropped dark hair is reminiscent of the bob style popularized by the iconic Kiki de Montparnasse, muse of Man Ray and model for Chang Yu's contemporaries in Paris, the artists Tsuguharu Foujita (1886–1968) and Chaïm Soutine (1893–1943). Straight horizontal lines in the painting are gently offset by the rounded curves of the body's outline, and the human shape is reduced to torso and legs, aside from the facial detail of one elongated eye peeking through the crook of her elbow. Chang Yu's nude paintings of "cosmic thighs" traveled back to Shanghai and were fondly recounted, for instance, in a letter from modernist poet Xu Zhimo in Shanghai to Liu Haisu in Paris dated February 9, 1931 (Xu 1983, 145).

The space where the viewer is accustomed to seeing detail, or expects to find detail, is surprisingly free of facial or anatomical features. Instead, the viewer's attention is drawn to the minutiae of the fabric, Chang Yu's transposition of Chinese silk textile design; through the centrality of the textile, the painting invokes the invisible artist, whose studio mise-en-scène implies the active artist's agency, as confirmed by the model's steady eye contact with the viewer.

In another painting from the same period, *Reclining Nude*, Chang Yu dismisses outright any clear delineation between human figure and space, hav-

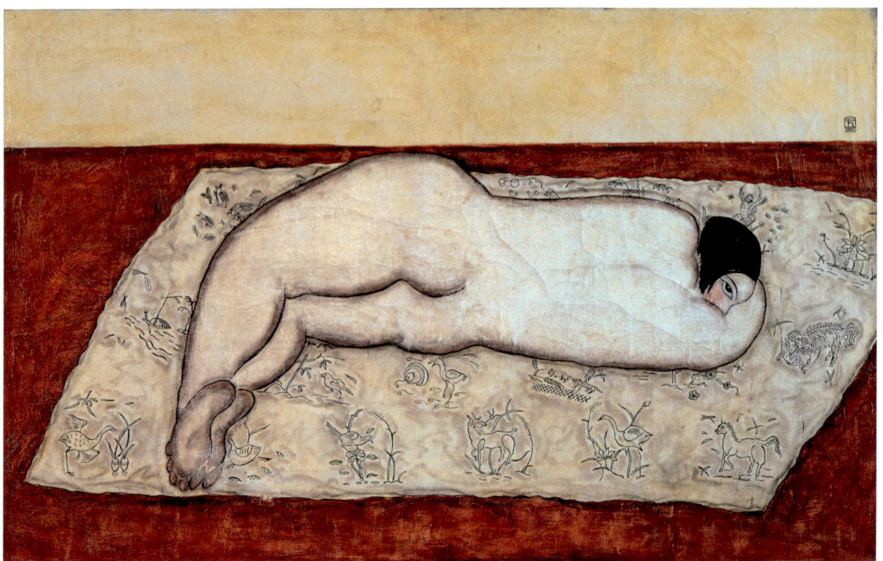

Figure 6. *Nude on Tapestry* (Huatan shang de cewo luonü 花毯上的側臥裸女), oil on canvas by Chang Yu 常玉, 1930s, 79 x 127.5 cm. Courtesy of the Li Ching Cultural and Educational Foundation.

ing gotten rid of the black outline of his *Nude on Tapestry*. The soft curves of the undulating body are offset by the sharp edges of the black tapestry, and the viewer is forced to make sense of the phallic-shaped rounded mass, to fill in and imagine the details that have purposely been left out. The faceless figure with her arms reaching behind her head is a fleshy mass of pink, and the only break in her smooth torso and curved limbs draws the viewer's eye to the pubic region: a lone black triangle that breaks up the otherwise almost amorphous surface.

As with most of Chang Yu's nudes, the female figure takes up almost all of the space in the composition. The force of the body's twisting movement does not come from the obvious movement created by the brush-line, or any underlying concern with three-dimensional perspective. The painting's flatness also allows Chang Yu to achieve the painting's aim of self-expression, and the body's natural vitality and relaxed spirit are captured by the artist's ability to capture the mood of emotional solitude at one particular moment in time. In an earlier article, I showed how Chang Yu used exaggeration and distortion of difference as way to advocate for the appreciation of a new stan-

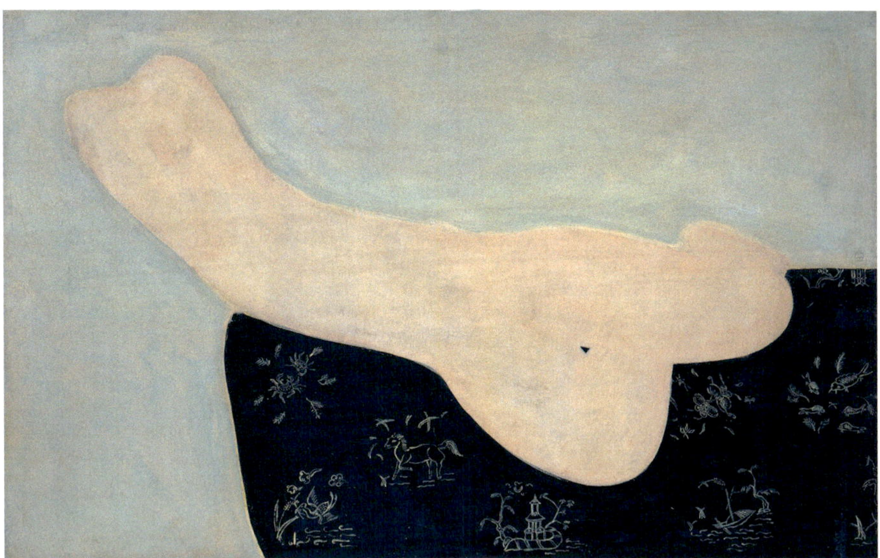

Figure 7. *Reclining Nude* (Quxian luonü 曲線裸女), oil on canvas by Chang Yu 常
玉, 1930s, 81 x 130 cm. Courtesy of the Li Ching Cultural and Educational
Foundation.

dard of aesthetic beauty; for the Chinese artist, white woman's otherness
enabled a process of self-definition for wenren affiliates (Chau 2017, 45).
Through distortion and exaggeration, Chang Yu's nude paintings of white
women challenge conventional ideals of feminine beauty and also the relationship between Western painting and realism.

At first glance, Chang Yu's nude paintings may seem imitative of works
by his European modernist contemporaries, such as the Cubist painters
Picasso and Georges Braque (recall, for example, the 1948 article that called
him a "second rate" Matisse). However, his connection to wenren culture,
combined with his belief in a subjective appreciation of aesthetic beauty,
invite a more nuanced interpretation. Eugene Wang's discussion of the relationship between realism (*xieshi*) and sketch conceptualism (*xieyi*), the anti-
thetical binary briefly discussed in my introduction on p. 23, is instructive in
exposing the fraying boundaries between these two representational modes.
Drawing on Xu Beihong's well-publicized comments on contemporary Chinese art written upon his return to China in 1926, Wang notes, "Realism
emphasizes images and objects, while conceptualism concerns itself with

mental states and emotions. Realism stems from close observation, while conceptualism thrives on sensation" (Hearn and Smith 2001, 111). In discussions about the development of modern Chinese art practices, realism and sketch conceptualism are frequently set up as two opposing categories. The latter, the key philosophy in traditional Chinese art, relies on the artist's spontaneity and expressivity that is possible only through literati amateurism. This subjective approach requires an interaction that calls for the viewer's active participation and interpretation. Realism, by contrast, is cast as a modern, scientific approach, by which the artist faithfully conveys his or her objective vision of reality. In this mode, the artist's skill is evaluated by achieving technical *gongbi* verisimilitude, not the ability to capture the subject's spiritual essence or "intention."

Surely Chang Yu was well aware of the intellectual debates about nude models taking place in China, because he was close friends with Xu Beihong and stayed connected through his relationships with other Chinese artists and writers, such as Pang Xunqin and Shao Xunmei, who were either passing through or residing in Paris. And the issue of race was never far from his mind. In 1945, Chang Yu published a review of a Picasso exhibition in the *Parisien libéré* titled "Opinions d'un peintre chinois sur Picasso," in which he recounts a conversation with a female observer about whether the nose and eyes can move on a human face. He tells her that Picasso never claimed that the painting in question is supposed to represent a certain "Mme la comtesse X" or any actual member of the female sex for that matter. When the woman protests that the God who created the human body created a beautiful not ugly body, Chang Yu retorts, "Madame, beauty is not a thing fixed by law. It is merely a matter of habit. If for example you lived in the wild in Africa, your clothing and your beauty would be, in the eyes of the blacks, like how you see Picasso's paintings. It is not that you are ugly, but that your beauty is not what they are accustomed to" (Sanyu 1945). Chang Yu argues that in order to appreciate something unfamiliar, an observer must imagine oneself in another's shoes and then look back at his or her own reflection as Other.

One can imagine that Chang Yu experienced this defamiliarization process himself as an outsider in France and that now he was able to appreciate a new kind of beauty, markedly distinct from what he was accustomed to in China. This re-created dialogue between the artist and the female viewer, who is presumably a white French woman, concludes with a surrealist prophecy of race:

> Deformation in Picasso's painting is only the first step. Our race is too ancient, our bodies too frail, our lives too short. We must find a new God. He will give us eternal youth and power. . . . We will be able to live in the air or underwater. . . . We will go to Asia like we go to Versailles, we will spend a weekend on the moon. Humans will be made however we wish, whether it's with four eyes, two in the front, two in the back, or with four arms or four legs. In terms of size, they could be as big as King Kong. (Sanyu 1945)

In Chang Yu's fantasy, Asia acquires the status of an international tourist destination like Versailles. His aestheticization of race begins as a way of justifying Picasso's disfigured human subjects and ends up as a grotesque vision of the new posthuman race. The title of this review recalls the subheadings of the aforementioned article about Chang Yu that appeared a year later in the same Parisian newspaper: "peintre chinois de Montparnasse" (Chinese painter of Montparnasse) followed by "ne peint ni en français ni en chinois" (paints neither in French nor in Chinese). The significance of Chang Yu's opinion of Picasso hinges on his identity as an ethnic Chinese ("un peintre chinois"). Amid a public sphere awash with French opinions of Picasso's artwork, readers want to know, what does a Chinese artist think about Picasso?

Chang Yu anticipates the curiosity about the Chinese perspective by bringing together two unlikely figures—the controversial Cubist Spanish expatriate painter and the ancient Chinese philosopher. Alluding to Laozi's famous anecdote about Butcher Ding in the foundational Daoist text the *Zhuangzi*, Chang Yu writes: "I imagine Picasso when he places his brush on the canvas. It reminds me of one of Laozi's anecdotes" (Je m'imagine Picasso quand il fait jouer son pinceau sa toile. Il me rappelle cette anecdote de Lao-Tseu; Sanyu 1945). The story he cites is about the concept of *wu wei*, action through inaction, or trying not to try. Likening the butcher's knife to the artist's tool of paintbrush, Chang Yu emphasizes the perspective of the butcher, who no longer feels or sees the animals about to be slaughtered: "I don't feel the animals, I don't see anything, and the knife in my hand, I don't feel that either" ("je ne sens pas les bêtes, je ne vois rien et mon couteau dans ma main, je ne le sens pas non plus"). The story illustrates the achievement of harmony and efficacy through effortlessness; but in Chang Yu's interpretation, it's about endorsing a new way of understanding and appreciating art. Complaining that complicated theorizing about Picasso's work has rendered it more confusing and muddled, Chang Yu pushes for a return to simplicity. The reference to Laozi allows Chang Yu to share his vision for the future of painting, in which the brave artist breaks habits and shatters viewer expectations by the creation of something new, while also providing curious readers with insider knowledge of a Chinese painter's perspective: "The artist creates the human form just like God does, he creates the world he wants" (L'artiste crée la forme humaine, c'est comme le Dieu. Il crée le monde qu'il veut). This isn't really what the Butcher Ding is saying about the beauty of ease or habit, but Chang Yu brings together two seemingly disparate icons to celebrate the courage of Picasso—and any artist for that matter—to redefine beauty and nature.

THOSE POOR CHRYSANTHEMUMS

The image of the female nude in modern art was openly debated and criticized along moralistic lines among Chinese intellectuals, leading Lin Yutang to explain to Western readers in 1935 that "with the seclusion of women, the exposure of the female form, both in art and in everyday life, seems indecorous to the extreme, and some of the masterpieces of Western painting in the Dresden Gallery are definitely classed under the category of pornography. The fashionable modern Chinese artists who are aping the Western dare not say so, but there are Continental artists who frankly admit the sensuous origin of all art and make no secret of it" (Lin 1939, 149–50). As a subject of visual representation, the chrysanthemum flower may appear to fall on the opposite side of the spectrum, given its cultural legacy in Chinese art history and the long tradition of flower-and-vase paintings in Chinese art. However, in Chang Yu's paintings, the two motifs allow Chang Yu to entirely subvert viewer expectations of the nude and still-life genres, since both the nude and the chrysanthemum serve as ideal visual icons for experimenting with the art of transposition.

In classical Chinese painting, "bird and flower painting" (hua niao hua 花鳥畫) as a formal category emerged in the tenth century and reached its height of popularity during the Song dynasty. Characterized by attention to detail over that in modes of landscape painting and figure painting, the genre's use of color varied in relation to each artist's approach to *xieyi* and *xiesheng,* and which kinds of meanings could be suggested by visible surfaces and colors. Composition was also a significant point of comparison in conveying both motion and the preservation of a moment in time. Comparing the act of artistic composition to the poetic process, art historian Richard Barnhart claims that for the greatest artists, "a quality of mind that perceives meanings in phenomena" is required in addition to skill (Barnhart 1983, 31), and certainly Chang Yu's experiments with the well-established genre of bird and flower painting indicate a fluency with expectations regarding color, composition, and the outside world.

The chrysanthemum was cherished by classical poets such as Tao Qian, and has a rich history in Chinese painting.[4] The thirteen-book canonical painting instruction manual *Mustard Seed Garden Manual of Painting* (*Jieziyuan huazhuan* 芥子園畫傳), which appeared between 1679 and 1701 during the rise of the Qing dynasty, was intended as a guide for beginning painters, and included sections devoted to each of the "four gentlemen," popular painting motifs in Song literati culture. The chrysanthemum was renowned for being "defiant of frost and triumphant in autumn," for its lingering fragrance, and the endurance of its numerous petals: "The chrysanthemum is a flower of proud disposition; its color is beautiful, its fragrance lingers. To paint it, one must hold in his heart a conception of the flower whole and complete. Only in this way can that mysterious essence be transmitted in a painting" (Sze and Wang 1956, 435). Following pages of principles and rules to be memorized on painting stems, flowers, leaves, and buds, the manual provides detailed illustrations and diagrams of multiple views depicting flowers in various stages of blossom.

For Western audiences familiar with the eighteenth-century chinoiserie aesthetic, the significance of the chrysanthemum in Chinese culture could not have been lost. For example, the *Decorator and Furnisher*, a late nineteenth-century American monthly publication based in New York, featured an article titled "The Chrysanthemum in Chinese Art" (1889) in which the unnamed author informs readers of the flower's fabled power in China "to have the power of conferring immortality" (22). While Chang Yu's poetic ode to the chrysanthemum that opened this chapter also touched on the theme of mortality and the divergence of everyday practices, Chang Yu's chrysanthemum paintings remove the flowers from their natural environment, playing with the mythological notion that the blossoms are somehow immune from decay and the passage of time. In his oil paintings of chrysanthemums, Chang Yu adopted the Western convention of grounding his flowers in a vase, unlike blossoms depicted in the classical tradition, which typically appear on the branch as if in nature. Like the nude model posing atop a piece of draped fabric, the chrysanthemum blossoms in their pot are emphasized by Chang Yu, who points out the mediated posing of the artistic subject in an unfamiliar context. Yet the flowers remain a subject for intense contemplation, placed squarely in the center of his paintings atop a flat surface.

Chang Yu's 1940s-1950s oil *White Chrysanthemum in a Blue and White Jardiniere* is just one example of the numerous chrysanthemum paintings that the artist produced beginning in the 1930s. Painted on masonite, a smoother surface than canvas, the work's vertical orientation draws the viewer's eyes up and down the length of the chrysanthemum plant's long stems, reaching down to a shallow, rectangular blue and white ceramic pot atop a wooden stand. Defying the viewer's expectations of attention to detail in the still-life genre, in which the subject matter is seemingly magnified, Chang Yu's use of color is most striking here, as the chrysanthemum in its entirety—including blossoms, stems, and leaves—is painted all in white, which stands in dramatic contrast with the deep red background and the yellow expanse on which the jardiniere rests. The base of the chrysanthemum disappears into the white interior of the planter, and while the jardiniere is rendered with attention to perspectival dimension, the flowers themselves are surprisingly flattened, the blossoms speckled with light red flecks and creating a detailed impression of Chinese paper-cutting or lace doilies. The bright yellow surface at the bottom of the painting is divided from the red background with a simple, thick, light yellow horizontal line, inviting the viewer to ponder the tenuous relationship between surface, foreground, and background. Chang Yu's highly visible brush strokes do not attempt to blend the colors smoothly but instead show the subtle variations of white, red, and yellow. The vibrant colors of this oil painting give it more vitality than most of Chang Yu's other chrysanthemum paintings, and here the sense of drama arises from the vividness of the table and the background—not the relatively muted blossoms, leaves, and stems of the actual plant.

Chang Yu's repeated efforts to depict the flower prized for its golden color in new ways indicate his interest in and attentiveness to exploring the chrysanthemum's potential, as a challenge to the vigor and vitality carefully prescribed in the *Mustard Seed Painting Manual*: "Brush should be pure and noble, and one should be careful to avoid too few leaves with too many flowers, vigorous stalks on a weak main stem, flowers not properly attached to stems, petals without peduncles, a clumsy brush, dead color, a confused conception and thus an obstruction (of mind and brush, heart and hand)" (Sze and Wang 1956, 440–41). Chang Yu's chrysanthemum paintings demonstrate that "a

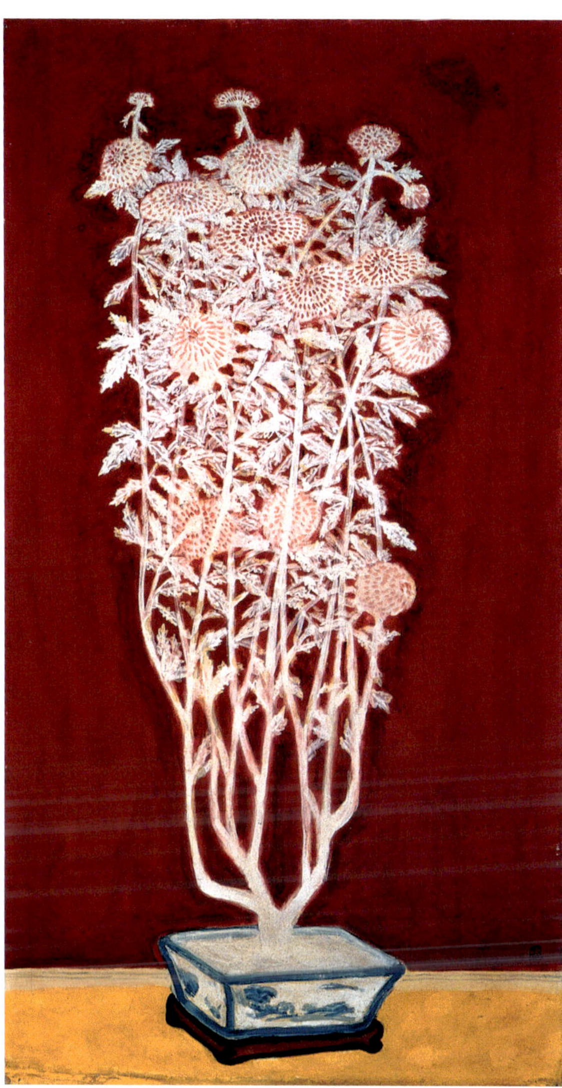

Figure 8. *White Chrysanthemum in a Blue and White Jardinière* (Qing huapen zhong shengkai de juhua 青花盆中盛開的菊花), oil on canvas by Chang Yu 常玉, 1940s/1950s, 152 x 78 cm. Courtesy of the Li Ching Cultural and Educational Foundation.

confused conception," what may be initially misinterpreted as an obstruction, might constitute a cleaner, clearer vision of the essence of things. Furthermore, the chrysanthemum paintings are a reminder of the incommensurability of two cultures. Chang Yu's concern, which he eloquently and succinctly expressed in his poem, reveal a crucial challenge in the project of intercultural encounter, but this disparity, once recognized and addressed, can inspire artistic creation and bring about deeper aesthetic appreciation.

On July 10, 2020, *White Chrysanthemum in a Blue and White Jardiniere* was auctioned for $24.6 million at Christie's Hong Kong. Because of the record-high prices Chang Yu's paintings have been selling for on auction, academic attention to his work has extended beyond the borders of Taiwan, and recent mainland PRC publications by Hu Yixun (2013) and Du Dakai (2012), for instance, insist that more attention should be paid to the "lonely artist." In April 2021, Sotheby's Hong Kong held an auction of five pieces in a collection titled "ICONS: Masterpieces from across Time and Space," featuring a Song dynasty wooden sculpture of the bodhisattva Avalokiteshvara, along with a bronze bust by Alberto Giacometti, a self-portrait of Zhang Daqian, a matador painting by Picasso and Chang Yu's oil painting *Nude with a Pekingese*. The auction catalogue calls the two latter works, *Buste de matador* (1970) and *Nu avec pékinois* (1950s) "important post-war works by two pioneers" and claims that the paintings link East and West, in particular "looking at Asian modern art as it grew from a regional to a global phenomenon and redefined modern art as a whole from an Asian perspective" (Sotheby's 2021, 22). The pairing in fact serves as the basis for the auction's theme as a whole, which promises that "to see these two masterpieces is to see the fates of the two artists intertwined across time and space," but it's not clear how their fates are "intertwined," considering that Chang Yu's fame has not reached even close to Picasso's (Sotheby's 2021, 26).

The auction houses do help perpetuate the myth of Paris, by writing, as curator Melissa Walt does for Sotheby's, "Paris, then, transformed the works of Sanyu, Chu Teh-Chun and Zao Wou-Ki. New media, forms, and styles have suggested avenues of creative exploration for generations of Chinese artists, each in their own way. Of equal importance, Paris allowed some of them the distance and confidence to re-evaluate their relationship to traditional Chinese painting and create bodies of work that pay homage to that past even as they speak to the present" (Walt 2018). The romantic image of Paris promoted on the auction circuit dovetails conveniently with the same image promoted by art institutions and embraced by art lovers. This chapter has shown, however, that Chang Yu's career and artist persona challenge the promise of expressive freedom associated with Chinese artists studying abroad in Paris during the first half of the twentieth century, during a period when cultural difference was seen as desirable and liberatory, but also something to be contained, and made recognizable or easily identifiable. Su Shi's oft-cited poem about the relationship between life and art in this chapter's epigraph was composed to accompany a painting of a plum branches in blossom, and the poem continues past its famous first lines, "Poetry and painting share a single goal—clean freshness and effortless skill" (Mair 1994, 249). Chang Yu's painting philosophy similarly aspired to the goal of appearing effortless, but his creative acts of transposition required skills of negotiation, strategy, and active engagement with multiple sets of audiences.

CHAPTER 3

Fu Lei the Critic

Looking at paintings is like judging beautiful women: their spirit and
bone structure are more important than their flesh and limbs.
Contemporaries who judge masterpieces are certain to look first for
formal likeness, then coloring, and then the subjects illustrated; and
this is definitely not the proper method of connoisseurship.

—TANG HOU 湯垕, HUA LUN 畫論, YÜAN DYNASTY, IN MEISHU CONGSHU 美術
叢書 SERIES III.7.IA 3A–3B, COMPILED BY TENG SHIH 鄧實SHEN-CHOU
KUO-KUANG SHE, 1923, AND TRANSLATED IN BUSH 1978, 127

Aboard the ocean liner *André Lebon* on the way to France in 1928, the obser-
vant twenty-year-old Fu Lei was drawn to some of the ship's more colorful
passengers. Describing an English musician playing the piano, Fu Lei noticed
the withered backs of the old man's hands, veins pulsing: "Even though his
fingers were a bit stiff, he was old but proved himself to be an impressive
musician" (Fu 2000, 31). Fu Lei's one complaint—that the man never finished playing an entire song—was quickly followed by his modest suspicion,
"This is probably because we—the ship's passengers—are all mere commoners [fanfu suzi 凡夫俗子] who can't understand what can be called the reasons for music, so we aren't worth wasting his precious energy, to perform
refined music would be like 'playing the *qin* to cows' [duiniu tanqin 對牛彈
琴], right?" Fu Lei's letter "Traveling Companions" provides critical analysis
of the implications of the artist as performer in relation to a public audience,
and was published as part of a series of travel letters titled *Letters on the Way
to France* (*Faxing tongxin* 法行通信) on his way from Shanghai to Marseille.
The collection of letters, consisting of a total of fifteen pages, first appeared
serially from January 2 to February 9, 1928 in the first issues of *Contribution
Daily* (*Gongxian xunkan* 貢獻旬刊), a journal edited by the brothers Sun Fuxi

and Sun Fuyuan that was published once every ten days. Unlike the travel accounts of similar voyages made by Fu Lei's literary contemporaries Xu Zhimo and Ba Jin, in which the writers focus more on imparting the details of their trip and their new surroundings than their own personal reflections or practical applications of that experience, Fu Lei's letters to curious readers in China relay the experience of overseas travel and include his pointed opinions and observations about food and meals aboard the ship, ship passengers, seabirds, and his lamentations about missing his beloved mother and friends.

Born in Jiangsu on April 7, 1908 and educated in Shanghai, Fu Lei participated in the labor and anti-imperialist demonstrations of the May Thirtieth Movement as a student at Datong University in 1925. He studied art theory and art criticism in France from 1928 to 1932, during which he attended lectures on art and literature at the Louvre and the Sorbonne, served as Liu Haisu's personal translator, and lived in the suburbs with another young Chinese artist, the painter Liu Kang (劉抗 1911–2004). After returning to China, he taught French and art history at the Shanghai Academy of Art, which was founded by his close friend Liu Haisu, before turning to work as a translator and critic. Labeled a rightist in 1957, Fu Lei, along with his wife Zhu Meifu, committed suicide at the beginning of the Cultural Revolution. In the literary canon, Fu Lei is best remembered for his two roles as an ideal father figure and linguistic translator, although his expertise and interests also included classical music and art. His *Family Letters* (*Fu Lei jia shu* 傅雷家書), the bestselling compilation consisting of over two hundred letters he wrote to his son Fu Cong (傅聰 1934–2020) between 1954 and 1966, share advice and impart knowledge on topics like music, literature, and romantic and familial relationships.

Fu Lei first began translating French short stories while he was abroad and was later celebrated for his prolific work as a linguistic translator, including his 1937 translation of Romain Rolland's revolutionary novel *Jean-Christophe*. He presented his esteemed theory of translation in the 1951 preface to the second edition of his translation of Balzac's *Le pere Goriot*, which broke from his predecessor Yan Fu's (嚴復 1854–1921) "three principles" (xin, da, ya, 信達雅 "faithfulness, comprehensibility and elegance") (Chan 2004, 69). Instead, Fu Lei argued for the importance of *shensi* 神似, or likeness in spirit, an aesthetic philosophy rooted in traditional painting: "In terms of effect, a translation, like an imitated painting, should seek after resemblance in spirit rather than in form" (Chan 2004, 102). The annual Fu Lei Translation Award, inaugurated in 2009 and established by the French embassy to China, continues to commemorate his contributions to the field of translation by recognizing the best works that have been translated from French into Chinese.

There is no other well-known modern Chinese writer who has written so prolifically on both Western and Chinese literature and art, and rather than promote the more accepted forms of patriotism such as the essay or even fiction, Fu Lei chose to champion the cause of modern art, an astounding move for someone who was not an artist himself. This chapter reveals how Fu Lei's observations about cultural misunderstanding and exchange inform his conceptualization of the ideal purpose of art and the ideal artist. In particular, his essays on art criticism, "La crise de l'art chinois moderne" (1931; Fu 2018) and "Xunqin's Dream" (1932; Fu 2000), when read alongside *Letters on the Way to France* (1928; Fu 2000), reveal that for Fu Lei the art of transposition was something that could bring together aesthetic appreciation and pleasure with personal vision. While Su Shi's poem about painting did not discriminate between reader or viewer and critic, for Fu Lei, there was an important distinction between the two roles. As an art critic, Fu Lei developed his practice of transposition as a way to recognize cultural difference toward the path to intercultural appreciation. His published letters, addressed to Chinese readers back in Shanghai, acted as an intimate media platform for Fu Lei to voice his ambivalent attitude toward deeper cultural contradictions revealed in everyday modes of expression like music, games, and food from abroad.

In "Traveling Companions," Fu Lei's affinity for music shines through, as does his empathy for the artist who toils in vain to be understood and appreciated by an oblivious audience. By invoking the Chinese idiom about an artist's ability to find the right mode of engagement with his audience, Fu Lei reveals his own position as critic, someone who navigates the in-between space that separates the musical performer from the cows. Fu Lei's attentiveness to language can already be detected, as he details a conversation with his Russian shipmate about their fellow passenger, an older Englishman who turns out to be the musician. When Fu Lei interprets the elderly man's hesitant physical maneuvering on the deck stairs as a sign of old age, the Russian friend informs Fu Lei that the Englishman's problem is he has "too many reasons for talking" before further elaborating: "This Englishman says that he is a musician, *musician* [original in English, ital. added], he can speak all kinds of languages, not only *European language* [original in English, ital.

addcd]; his Chinese is good although he's forgotten it now. He also says that he's studied everything, philosophy, literature . . . he's learned almost everything." Upon hearing the Russian friend's explanation, Fu Lei concludes, "I finally came to understand what he meant by 'I think this is because he has too many reasons for talking'" (Fu 2000, 31). The musician's far-reaching expertise and linguistic abilities greatly impresses Fu Lei, whose own sense of insecurity about insufficient linguistic expertise and Western knowledge is heightened in contrast. As he works to converse with his Russian friend, Fu Lei tries to interpret the bodily movements of this English musician, but is then corrected by his friend who provides crucial biographical context in order to critique the elderly man's learnedness as a backhanded compliment. An additional layer of mediation is added by the Russian friend who interprets the Englishman's identity, by using the word "himself" (ziji 自己) to preface each of the musician's self-proclaimed skills. Furthermore, the conversation raises the larger question of why people talk, and what it means to have "too many reasons" to talk.

The experience with the English musician, beyond its obvious significance in signaling Fu Lei's apparent interest in language and music, is formative because it encourages Fu Lei to recognize a key contribution that he offers as an interpreter and critic. He may not have the cosmopolitan savvy of the seasoned musician yet, but neither does Fu Lei see himself as one of the common "cows." Heartened by the promise of a potential reunion one day in Paris, the friendship takes a dramatic and unexpected nosedive when Fu Lei's Russian shipmate sets him straight again—this time, by informing him that the father-daughter pair are actors, as seen by their props. Fu Lei admits near the end of "Traveling Companions," albeit reluctantly, that "they did have a kind of condescending expression [qingshi biaoqing 輕視表情]. I couldn't help but remember that once Shakespeare too was nothing more than a traveling performer" (Fu 2000, 33). After lamenting the dismal state of world affairs, Fu Lei declares, "I didn't necessarily feel any kind of emotion for him or admire his musical skills or talent, nor am I saying he could be the next Shakespeare. I didn't harbor any such fantasy, only I felt that mankind in this world is too horrible! Their acting eyes and praising mouths, ah, ah!" Concluding this section of the letter, he adds by way of reflection, "After writing this, I read it once and discovered that in my description of this musician, there are many moments where I couldn't avoid indulging in affection, contradicting what I eventually said. But forgive me—after all, I am one who makes a living out of contradiction and conflict!" (我本是矛盾冲突中討生活的人! Fu 2000, 33). As this chapter demonstrates, according to Fu Lei, the role of a worldly critic depends on the recognition of contradiction and conflict, productive elements necessary in the process of intercultural exchange. In this case, by likening the old man to Shakespeare, Fu Lei reconciles his aesthetic appreciation for the musician's performative talent as artistic skill and creative expression with his Russian friend's more literal understanding of acting as having no value other than pretense.

Until now, Fu Lei's contributions to art and music theory have received relatively little attention, perhaps because his early writings are difficult to categorize in literary historiography, and his time abroad did not result in a set career path upon returning to China. Nicolai Volland argues that Fu Lei's unproductive stint in Paris led to professional setbacks down the road back in Shanghai: "His failure to obtain a regular degree from the Université de Paris after three and a half years of study turned out to be a major obstacle for a career in the increasingly professionalized world of teaching and research" (Volland 2014, 134). Describing Fu Lei as embodying the "aura of a mandarin connoisseur" (Wang 2017, 656), Guangchen Chen writes, "Today Fu is remembered mainly as a translator; this reputation has prevented people from recognizing the full range of his cosmopolitan vision. Apart from the fact that his translations have been immensely influential, there is another reason why he is known as a translator: his career was eclectic but fragmentary, and presented a mode of intellectual engagement that is difficult to define" (Wang 2017, 655). Instead of reading his time in Paris as unproductive, I argue that the "fragmentary" experiences of his stay in Paris provided Fu Lei with the opportunity to develop his ideas about intercultural encounters and conflict. In particular, my analysis builds on Chen Liu's assertion that Fu Lei's "observations were first and foremost based on his perception of the inter-communicability between various forms of expression, the correlation between various senses, or synesthesia. He delighted in and benefited from unrestrained explorations in the world of literature, art, and music" (Liu 2017, 359). By carefully examining Fu Lei's writing on art, the ideal artist, and the role of the art critic, this chapter looks more closely at this "eclectic but fragmentary" body of work, not with the aim of defining Fu Lei's mode of intellectual engagement but rather to show how he used transposition to expose the porous boundaries of artistic fields and media forms.

The letters and essays in this chapter suggest that Fu Lei's attitude toward the relationship between China and France is more ambivalent than has generally been accepted. In particular, my discussion pushes back on Guangchen Chen's assessment of Fu Lei as a "Chinese" critic: "His interpretations shed a typically Chinese light on European texts, paintings, and music; enrich the expression of both cultures; and unveil their surprising parallels" (Wang 2017, 651). Chen concludes, "Fu's description of Western art was accurate and scholarly, but his judgments, Chinese" (Wang 2017, 654). Fu Lei may have promoted the image of the artist who turned back to China, but this does not mean that his judgments were especially "Chinese." In these examples of transposition across media, time, and languages, Fu Lei aimed to highlight cultural difference and contradiction by emphasizing the intercommunicability of senses; but as a critic, his artistic and cultural judgments failed to make a lasting intellectual impact, probably because they were not perceived as Chinese enough.

ART AS DIRECT ENCOUNTER

Analyzing the pros and cons of at-sea dining in a letter titled "Tidbits from Life at Sea" (Haishang shengya lingshi 海上生涯零拾), Fu Lei expressed dissatisfaction with the tea and coffee on board, his distaste for half-cooked dishes, and an affinity for ice cream. He introduced readers to a new kind of mango fruit (which he likes), and a fruit he doesn't know the Chinese word for (manquostant in original, referring most likely to the mangosteen fruit). Many of his explanations were written specifically for his Shanghai readers, such as the clarification that what was called "yellow pear" (huangli 黃梨) in Singapore is what Shanghaiers call *poluomi* 坡羅密 (Fu 2000, 48). He patiently informed readers that "dessert" is what Westerners call *dianxin*, the sweets that come after a meal, and complains repeatedly about the coffee that follows each meal, which pales in comparison to the coffee he was accustomed to in Shanghai (Fu 2000, 48). However, Fu Lei's most striking observation is not about the poor quality of food or these linguistic curiosities, but rather about the dining room menu, as he described the mundane yet nuanced process of scanning the menu: "Every time the announcement for the dining room comes on, the first thing is to grab the menu and take a look. If I see Roti-this Roti-that, I expect the worst, or Mouton-this Mouton-that, not for me. By the time the first cold plate or soup is finished, I'm already sick of looking at that menu. But as I await the arrival of the second course, I read it leisurely as I would a magazine" (Fu 2000, 48–49). Fu Lei's narration hints at the challenges of reading in a second language, as readers can infer his struggle with identifying the menu items in French while recognizing certain keywords indicating an exotic mode of preparation or type of meat. The observation also fits neatly with the overarching theme of contradiction in Fu Lei's writing, as he recognizes how quickly anticipation turns to distaste, transforms into boredom, then returns to interest and appreciation.

Fu Lei's internal conflict about the relationship between images and text, and how they shape viewer expectations, gets highlighted as he recounts in the letter: "As I wait for the food to come, I look at the landscape illustrations on the menu, but seeing those same four or five images repeatedly gets boring fast—whether it's Pothos a Saigon, Paul-Lecat a Port-Said, the Xiannongtan [Altar of Agriculture] in Beijing, or the Louis Bridge in France [Pont Saint-Louis] . . . the names of the dishes are written below, like this, main course on one line, side dishes on another line. For example, roast beef with potatoes would read cooked beef on one line, followed by roasted potatoes on the next, so even though there are only three dishes, they take up a full page, giving off the appearance of a little banquet. Humph, too bad, it only looks good but doesn't taste good!" (Fu 2000, 49). Fu Lei is especially interested in the alignment of the menu because of its deceptively misleading nature, giving off the impression that the meal is much more complex and tasty than it is. His professed anxiety of sitting in the ship's dining room waiting for the next course to arrive is reminiscent of Eileen Chang's characters in the short story "Sealed Off" (Fengsuo 封鎖, 1943) who, as passengers stuck on the tramcar during a wartime air raid in Shanghai, are desperate to read anything they can find: "They simply had to fill this terrifying emptiness—otherwise, their brains might start to work. Thinking is a painful business" (Goldblatt and Lau 2007, 190). Fu Lei's analysis of the viewing experience, even though the ultimate result of eating is disappointing, highlights how images that seem compelling (either landmarks on their route, or iconic images of China and France) can fail to deliver. Yet visual images and appearances are incredibly powerful in their ability to entice, heighten anticipation, and entertain.

Viewing the ship dining menu as a work of art may be a bit of a stretch, but Fu Lei's account of the inherent contradiction and conflict that accompanies one's encounter with new and unfamiliar views illustrates the importance of art as site of encounter and reflection. In 1932, Fu Lei identified imitation as a main problem with contemporary Chinese art in an essay titled "I Will Say It Again: Where Are We headed? . . . To the Depths!" which was published in *L'Art* (*Yishu xunkan*, 1931–32). He criticized artists for either copying "the ancients" or foreigners, declaring provocatively, "It may sound like blasphemy, but when contemporary Chinese artists paint in Western styles, most of them have forgotten about themselves" (如果我說一句冒瀆的話，現代的中國洋畫家在創作的時候，多少是忘掉了自我 Fu 2017, 189). His criticism about the artist's cultural identity echoes the difficulty and discomfort that critics faced when trying to categorize Chang Yu's work. The trope of "forgetting" oneself in both cases is perceived to be linked to being outdated and out of step with socially ascribed conditions.

Emphasizing that the ideal art not only reflects the present time (biaoxian shidai 表現時代) but also predicts the future (yuyan shidai 預言時代), Fu Lei compares art to "a mirror that never reflects a real image of the actual thing," but instead allows for the artist's individual self-expression (藝術是一面鏡子，但絕不會映出事物的現實相 Fu 2017, 189). Encounters, even conflicts, between different views and experiences is what produces art, and gives meaning to the human experience. Fu Lei voiced his "hope that artists can experience this kind of transformation, only that on their life's journey they gain one more experience, especially one that they may have spurned in the past. This allows the different life experiences and world-views of the East and the West—the primary factors that contribute to art—to have a more direct and meaningful encounter" (我所以希望藝術家有這種轉變，無非是要他在人生的途程上，多一番經歷─尤其是一向所唾棄的經歷。而且，由這種生命的體驗上，更可以是東西種不同的人生觀，宇宙觀─藝術的主要成因─做一番正面的衝突 Fu 2017, 190). According to Fu Lei, the vital act of turning-changing (zhuanbian 轉變) one's position (transposition) is possible only through the artist's experience of conflict and encounter; a shift in perspective and positionality is what makes self-expression possible.

Fu Lei's essay "I Will Say It Again" ended on an anticipatory note: "Art should be prophetic and suggestive. But what should it foretell? What should it suggest? At this point I cannot yet say" (藝術應當預言，應當暗示。但預言什麼？暗示什麼？此刻還談不到 Fu 2017, 190).[1] Fu Lei used the French phrase "en attendant," an alternative take on Valéry's 1933 Musée de Jeu de Paume exhortation about China as "on n'est pas en train," both descriptions of modern Chinese art as a movement frozen in time and space. Referring to interactions that span historical time and cultural boundaries, Fu Lei conceived of a meaningful, artistically productive conflict (chongtu 衝突) that could still accommodate individual expression, creating innovative art based on the diversity of perspectives resulting from new experiences. Even the casual act of reading a dining menu, which may seem mundane to the average traveler, becomes a generative experience for the artist, but it takes a critic sharing his observations with curious readers to reveal the creative potential of an initially disappointing intercultural encounter.

THE TURNED BACK ARTIST

Writing to his son Fu Cong on May 27, 1965, Fu Lei responded to a comment from an earlier letter about the transformation of the Chinese nation by recounting his long-held belief that "the more I study Western culture, the more I appreciate the beauty of Chinese culture and find it more suited to my personality" (Fu 2001, 493). In a much-cited line, Fu Lei continued, "I first fell in love with Chinese art when I was twenty-one or twenty-two, studying Western painting at the Louvre in Paris."[2] The paragraph that follows his autobiographical reflection provides advice to Fu Cong about how to be a successful artist: "The only way an artist will always have fresh content to understand and not get tired of his own art is to always maintain an open mind and fresh sensations, even if some people think that is hard work" (Fu 2001, 493). Written on the eve of the Cultural Revolution, Fu Lei's story of how he came to appreciate Chinese art may come across as a bit of revisionist history, told from the perspective of a middle-aged (fifty-seven-year-old) father trying to inspire, encourage, and support his thirty-one-year-old musician son who was performing and living overseas in Europe. The account certainly challenges conventional narratives that emphasize the causal relationship between studying Western art as the requisite first step in Chinese artists' admiration and imitation of Western art, and for this very reason accounts for why this quote is so loved by historians. At the same time, Fu Lei's story preserves the centrality of Paris, adding to its imagined role in the development of modern Chinese art. His advice to Fu Cong also foregrounds a vision of the ideal artist as someone who actively seeks out being exposed to new sensations and experiences, then is able to use new content to appreciate and create new art without forgetting or losing his sense of self (Chinese artistic heritage).

Fu Lei shared his image of the ideal artist in one of his earliest pieces of art criticism about the French postimpressionist painter Paul Cézanne. Origi- nally published in the October 10, 1930 issue of *Eastern Miscellany* (*Dongfang zazhi* 東方雜誌), Fu Lei's essay "Cézanne" (Saishang 塞尚) was included in the posthumously published *Lectures on Twenty Masterpieces of World Art*. In his admiring portrait of the artist, Fu Lei highlighted key tenets of his artistic philosophy. Of course Paris played a pivotal role in the development of Cézanne's artistic journey as he traveled back and forth from Paris to his home in Provence (Fu 2018, 169–70). The true artist, according to Fu Lei, was one who "is definitely a pioneer of his time, his vision is insightful, causing him to gaze steadfastly far into the future, and giving it a penetrating feeling, makes him feel constantly unsatisfied with reality" (Fu 2018, 168), even if it meant that the artist would necessarily be misunderstood by his contemporaries (Fu 2018, 173). Another sign of Cézanne's artistic talent is his ability to respect the traditional artistic spirit, which, for Fu Lei, is manifested in the artist's willingness to turn back: "Standing at the ideological trend of his own time to establish the foundational etiquette for the sake of new 20th century art—this is the difference between respecting tradition versus serving tradition, knowing that creation is not just adding stilts to existing pavilions, this is the most impressive part" (Fu 2018, 171). The recognition of difference or seeming contradiction is also apparent in Fu Lei's description of Cézanne's relationship with nature and scientific observation versus artistic expression: "Be true to nature, but use your own eyes (don't be influenced by other people's eyes) to observe nature. In other words, you must purify your own vision, freshen it, rejuvenate it, as if you were using the strange new eyes of a child to stare at nature" (Fu 2018, 171). As this chapter shows, according to Fu Lei, as effective artists, Liu Haisu and Pang Xunqin were able to "freshen" and "rejuvenate" their artistic vision by experiencing life in Paris, then turning back to appreciate Chinese art.

"Cézanne" also emphasizes the importance of the artist's personality (renge 人格), and its relationship with the work of art: "A work of art must not only express truth and beauty in appearance [biaoxian waixing de zhen yu mei 表現外形的真與美], moreover it must express inner truth and beauty [biaoxian neixin de zhen yu mei 表現內心的真與美]; the latter is the objective, and the former is the method and we must never mix these up" (Fu 2018, 171–72). In order to achieve the highest level of expressing inner and outward truth, the artist must have his entire personality "penetrate the core of the universe, to awaken the mystery of nature, then take his pure vision and grab on to nature's external form" (Fu 2018, 172). This seems really difficult if not impossible to achieve, as it involves being sure of one's artistic identity and vision (shijue 視覺), then finding the proper tools for artistic expression in order to achieve outward "truth and beauty." Finally, Fu Lei identified Cézanne's principal technique as the use of secondary color (zhongjian se 中間色) as similar to the semitone or half step (banyin 半音) in musical theory: "Here secondary colors are like the harmony or dissonance in music between the semitone and the melody. The full vision depends on whether the arrangement of the semitone fits or not, and tone in painting also similarly shares this attribute" (Fu 2018, 172). Likening Cézanne's painting process, specifically his complementary color system of modulation to that of music composition, Fu Lei explained, "He doesn't follow his predecessors, but employs two tones of light and dark to compose a melody [zucheng xuanlü 組成旋律], using only one or two kinds of symmetrical or harmonious colors to assemble a scale [yinjie 音階]. He uses all sorts of complicated colors, first, stroke by stroke juxtaposing them side by side, then stroke by stroke piling layer upon layer, until the color of the entire painting becomes brilliant, dense, and stimulating, as resounding as the harmony in music [ru yinyue shang hesheng zhi xiangliang 如音樂上和聲之響亮]" (Fu 2018, 172). Turning back is not simply a matter of following a well-established path, for it requires incorporating something new. For readers who may not have access to color reproductions of Cézanne's paintings, Fu Lei's finesse at transposing visuality into auditory description is remarkably inventive, and the musical metaphor aptly illustrates both Cézanne's unique artistic vision and Fu Lei's contribution as a critic.

Fu Lei continued fine-tuning his image of the ideal artist and the inter-communicability of music and visuality in "Xunqin's Dream" (Xunqin de meng), an essay published in the avant-garde journal *L'Art*. The modern painter Pang Xunqin traveled to Paris to study art at the young age of nineteen, but he quickly returned to Shanghai in 1929 with the hopes of creating a modernist art salon in the Parisian style. In 1931, Pang cofounded the Storm Society (Juelan she 決瀾社) with the help of the writer Ni Yide (倪貽德 1901–70) who had just returned from Tokyo. In 1932, the society's manifesto was published in *L'Art*, Ni Yide's short-lived magazine for the arts group Muse (Moshe) whose members included Liu Haisu and Pang Xunqin. The Storm Society was the first attempt at a modernist, salon-style art association in China, with an emphasis on the avant-garde. The society's Manifesto employed the crisis discourse characteristic of its time: "Whither has gone our ancient creative talent, our glorious history? Our whole art world today is decrepit and feeble" (Sullivan 1996, 62). In the climate of national crisis, the group of like-minded artists, many of whom had been educated abroad in Japan or France, wholeheartedly believed in the potentially revolutionary power of visual art. The legacy of Chinese art had reached an all-time low point and Western modernism was called upon to rejuvenate it.

The same year in 1932, Fu Lei curated Pang Xunqin's solo exhibit in Shanghai. The narrator of "Xunqin's Dream" began by describing the artist's youthful dreams as a medical student at Zhendan University (L'Université l'Aurore) in Shanghai: "One day, he suddenly wanted to go to Europe, so he left war-enveloped China, crossing over to the polyphonic motley West—this was more or less a paradise for him" (Fu 2000 95). The sounds and images evoked by "polyphonic" (fansheng 繁聲) and "motley" (zase 雜色) refer very literally to the music that Pang Xunqin was immersed in, after abandoning all the trappings of "tedious, mechanical, theoretical, and pragmatic science." Listing Frédéric Chopin, Felix Mendelssohn, Ludwig van Beethoven, among other classical composer greats, as sources of artistic inspiration for Pang Xunqin's "dream of music," the narrator asserted that Pang "thinks amidst musical notes, borrows emotional expression from melody" (Fu 2000, 95). Fu Lei's description of the contrast between China and France echoes a passage from an earlier letter published in *Letters on the Way to France*. In "Letters to Friends after Arriving in Paris" (到巴黎後寄諸友), written on February 6, 1928, Fu Lei admits, "Not much to report after two days in Paris, except that everywhere there is a kind of peaceful, happy atmosphere; plucked out of a seething, terrified China, I feel myself in an extraordinarily peaceful, leisurely mood" (Fu 2000, 67–68). Ironically, the "the polyphonic motley West" represented by Pang Xunqin's Paris as a physical site of sensory overload barely resembles the traveler Fu Lei's internal mood; but no matter how chaotically exotic the City of Lights appears, its greatest advantage is that it offers an opportunity to escape China.

Fu Lei enthusiastically captured the fragmentary simultaneity of urban life: "In Paris, crumbling structures stand alongside brand-new buildings . . . the new, the old, the ugly, the beautiful, things to see and things to hear" (Fu 2000, 95). Enumerating the gritty and glittery attractions of Paris, Fu Lei's stream-of-consciousness narration ranges from mentions of the city's diverse and seductive inhabitants to iconic landmarks such as Montparnasse, the Eiffel Tower, and the secondhand book stalls along the Seine. For Chinese travelers such as Fu Lei and Pang Xunqin, Paris was a composite of many diverse elements: its eclectic population, landmarks, extraordinary sights, nightlife, all of which envelop its inhabitants in a whirlwind of sensation. Fu Lei listed alongside other attractions the "pretty and seductive demon-women," "dancing girls," "*poule* (floozies)," and "charming and elegant maidservants, disgusting landladies," all circulating in an urban space that is half modern and half ancient, surrounded by "the historical remains of an ancient culture, the passion of a new culture." The dreamlike images evoked in Fu Lei's montage about city life, visually depicted in Pang Xunqin's collage painting *Such Is Paris* (Ruci Bali 1931), always exist in a feminized space, but this is merely the backdrop against which the detached artist Pang Xunqin finds himself.

Meanwhile in the middle of this chaos—"all of this spinning and spinning around in the whirlwind in his [Pang Xunqin's] mind"—the lone figure of the artist emerges: "He, in his black velvet jacket, hat at a half-slant, both hands hidden inside his pants pockets, from morning to night, in a half-conscious daze, subsumed by this huge vortex of a world" (Fu 2000, 95–96). As much as "Xunqin's Dream" can be read as a celebration of the "exuberance of Paris," and the marginalized social position a traveler occupies in a foreign city, it is at the same time about the detachment required of an artist, or the ideal position of an artist in modern society. Fu Lei introduced the painter by claiming, "From childhood to adulthood, he is the same as all young people; he has dreamed many innocent, magical dreams. His silent disposition, his fanciful sense of humor, cause him to drift further away from reality each day." Fu Lei concluded with the Chinese saying, "One cannot see Lushan [mountain]'s true face by standing in the middle of the mountain" (Bu shi Lushan zhen mianmu, zhi yuan shen zai ci shan zhong) and applauds Pang Xunqin for his dream: "'Xunqin's Dream' is perfectly situated outside the mountain. This is like Rodin's so-called 'human paradise.' Xunqin, you are so blessed!" (Fu 2000, 97). Being situated outside the mountain or detached from social reality allows Pang Xunqin to view that reality more clearly; the artist's identity and vision depend on his mental detachment, which leads to a more accurate and perceptive vision of reality. As a critic who recognizes Pang Xunqin's artistic contribution, Fu Lei drew on an assorted sprinkling of references ranging from jazz music and Josephine Baker to French sculpture and Claude Debussy, but pointedly concluded with a line from the Song dynasty poet Su Shi about the required distance for an artist to turn back to his Chinese cultural heritage in order to "purify" his vision.

Another essay in which Fu Lei insisted on the dialogue between painting and music and further developed his image of the artistic genius is the first of two lectures on Leonardo Da Vinci in the *Lectures on Twenty Masterpieces of World Art* series. Fu Lei focused on the Renaissance master's famous paintings, the *Mona Lisa* (La Gioconda) and *The Last Supper*, and analyzed the Mona Lisa's beloved facial expression. Comparing her sense of mystery to the soul-stirring power of music, Fu Lei wrote: "One melodic phrase, two beats, four notes, have the ability to change our mood, to make us restless; they can awaken our heart's hidden consciousness. A sound in our soul can be extended forever without limit, even to the point of inciting infinite vibrations of ideas and sensations" (一個旋律的片段，兩拍子，四音符，可以擾亂我們的心緒以致不得安息。它們會喚醒隱伏在我們心底的意識，一個聲音在我們的靈魂上可以連續延長至無窮盡，並可引起我們無數的思想與感覺的顫動 Fu 2018, 104). The musical theory terminology Fu Lei employs makes it seem like the Mona Lisa is merely an excuse to talk about his true love, music. Again, the motif of the turning back artist reappears, as he cited the musical requirement of a conclusion: "Many professional musicians make use of this trait, purposely extending the note that leads to the conclusion especially long, forcing listeners to wait impatiently for that response, so the 'soul-stirring power of music' is located in this uncertain and vague note; it calls out, waiting for another note to respond. This call possesses the magic of ecstasy and agitation" (Fu 2018, 105). Likening the Mona Lisa's enigmatic smile to this musical "call," Fu Lei compared Da Vinci's skill to that of Mozart.

The essay continues with an anecdote about a social gathering at Mozart's home, during which a guest was interrupted while casually playing the clavichord and joined his friends in conversation. Fu Lei recounted, "After awhile, all of the guests went home on their own ways, and Mozart went to bed, but he couldn't fall asleep, for a kind of indescribable irritation and unease assailed him. He got up suddenly and went to the clavichord to play the coda's harmony, then returned to bed and fell fast asleep, now that he had satisfied his spirit" (Fu 2018, 105). According to Fu Lei, the act of artistic creation serves to satisfy the artist, for whom artistic expression is the natural and absolutely necessary resolution to an innate drive. Fu Lei told the story of Mozart in his role of art critic, affirming that music's "soul-stirring power" is related to the artist's unique ability to elicit an intense desire on the part of the viewer or listener to respond, either visually or musically (Fu 2018, 105). Therefore, the critic's job is to identify and recognize this artistic latency, in order to properly appreciate the power of hidden mystery suggested in the Mona Lisa's smile.

CULTURAL MISUNDERSTANDINGS AND THE ROLE OF THE CRITIC

In another letter written at sea dated January 22, Fu Lei described some of the games they play aboard the passenger liner *André Lebon,* including a new version of hide-and-seek: "The way they play hide-and-seek is slightly different from ours. According to our rules, as long as you've been tagged by the blindfolded player, you're out, even if it's only a light touch. Not for them—even if you've been tagged it doesn't count. As long as you can manage to get free, you can even do secret things to the blindfolded person who's 'it,' this is something that's not allowed in our version. Some of the players even warn others, could this be a way of showing a bit of compassion?" (Fu 2000, 42). The two distinctive ways of playing hide-and-seek come to represent deeper cultural differences for Fu Lei. "From comparing these two ways of playing, we can see clearly that they value strength, as long as you have physical might you will never get caught. . . . We on the other hand value wisdom, so when they play hide-and-seek they are like 'pingping pangpang' completely relying on brute force. We play lightly, quietly, nimbly, tiptoeing, not making a single sound, you can't even hear the seeker's footsteps" (Fu 2000, 43). In his final analysis Fu Lei connected his observations on deck to hearsay about cultural characteristics: "I often hear people say eastern culture is still, western culture is moving—I don't know if these two statements are true or not, yet it makes sense in the context of hide-and-seek" (Fu 2000, 43). His skeptical attitude about cultural essentialism avoids being completely critical, and he effectively established empathy for his foreign shipmates by acknowledging the potential benefits of an alternative playing strategy. Fu Lei's approach toward identifying and appreciating cultural difference in this seemingly trivial instance of a leisure activity reveals a deeper effort to carve out the critic's social role as one whose responsibility is to navigate the misunderstandings that inevitably arise between the artist and his audience.

The danger of misunderstanding art and, even worse, misunderstanding its creator the artist, is a pervasive theme in Fu Lei's art criticism. Like Pang Xunqin, Fu Lei's friend Liu Haisu turned back to Chinese culture after receiving a Western art education: "After researching the history of European painting for a short period of time, his national soul and individual identity started to awaken" (Fu 2017, 185). This description echoes his view of Fu Lei's own circular journey to appreciating Chinese painting, and also emphasizes the connection between national spirit and individual personality. But artistic identity and vision did not guarantee critical or popular success, as Liu Haisu quickly discovered. Fu Lei's essay "Liu Haisu," dated November 26, 1931, included in volume 2 of *A Collection of World Famous Paintings* (*Shijie ming huaji* 世界名畫集), begins by quoting Rainer Maria Rilke's biography of the French sculptor Auguste Rodin (1840–1917) about fame and status: "Although he was acclaimed, he was still new, and therefore was surrounded by only total misunderstanding" (cuohui de zonghe eryi 錯會的總和而已) (Fu 2018, 79). As a critic, Fu Lei explained why this reading of Rodin resonated with Liu Haisu who felt similarly surrounded by misunderstanding and relied on Fu Lei as a mediator.

Fu Lei linked the source of misunderstanding to the exposure gained by travel and the circulation of Liu Haisu's art, which occurred "after returning to China from overseas where his long world-famous artwork encountered its compatriots" (Fu 2018, 80). Liu Haisu is depicted as having to defeat all of his enemies in society at large and in the art world: "He interacted with everyone in the world, mentored students all over China, then was misunderstood, not only by his enemies but worse, by his friends. Today, Haisu's name is no longer isolated, instead, that people from all over the world know his art is even more isolating." Subverting the narrative that global recognition necessarily leads to intercultural exchange and tolerance, Fu Lei's account of Liu Haisu's stigmatized status back in China shows how, in some cases, increased circulation actually decreases understanding. Fu Lei's essay draws a fine distinction between knowing (renshi 認識) and misinterpretation (cuohui 錯會), pointing out that "knowing of" (having heard of) an artist or seeing artwork is different from truly understanding it. Fu Lei's cynical attitude toward global acclaim and fame in the "Liu Haisu" essay may appear surprising, coming from the editor of a collection of essays specifically designed to highlight "world famous" paintings and Fu Lei's particularly ambitious mission to insert Liu Haisu in the company of international art masters.

In his preface for the unpublished volume authored in 1934, Fu Lei wrote: "Today, in eastern and western artwork, techniques and forms are so different, they have been produced from such unlike states, and they express sentiments from the soul. Furthermore, each has a distinct national style at its foundation, so when I see these so-called slogans for merging Chinese and western art—it's too premature. Today's artists, if they can't even resolve the contradiction between Chinese and western culture, there's no way to escape from this whirlpool, so how can they say reconcile [tiaohe yun he zai 調和雲何哉]? Moreover, since we [Chinese art] have yet to attain complete understanding of the field of western art, what creation could possibly result from hasty words [huang yan chuangzao hu 遑言創造乎]?" (Fu 2018, 7). Adopting the image of the swirling vortex used to describe the milieu surrounding

Pang Xunqin in Paris, Fu Lei pointed out the conflict between words and slogans and the failure of conventional language to reconcile contradiction and eliminate misunderstanding. Reconciliation—the alternative to conflict—is an impossible and reductive goal, according to Fu Lei, and it fails to take advantage of the intercultural encounter, to the extent that critics' "hasty words" can even be fruitless or worse, potentially damaging, to the artistic field.

Instead of expressing sorrow for Liu Haisu in the essay, Fu Lei was disappointed at the Chinese people, blaming them for the fact that "a true genius that has been misunderstood—especially an artistic genius—is a sign that the masses are outdated" (Fu 2018, 80). Like the "cow" commoners on the ship who cannot appreciate the piano music they hear, the Chinese audiences who misunderstand Liu Haisu occupy the opposite side from the artist, and Fu Lei positioned himself as the mediating critic. He cited Xu Zhimo's earlier defense of Liu Haisu in 1916, "Haisu has already decided to leave the country for a few years, so we can anticipate that he will not return empty-handed, given the kind of preparations he has made for this treasure hunt, let's wait here for his news!," as a way to highlight the disparity between the anticipation of the past and the poor reception of Liu Haisu's "news" upon return from "treasure hunting" after three years in Europe, after having achieved everything that Xu Zhimo had encouraged him to accomplish (Fu 2018, 81). Fu Lei quoted excerpts from Liu Haisu's letters to him about financial hardship in France, as well as autobiographical accounts from their life together, such as visiting Liu Haisu's room on the fourth floor of a hotel in the Latin Quarter near the Sorbonne where the artist would return from a day at the Louvre and chat with Fu Lei about Rembrandt, despite not having enough money to pay for meals in the hotel.

Listing the exotic places Liu Haisu traveled, including Florence, Venice, and especially "in Paris where artists from all over flock, where he was immersed, where he bathed in artistic air too dense," Fu Lei called China a "wasteland of talent" in need of Liu Haisu's creative and pedagogical intervention: "Finally he endured the pain of departure and separated from his artistic paradise, Paris" (Fu 2018, 83). Under Fu Lei's pen, a burdensome sense of national duty and social (paternal) responsibility compel Liu Haisu to return to China: "Haisu, deep within his chest, nevertheless felt a kind of inexpressible dejection in his travels as he painted, frequently receiving telegrams from his homeland; after all, he was propping up his beloved son, Meizhuan [Shanghai Academy of Art], who needed him to come back, with one arm" (Fu 2018, 83). To compound the guilt of Chinese readers critical of Liu Haisu's aesthetic project, Fu Lei added that prior to his return to China, he organized two exhibits of *guohua* traditional painting in Germany and France. The shows, albeit commended by the western European critics, should horrify and make Chinese critics blush from shame that "the true value of our modern Chinese artistic renaissance master had to be first recognized by our Western neighbors" (Fu 2018, 83), the same causal relationship that allegedly plagued Chang Yu in the previous chapter. Fu Lei's description of Liu Haisu's inability to truly enjoy himself while abroad echoes the ambivalence expressed in his own letters about leaving China. In "Traveling Companions," written on January 22, 1928, Fu Lei exclaimed, "Departing from my China, how far away it is! No matter what, when I was back at home I cursed China every day; however since leaving I long for her daily, thinking back nostalgically and cherishing my memory of her: ah my China!" (Fu 2000, 41). His critique of China is closely linked to the act of turning back, the cultural pull that unavoidably arises when one arrives in a foreign setting. The persistence of remembering one's cultural roots can be painful but only through the encounter of new experiences abroad can one gain fresh perspective to transform oneself.

Having felt firsthand the double-edged emotions of guilt and excitement at being in Europe while the political situation in China continued down a path of uncertainty in the late 1920s and early 1930s, Fu Lei was well suited to address both Chinese and French readers. In the summer of 1931, the same year as Pang Xunqin's exhibit, Fu Lei's article "La crise de l'art chinois moderne" was published in the Paris magazine *L'Art Vivant*.[3] Solicited by the magazine's editor, Florent Fels, to write about the state of Chinese modern art, Fu Lei (publishing under the name Fou-Nou En) explained to French readers about the challenges China faced upon being inundated with "the tremendous tidal surge from the West": "Today in China, after thousands of years of living in wisdom, harmony and the Golden Mean, people are finding it increasingly difficult to hold on to their quiet and deep pondering dream in the face of Western mechanization, industrialization, science and the temptations of material culture" (Fu 2018, 187). The image of China's timeless past is depicted as being disrupted by the encounter with the West, and in stark opposition, the modern material world is alluring but inadequate, ineffectual and shallow, making it difficult for (Chinese) artists to maintain their vision and identity in the face of attacks from both proponents of Western-style art education and New Movement reformers in China. Adopting a tone of urgency, Fu Lei warns, "Whether in politics or art, to really explore the reasons for the present crisis, it's necessary to look beyond the surface underneath to the innermost core" (Fu 2018, 183). Here, Fu Lei as critic again reiterates the importance of audiences truly understanding the art they encounter, for this is the only way to avoid misinterpreting the reasons for the crisis in modern Chinese art. The problem can be traced to the movement's inability to preserve a "knowing quietude," which, Fu Lei admits, is only a "dream-like" fantasy.

As an act of transposition, Fu Lei brings up the work of late Qing literati master painter Wu Changshi (吳昌碩 1844–1928), which "conveys a spiritual sense that is wholly distinct from the material world, giving his paintings an atmosphere that is at once both simple and charming [you gupu you fu yunwei 又古樸又富韻味]." Wu Changshi's commercial calligraphy and painting during the transitional period is considered "a last effort to save the so-called tradition of literati painting" (Andrews and Shen 1998, 82) by art historians, but Fu Lei holds him up in the essay as a successful counterexample to contemporary Chinese artists who blindly follow earlier imitators and also those who emulate the latest newcomers: "Many young people, however, crave all that is 'new' and 'Western', moving too far from their own time and place." The artists are only partially to blame though, as the bulk of the problem lies with the masses and their misunderstanding of art.

On why the Western art aesthetic did not catch on with Chinese artists, despite previous foreign encounters during the late Ming–early Qing with missionaries, Fu Lei surmised, "When it comes to understanding and appreciating 'foreign sentiment' [yiguo qingdiao 異國情調], ordinary people still have a ways to go" (要談到民眾對於這種異國情調之認識與鑑賞，還相差很遠 Fu 2018, 184). His theory of why Chinese art has finally reached its breaking point sets up the opposing parties of artists versus "ordinary people" (minzhong 民眾), and implies the presence of an invisible third party of the critic, who is able to properly "understand" and "appreciate" artistic expression. Late nineteenth-century political turmoil is seen as the last straw, causing Western aggression to assert control over China, with military power and physical invasion equated to cultural domination, a sentiment addressed also in Xu Xu's writing in chapter 5.[4] For Fu Lei, the only way to understand and appreciate a new and unfamiliar "sentiment" was through the cultural exposure gained during the experience of traveling, even at the risk of painful reminders of how far behind China lagged.

Two days after his arrival in Paris in 1928, the young writer described the appearance of such "lavish enjoyment of abundant and prosperous living" in France that it would seem "unreal to the spiritual civilization of China, who could not even dream of such material waste" (Fu 2000, 67). Several paragraphs later, Fu Lei added the following demographic observation: "There are hundreds of Chinese students here, and you bump into them quite frequently on the streets (those that are definitely not Japanese). The study abroad situation is less than ideal, though, and those that are actually studying make up less than one-tenth [of that number]!" The piece titled "Letters to Friends after Arriving in Paris" ends with the Tang dynasty poet Zhang Gu's (張固 1395–?) famous proverb about the difficulty of life in the big city, as Fu Lei questions his position as a Chinese student studying abroad in Paris. Fu Lei quickly realized the city's inherent contradiction; at the same time as he celebrated Paris for its cosmopolitan status, he finally consciously acknowledged its paradoxical relationship with wealth, class, and race. He lamented, "To live a peaceful life is not easy; moreover in world-famous Paris how is an impoverished student to find paradise?" (長安居，大不易；何況名聞世界的巴黎怎是窮學生的樂土呢？). If it was already difficult enough for mankind to live a peaceful existence, surely the cultural capital of the Western world posed an even greater challenge for a young student from China—someone who was lacking in not only age and experience, but also money and social status as a complete outsider. In a legendary city renowned for its revolutionary spirit, where did an individual like Fu Lei fit?

By February 9, a mere two days later, the initial exhilaration of being in the artistic capital of the world had already lost some of its appeal. Fu Lei's "Dejected at the Luxembourg Garden" (Zai Lusenbao huayuan changwang 在盧森堡花園悵惘) is the last letter in the *Letters on the Way to France* series. The title suggests to readers that the scenic spot does not fulfill Fu Lei's expectations, but this is misleading in a way; Fu Lei is not disappointed in the Luxembourg Garden itself, only when he imagines the figure of the Chinese artist in this idyllic landscape. As he muses about the young French children playing in the park, he thinks of the youth in China: "The children back at home in China during this cold harsh winter are traditionally prohibited to leave the house; not many of the most loving protective mothers will even allow a little recreation in the courtyard, and I do truly feel the true love of those mothers" (Fu 2000, 71). But faced with the "lively, strong and healthy" French children, Fu Lei admits feeling "a sense of dejection" at the thought of China's "gentle and delicate" youth. He is quick to point out the good intention of Chinese maternal care, yet in the process cannot help but fault the generation of women who have raised such a fragile younger generation: "Frailty and daintiness, words once used by Chinese people to describe a gentle and refined demeanor, now this weak literati scholar has turned the family's eldest son into a sickly old man! Our children of the rising sun, who until now are still being forced to hold back their radiant splendor" (Fu 2000, 71–72). Rather than inspiring him to produce art, observations of children at play filled Fu Lei with regret and worry, presumably as he wondered about the implications of his own upbringing on his future and imagined a dismal future for a generation of old-fashioned Chinese artists.

"Dejected at the Luxembourg Garden" praises the park's "three or four large grassy areas, in which there are many trees and flowers, beautifully carved stone sculptures, chairs for resting, places for young children to stroll and play after school hours for a change of atmosphere," but the added perspective on city planning only agitated Fu Lei's worries about China: "Outside Paris in the suburbs there are even more wooded forests, all for the use of the city dwellers. So Paris, whose industry flourishes hundreds of times greater than in Shanghai, is actually far cleaner and more sanitary. Oh, have some consideration for our China!" (Fu 1981, 72). For Fu Lei, the setting of Paris provided him the necessary critical distance to compare France's celebrated civilization with a China on the brink of collapse. In essays about travel and art criticism, he was especially fascinated with transmediality. Transposition in his writing implied recognition of the countless connections and movements between different artistic identities and media forms, and in his self-appointed role as critic, Fu Lei experimented with a new method of connoisseurship that relied on appreciation of cultural difference made possible through conflict. But not everyone was qualified to be an artist or critic.

CHAPTER 4

Li Jinfa and the Muse

Everyone considers themself a poet and a philosopher, yet their work is
honestly just ordinary.

(個個自命為詩人與哲學家，而且作品，只是老老實實地平凡而已)

—FU LEI, AN OLD DREAM OF MY HOMETOWN IN JUNE

Writing about his experience studying abroad in France, the symbolist poet
Li Jinfa (né Li Shuliang) explained the origins of his peculiar pseudonym,
"Jinfa" or "golden hair": "How my pen name came about was entirely the
result of a dream," he recalled one day spent with friends in Paris's Hotel Sen-
ate in the summer of 1922 (Yang 1986, 57). Suddenly overcome with dizziness
while taking a walk, the young man was struck with a fever for days, during
which a "golden-haired goddess dressed in white" visited his dreams numerous times and led him on hallucinatory journeys through the heavens. After
his miraculous recovery, Li Jinfa attributed his survival to the anonymous
female divinity, and thought it only fitting to honor her by referring to the
image of her golden tresses in his pen name Jinfa—a move recognized by his
friends as "fresh and clever" (Yang 1986, 58).

Li Jinfa was born in Meixian, Guangdong Province, and arrived in France
in 1919 at the age of nineteen, after one year of schooling in Shanghai. As
part of a work-study program, Li studied sculpture in Paris and Berlin,
returned to China in 1925, and taught art from 1928 to 1930 at Hangzhou
Academy. His three major volumes of poetry—*Light Rain* (*Wei yu* 微雨, 1925),
A Visitor in Hard Times (*Shike yu xiongnian* 食客與凶年, 1926) and *Singing for Joy*
(*Wei xingfu er ge* 為幸福而歌, 1927)—were composed during his stays in Paris
and Berlin from 1920 to 1924. Li Jinfa's translations of Western poetry
appeared most notably in *Light Rain* as an appendix of twenty-eight poems

translated from a wide range of non-Chinese poets, including Lord Byron, Baudelaire, Rabindranath Tagore, and Paul Verlaine. Yet remarkably, before arriving in France, Li had never written poetry or spoken French, although he did have a limited understanding of English. Upon arrival, he and his fellow Chinese work-study compatriots were sent to a middle school in Fontainebleau to learn French from a shared French-Chinese dictionary.[1]

Li Jinfa's tale of being saved by a blonde goddess reveals the loneliness of a penniless young man in a foreign land who spent his days and nights reading novels and wandering around in museums. The supernatural anecdote further suggests that inspiration can strike anyone at any time in any form, as along as the artist is an active and receptive medium, open to risk. This chapter argues that Li's work reflects the potentially liberatory but also offensive idea of artistic inspiration. While the muse may provide individual inspiration to the modern poet, the belief that anyone without proper literary or language training can be a poet is perceived by the literary establishment as an act of betrayal. Starting from the line of linguistic critique used to attack Li Jinfa, I analyze a selection of poems from *Light Rain* and *Singing for Joy* using the lens of transposition to explain why his experiment failed to win over readers, despite meeting certain literary criteria of modern poetry. In this rereading, the concept of muse as source of inspiration provides further reflection on the tension between a democratized form of art for all versus art as an elite calling. Rather than debate the literary quality of Li Jinfa's poetry or rescue his work from the category of "bad" modern poetry, my discussion focuses on how the notion of poetic inspiration is closely linked to the city of Paris as a site that fosters artistic communion.

When his first poetry collection *Light Rain* was published in 1925, it was heralded as groundbreaking by prominent literary critic and poet Zhou Zuoren (周作人 1885–1967), brother of modern Chinese literature celebrity Lu Xun (魯迅 1881–1936): "Your poems are like nothing in China, they are truly original" (Cheng 2000, 76). Part of Li Jinfa's originality can be attributed to how forthcoming he was about his lack of poetic credentials. In his preface to *Light Rain*, Li began, "Even though it's said there is no higher calling than composing poetry [zuoshi 做詩], it is nonetheless difficult work, for someone like me, I'm not even worthy to compose poetry!" (Li 1986, 1).

A decade later, renowned May Fourth language reformer Hu Shih called Li Jinfa's poems "stupid riddles that can't be solved" (cai bu tou de benmi 猜不透的笨謎) (Chen 2018, 309). Was Hu Shih using *ben* (stupid, awkward, foolish) to describe Li's poems themselves, or were the poems stupid precisely because they frustrated any attempt at comprehensibility and made readers feel stupid? Hu Shih's 1921 composition "Dreams and Poetry," an expression of his "experiential poetic theory," offers a clue as to what a more "ordinary" understanding of poetic creation should look like:

夢與詩	Dreams and Poetry[2]
都是平常經驗	It's all ordinary experience,
都是平常影像	All ordinary images.
偶然湧到夢中來	By chance they emerge in a dream,
變換出多少新奇花樣	Turning out infinite new patterns.
都是平常情感	It's all ordinary feelings,
都是平常語言	All ordinary words.
偶然碰著個詩人	By chance they encounter a poet,
變換出多少新奇詩句	Turning out infinite new verses.
醉過才知酒濃	Once intoxicated, one learns the strength of wine,
愛過才知情重	Once smitten, one learns the power of love:
你不能做我的詩	You cannot write my poems
正如我不能做你的夢!	Just as I cannot dream your dreams.

For Hu Shih, dreams and poetry share the transformative, creative power of turning the ordinary into the sublime, and the act of transposition is located in the verb of transforming (bianhuan 變換) that produces (chu 出) an infinite number of new possibilities. But, like how Fu Lei imagined the ideal conditions to produce art, Hu Shih's theory similarly requires two qualities in addition to the lucky dream: experience and the artist's subjectivity or individuality.

Li Jinfa's own poetic philosophy did not depart entirely from Hu Shih's vision, except for on one crucial point: how to define "ordinary." Could anyone be a poet? If so, how could a poet avoid falling into the trap of producing merely ordinary work, as this chapter's epigraph by Fu Lei points out? Li Jinfa wrote in "A Record of My Own Inspiration" in 1933, "My poetry is a record of my own inspiration, a song sung aloud in intoxication, I cannot hope that everyone will understand it" (Denton 1996, 390–91). As he correctly predicted, no one could understand the "eccentric of poetry" (shiguai 詩怪) (Zhou 1987, 1), and Li's poetic contribution to Chinese literary history was long considered an "utter failure" (Bian 1982, 154), especially in comparison to his contemporaries such as Guo Moruo (郭沫若 1892–1978), Xu Zhimo, and Dai Wangshu (戴望舒 1905–50), whose poetry was more comprehensible, lyrical, and therefore palatable. Critics have explained the unpopularity of Li's poetry by way of his decadent themes that were just too strange for Chinese readers, but the bulk of negative critical reception consistently reflects an underlying obsession with the poet's lack of literary and linguistic qualifications in Chinese and French. Michelle Yeh's introduction to Li Jinfa's poems in English translation represents the most gracious example of this: "Much of the notorious obscurity of his poetry comes from its dense imagery and the mixture of classical and modern diction" (Yeh 1992, 32).

A survey of the mixed reception of his poetry from its time of publication in the late 1920s and 1930s to more recent evaluations reveals that Li Jinfa's ultimate offense is promoting the potentially liberatory idea of artistic inspiration to the limit—the idea that anyone without proper literary or language training can compose poetry. Given his lack of proper literary and linguistic credentials, Li Jinfa's poetry is perceived to cross the line from acceptable or even admirable experimentation to the realm of "language criminal," in the words of critic Sun Xizhen.

In 1930s literary circles, Li Jinfa was renowned for his incomprehensibility, and the critic Su Xuelin stated matter-of-factly in an essay for *Xiandai* journal in 1933, "There is not one poem by Li Jinfa that can be understood completely" (Hong 1936, 509). The writer Zhu Ziqing credited Li with introducing French symbolism to Chinese readers in Zhao Jiabi's 1935 *Compendium of Modern Chinese Literature*, comparing his poems to "many small and big beads with the connecting thread deliberately hidden by the poet, who expects the reader to supply the missing link" (彷彿大大小小紅紅綠綠一串珠子，他卻藏起那串兒，你得自己穿著瞧) (Zhao 1981, 7; English translation by Julia Lin in *Modern Chinese Poetry*, 152), an accusation in line with the "stupid riddles" Hu Shih accused him of composing. Zhu added in his widely cited assessment, "I don't know if Li's desire to create a new language is too strong, or his knowledge of his mother tongue is not adequate, in any event, his syntax is too Europeanized, giving one the impression that they are reading a translation; add to this a sprinkling of classical words and phrases and one finds the reading experience more uncomfortable still" (不知是創造新語言的心太切，還是母舌太生疏，句法過分歐化，教人像讀著翻譯；又夾雜著些文言裏的嘆詞語助詞，更加不像 Zhao 1981, 8). The factors that add up to the poetic effect of "reading a translation" are difficult to pinpoint, as Zhu's uncertain tone indicates above, but Li Jinfa's transpositional practice of picking key poetic elements from two renowned literary traditions—classical Chinese poetry and French symbolist poetry—to create modern Chinese poetry resulted in the discomforting, defamiliarization sensation for Chinese readers described by Zhu Ziqing.

Echoing Sun's assessment, Bian Zhilin (1910–2000), the Crescent School poet who coedited the journal *New Poems* 新詩 with Dai Wangshu in the late 1930s, described Li Jinfa's work as "worse than fruitless" and having a "pernicious" influence on modern Chinese poetry during a crucial period: "The fact is that his far from adequate knowledge of French and his no less inadequate mastery of his mother tongue, both in Baihua (the vernacular) and Wenyan (the literary language), did gross injustice to the French Symbolists. His 'translation' from them and his 'imitations' of them mystified the Chinese reading public as well as his followers so that so-called symbolist poetry was considered just a jumble of incomprehensible dazzling words devoid of meaning or logic" (Bian 1982, 154). According to Bian, who was himself a translator of symbolist writings, Li Jinfa's greatest crime was that his poor linguistic abilities in Chinese and French single-handedly ruined the literary reputation of French symbolist poetry in China, and therefore the development of modern Chinese poetry at large. Sun Xizhen also criticized Li's limited French and Chinese language abilities, writing in 1981, "He can't really speak or express himself in Chinese, he's read a bit of classical literature, it's just a *wenyan* hodge-podge that's lost all its clear purity. He did introduce Symbolism, it's true, but he also corrupted the language, he is the chief culprit"　(中國話不大會說，不大會表達，文言書也讀了一點，雜七雜八，文言的純潔性沒有了。引進象徵派，他有功，敗壞語言，他是罪魁禍首。Zhou 1987, 10).

In English-language scholarship, Li Jinfa has received less scholarly attention, often presented in contrast to his more agreeable successor Dai Wangshu. Julia Lin writes, "In Li Chin-fa's poetry one discovers little concern for the musical quality and richness of sound effects that characterize, for example, the verse of the Symbolist Tai Wang-shu. Li Chin-fa is primarily preoccupied with the darker, harsher, and bolder aspects in symbolism" (Lin 1972, 156). Bonnie McDougall likens Li Jinfa's poetic approach to "shock tactics," pointing out his "suspension of logical and grammatical relationships, bizarre imagery, and irony" (McDougall and Louie 1999, 59–60). Most recently Paul Manfredi recognizes the impact of traveling in France on Li Jinfa's progressive project, reminding readers that Li's poetic world "gives full reign to the chaos, the incommensurability of traditions, aesthetics, experiences. His poetry is an image gallery for the shards that remain, the observable remnants of post-impact cultural experience" (Manfredi 2014, 27). Critiques of Li Jinfa's poetry, while entertaining to read, raise the challenge of agreeing on any kind of objective criteria for determining an artist's linguistic competence. As Zhou Liangpei points out, it may be impossible to determine, or at least agree on, Li's French ability, and whether it is really "not great" (bu da xing 不大行) (Sun Xizhen's words in Zhou 1987, 10–11). When it comes to evaluating linguistic ability in creative expression, Li Jinfa challenges readers to seriously consider who has the authority to decide whether someone's usage of French language in poetic experimentation is "passable" (xing 行) or not, and what that criterion would look like.

CITY AS INSPIRATIONAL SENSORY OVERLOAD

Building on the origin story of his unusual nom de plume, the city of Paris plays a prominent role in many of Li Jinfa's poems as a place that inspires and transforms anyone into an artist. Specific locations, especially well-known landmarks, serve as a way to document Li Jinfa's authentic experience as a Chinese student studying abroad in France. Self-expression is possible in Paris, where everyone can be a poet. In the four-stanza long "Luxembourg Garden," Paris plays a central role even in the poem's title, which refers to Paris in a parenthetical as a "return" (chongui 重回) to remind readers of the famed garden's location in the city, and its status as a premier Parisian landmark. The famed city's impact is strongly felt, likely a nod to Baudelaire's famous practice in *Les fleurs du mal* of allegorizing Paris and reading the modern city as a psychological space. "Luxembourg Garden" begins by describing a dreamy setting, among wild birds and elegant women.

盧森堡公園（重回巴黎）

"你沉睡在野鳥之翼下，
張著廣大之盛服，
任世紀循環桑田滄海，
你總帶著閑靜而眺望。

"微笑呵！不可捉之友情，
我所愛之綠葉，既無力搖曳；
野花之菜色，適為你之環佩，
無味的昆蟲之，永不授你於深夜之侯？

"任牆陰之一角，
存留著詩人之嘆息，少年之愛慕，
與逃遁著之眼淚，長襯鐘聲而諧和也。

"我們遠去脫此殘暴之監察，
遙望之颶風，滿貯著溫熱之雨滴，
如幕面之女人走過，不願意還帶點羞。"

Luxembourg Garden (Return to Paris)

Sound asleep under the wings of wild birds
With your splendid dress spread out
Let the century cycle, the mulberry fields become the deep blue sea,
You always bring tranquility and a view from afar.

Oh, a smile! Friendship that is out of grasp,
The green leaves that I love lack even the strength to sway
The colors of the wildflowers are fit to make you a ring
The tasteless chirping of insects, will they ever be awaited by you in the deep
    night?

Let the shady window corner
Preserve the poet's sigh, the youth's admiration,
And the escapee's tears, lined in harmony with the clock bells.

We will go far away from this cruel surveillance,
A distant hurricane, full of warm raindrops,
Like a veiled woman passing by, apparently reluctant and rather shy.

Addressed to an unnamed woman who has fallen asleep in the park, the
second-person speaker in the first stanza conveys a tension between stopped
time and passing time, while the stanza's last line expresses an ambiguity
about the sleeping woman's presence. She brings forth both a sense of leisure
and a kind of restlessness in the natural yet manicured environment, with
the verb "overlooking" (tiaowang 眺望) implying a bird's-eye view from
above that foreshadows the "cruel surveillance" (canbao zhi jiancha 殘暴之
監察) in the last stanza from which the speaker urges the woman to escape
near the poem's conclusion. Although the poem begins with the woman's
state of sleep, the last line in the first verse quickly hints that tranquility is
always short-lived and the park can only provide temporary relief. The four
verses reflect some of the typical images and themes of Li Jinfa's other poems,
such as the ocean, the poet's sigh, youthful adoration, and yet "Luxembourg
Garden" has a distinctly encapsulated feel, as if all that occurs takes place in

a contained amount of time and space, related to the garden's setting as an artificial, man-made refuge from the city.

The second stanza builds on the park setting established by the title and the first stanza, by referring to the colorful flora and fauna in the garden, but these images and sensations (colors, sounds) are countered by a sense of lack that seems to negate their power (the "out of grasp" friendship, the leaves that "lack strength" to sway, the "tasteless" chirps). The unnamed woman is still depicted as a potential object of desire, but her ineluctability is linked to the poetic speaker's relative lack of power in the face of natural forces. While the first two verses set up the relationship between the anonymous woman and the garden landscape, a new subject appears in the third verse in the figure of the poet: "Let the shady window corner / Preserve the poet's sigh, the youth's admiration, / And the escapee's tears, lined in harmony with the clock bells" (III.9–11). The modernist poet's distinctive mannerism, a sigh, is described as mundane and cliché—his sentimental remnant can be everywhere and anywhere. The third verse confirms that in the Garden, all of the human senses, including auditory, visual, and emotional, are awakened. The female object of desire combined with the natural elements of the park serve as typical sources of poetic inspiration, but the poet's ability to appreciate them manifests itself only in his useless sighs of admiration without consequential action until the poem's conclusion.

In the last verse, the speaker tries to convince the woman to escape far from "this cruel surveillance" (ci canbao zhi jiancha 此殘暴之監察), confirming that the garden is not an idyllic paradise after all. The element of supervision and control in the verb *jiancha* echoes the *tiaowang* at the end of the first stanza, indicating that despite the casual outward appearance of the sleeping woman, she nonetheless exerts some power through seeing, just as the park may seem like an idyllic resting place but in reality is closer to being a place for "cruel surveillance." The poem concludes with a sense of ambivalence, as the speaker proposes that he and the woman disappear together into the distance, like a far-off hurricane—more comforting than threatening, and providing a storm of warm rain rather than pelting drops and torrid winds. The last line compares the vague nonthreat of natural disaster to another female figure: "Like the passing of a veiled woman, apparently reluctant and rather shy" (如幕面之女人走過，不願意還帶點羞). The image of a subdued and modest woman stands in contrast to the poem's opening lines about the woman being addressed, who falls asleep with her fancy clothes on display, but in his use of the conjunction "like" or "as if" (ru 如) in the poem's last line, Li Jinfa forces the reader to make a leap in comprehension: Is this modest woman like the "warm raindrops" in the preceding line or like the hurricane? Frustratingly for the reader, the poem relies on a series of contrasts, contradictions, juxtapositions of disparate images, sensations, and tropes, loosely joined together by the setting of the park. Yet through the series of *correspondances* the Luxembourg Garden becomes a physical and figurative space that brings together individuals for observation, rest, fantasy, imagination, and appreciation of beauty and nature. Architectural details like the window corner become repositories for poetic creation and preservation of art, emotion, and admiration.

"Luxembourg Garden" from *Light Rain* can be considered a representative work of Li Jinfa in its ambiguous treatment of the relationship between the natural environment, sentimental emotion, and physical sensuality. Li Jinfa's experimental poetry borrows elements from classical poetry, most obviously the *zhi* 之 construction that emphasizes the contrast between the awkwardness of outdated literary language with the purportedly modern and exotic setting of the Parisian park. His use of the traditional idiom, commonly translated as "the vicissitudes of life" (sangtian canghai 桑田滄海) in the third line of the first stanza, refers to the monumental changes and transformations in the physical landscape that symbolize epochal shifts. These examples of transposition bring elements of classical Chinese literary tradition into direct contact with the foreign context of the Luxembourg Garden, whose urban-but-natural setting plays a central role, even in the poem's title, a reminder to readers that the famed garden's significance is inextricable from its location in the city and its status as a Parisian landmark, thereby lending legitimacy to the poet who has been there in person. The poem imagines the poet (shiren 詩人) then as a marginalized figure in this exotic outdoor space, symbolized by the barely perceptible remnants of a sigh (tanxi 嘆息). However slight or fleeting their impact, it was important for Chinese travelers to indicate in their work that they had been there, and as "Luxembourg Garden" reveals, the modern artist's education could take place outside of more official settings like the Louvre or art studios, including at public locations and city landmarks, which were equally invoked and used to showcase the modern artist's engagement with a new culture.

"Paris Somniloquy," the poem that immediately follows "Luxembourg Garden" in *Light Rain*, provides the most direct poetic account of Li Jinfa's impressions of the city of Paris and the social conditions of the urban dwellers. The title associates Paris with the place of talking in one's sleep (yiyu 囈

語), which refers to the crazed, incoherent rantings of someone who is probably dreaming, and gives the poem an imaginary, subconscious connotation, a reading that stands in stark contrast to the visceral details provided by the narrator; coincidentally, Li Jinfa may be playing with the homophone in the more expected foreign language (yiyu 異語) in Paris. The title's reference to language (yu 語) fits aptly with Li's declaration in "A Record of My Own Inspiration" of poetry as intoxicated rantings that others may find incomprehensible, whose purpose is one individual's record (jilubiao 紀錄表) of personal inspiration (geren linggan 個人靈感).

巴黎之囈語

陽光下之鬧聲，
無休止轉動著，
閉了窗戶
我為黃金的靜寂之王。

抱著鼻頭流汗，
既不是原始之人類了；
虛無之喝食，
為空間上可怖之勾留。

一刻友愛之聚會，
永不再見麼？
先生與後死，
既非我們之園地。

遠去！可愛的孩子，
巴黎城之霧氣，
悶寒了屛弱之胸膈，
你不覺已足麼？

情熱之燈光，
以本能之忠實而安排，
時將你的影兒，
倒照在行人之背而走！

不安睡的人，
全輾轉在上帝之肘子下，

用意慾的嬉戲，
冰冷自己的血。

此所謂人們之光榮，
值到地上之爬蟲類。
地窖裏之莓腐氣，
燻醉了一切遊客！

背上重負在街心亂走，
全不願棲息之所在，
車輪下之塵土，
滿沾在將睡之倦眼上。

如暴發之憤怒，
人在血潮上洗浴了！
不嘆息之奴隸，
長愛護半頒的襁褓。

人在羣裏張皇，
瘦馬在輀下喘氣
以可怖物掩其兩眼，
惟能羨慕道旁之腐水而狂飲。

神秘之沈睡，
全繞以金屬之長城，
多言之破布商，
在街道蓋頭呼喚著我們先帝之名字。

他預示天人之詛咒，
赭色晨光中之疾笑，
可愛之腰兒，
再不舞蹈在 Vieux Fauboury [*sic*] 之旁。

淡月下之鐘聲，
如夜猿長叫在空谷之側：
海潮與舟子細語，
而泣下，悽愴，戰慄。

在行星冷歇之日，
我們不能吃既熱之殘羹；
惟流動之地心，
倒影 Trocade'o 於廣漠之野？

女人的心，已成野獸之蹄。
沒勾留之一刻。
其過處之回音，
惟有傲骨之詩人能聽。

Paris Somniloquy

Noisy clam`or in the sunshine,
Spinning around without rest,
Closing the window
I find the silence of gold to be king.

Holding my nose and sweating,
Not like the early humans
With nothing to eat or drink,
For the sake of space, this horrible stay.

A moment of friendly gathering,
Will we ever meet again?
Born first and die later,
Neither is our domain.

Go away! Darling child,
The fog of Paris,
Stifles the weak chest,
Don't you think you've had enough?

The light of passion
According to instinct's faith and plan,
Time reflects your shadow
On the backs of walking pedestrians!

Restless sleeper,
Tossing and turning under God's elbow,

Using desire's sport,
Turns one's own blood ice-cold.

This so-called people's glory,
Until they become like crawling bugs on the ground.
The rotten basement air
Intoxicates all visitors with fumes.

Carrying a heavy load, roaming the streets,
Unwilling to rest at any building,
Dust beneath wheels,
Full of sleepy eyes ready to slumber.

Like anger about to explode,
People bathe in waves of blood!
Slaves that don't even sigh,
Long cherished half-issued swaddling clothes.

Flustered people in the crowd,
An emaciated horse pants under his yoke
Cover the eyes of this frightening beast,
Whose only desire is to guzzle the putrid gutter water.

Mysterious slumber
Completely coiled like the metallic Great Wall,
The chatty ragpicker,
Shouting the name of our old emperor at the intersection.

He prophesies the curse of heaven and man,
The brief smile of the reddish sunrise,
An adorable waist,
Never to dance again alongside the Vieux Faubourg

Sound of the clock bell under a waxing moon,
As an ape's long night call across the side of an empty valley:
Whispers of the ocean tide and boat,
Sobbing, wretched, shivering.

On the day of the planet's rest,
We can't even eat hot scraps;
Only the earth's rotating center,
Can it reflect invertedly the vast openness of the Trocade'o?

A woman's heart has already become the hoof of a wild beast.
It doesn't stay for a moment.
The echo of this passing place,
Only an unyielding poet can hear.

Reminiscent of Fu Lei's portrait of the artist Pang Xunqin in chapter 3, which also depicted an artist amid the urban cacophony of Parisian life, the first-person speaker of the fifteen-verse-long "Paris Somniloquy" finds himself at the center of a dynamic kaleidoscope of images, sounds, and smells. Shutting the window on the incessant noisy movements below for some precious stillness, his nose dripping with sweat, he resigns in the second stanza to remaining in the city: "For the sake of space, this horrible stay" (為空間上可怖之勾留). Two references in French—"Vieux Faubourg," the old Parisian city outskirts, and the "Trocade'o" (Trocadéro), a tourist area in the sixteenth arrondissement located between the Seine River and the Eiffel Tower—interrupt the poem's flow by grounding it in concrete details that convey the poet's familiarity with the city. Without these textual clues, the commonplace figures of ragpickers, visitors, pedestrians, and even a weary horse could belong to any metropolis at the beginning of the twentieth century.

Consistent with the bizarre incomprehensibility of Li Jinfa's poetic style, real-life details in "Paris Somniloquy" are periodically offset by surreal images, such as people bathing in blood (IX.2), and the coiling metallic Great Wall (IX.2), an icon of Chinese culture in the writing of Chang Yu. While at first glance these images appear to confirm Li Jinfa's strangeness, a closer look at the central role of Paris reveals that as in "Luxembourg Garden," the poetic thrust of "Paris Somniloquy" is focused on the image of the "unyielding" (aogu 傲骨) poet, who is the only one with the ability to hear the city's intoxicating calls (XV.4). Here, the artist's isolation may be the result of his arrogance, but it also provides a distinct advantage over the burdened masses. More than any other poem in *Light Rain* and *Singing for Joy*, "Paris Somniloquy" challenges readers' assumptions of modernity. Instead of celebrating the liberating revolutionary aspects of the Western capital city, Li Jinfa reveals its dark underside. The "restless sleeper" (VI.1), presumably the voice behind the somniloquy, represents the city's inhabitants as loudly inspired entities, shouting wildly with the incoherent lunacy of a madman: "The chatty ragpicker, / Shouting the name of our old emperor at the intersection" (多言之破布商，在街道盡頭呼喚着我們先帝之名字) (XI.3–4). Li Jinfa's dystopic, nightmarish hallucination of the capital of Western culture reveals his disillusionment with the social dissonance of urban modernity.

Not only a social commentary about the injustices of living in Paris, his poem highlights the burden of the poet-as-traveler. Unlike the classical poet who travels and appreciates the unknown scenery unfolding before him as a site of contemplation or possibility, the city impressions here are overwhelming and hallucinatory. He seems to be asking himself chidingly, "Don't you think you've had enough?" (你不覺已足麼?) (IV.4). But still the feverish chaos of Paris has an evocative power over all its inhabitants, ranging from the ragseller to the poet who hears. Li Jinfa's repeated use of the classical *zhi* construction, plus strange word choices like the literary character *wei* 惟 used at the start of two lines, has a jarring effect on the reader and obstruct any lyrical effect, succeeding in reproducing the kind of sensory dissonance and incoherence of someone talking in his or her sleep.

In both "Paris Somniloquy" and "Luxembourg Gardens" the image of the poet raises the question of how Li Jinfa positions himself in relationship to this figure, just like Chang Yu's poetic speaker in the untitled poem-painting about the wenren and his underappreciated chrysanthemum flower in France does in chapter 2. Is it self-referential, and does it include Li Jinfa in a heroic and celebratory stance? Or does the presence of the artist in the two poems imply a diminutive or self-critical attitude toward the modern poet? Reading the poems in the context of transposition reveals how Li Jinfa's poetry encompasses the range of these possible attitudes, and why his poems are effective in challenging reader expectations about poetic language and genre. According to Li Jinfa, anyone can speak, but the true artist is the one who can hear the inspirational sounds and smell the odors provided by one's surrounding environment. "Paris Somniloquy" and "Luxembourg Garden" highlight the city as provider of poetic inspiration by providing a fresh context whereby Li Jinfa can imagine the distinct artistic agency of the modern poet. Because of his outsider identity and his marginalized social status in a foreign country, the Chinese artist is in the unique position to observe and create art out of chaos and nonsense.

FOSTERING ARTISTIC COMMUNION

Li Jinfa's stay in France also gave him the opportunity to experiment with how to potentially achieve artistic communion in the sense of a shared intimacy with one's artistic colleagues or predecessors, whether through interlingual or intermedial transposition. In his foreword to *Light Rain*, dated 1923 from Berlin, the last paragraph suggests an alternative approach to artistic creation: "The original plan had been to create a sculpture for the book cover image, but there was not enough time, so Rodin's *L'eternelle idole* is taking its place [tidai 替代]" (Li 1986, 2). An image of the sculptor's work on the cover, most likely a reproduction by Li Jinfa, features a nude couple, with the woman's face and breast visible, and the side and back profile of a male figure whose face is buried in her chest, arms clasped behind him as if in submission. Originally conceived by Rodin in 1890–91 as part of his *Gates of Hell* project, the work was cast in bronze then in marble; the latter version graces the cover of *Light Rain* and was also the "human paradise" that Fu Lei referred to in the context of Pang Xunqin's "dream" in chapter 3.

Without providing any additional context, Li Jinfa's explanation of the image choice poses more questions than it answers. As part of the figures in Rodin's interpretation of Dante's *Inferno*, the piece makes an obvious reference to sexual lust but its title points to the ambiguity of human relationships and desire. Perhaps Li Jinfa felt a sense of affinity with Rodin as a similarly misunderstood artist, as Fu Lei pointed out in his comparison to Liu Haisu, and Li Jinfa could be admiring Rodin's willingness to dwell in this space of creative ambiguity, to leave viewers wondering about the multiple possible meanings this expression of bold sexuality imparted. In addition, the idea of Rodin's sculpture standing in for an original creation of Li Jinfa is also worth further reflection. Li Jinfa could be equating his reputation with Rodin's, who, once misunderstood and criticized, had reached critical acclaim by the early twentieth century and was celebrated internationally by intellectuals like Fu Lei. Or Li Jinfa could be suggesting that Rodin's *L'eternelle idole* shares the same spirit as what Li Jinfa's hypothetically unfinished work would have expressed, thus implying that the two artists' sculptural work is interchangeable. Either way Li Jinfa blames his failure to produce art in time as a way to justify his decision to use the image of Rodin's sculpture to open his poetry volume, immediately highlighting an intermedial connection between the reproduction of the nude sculpture with his love poems.

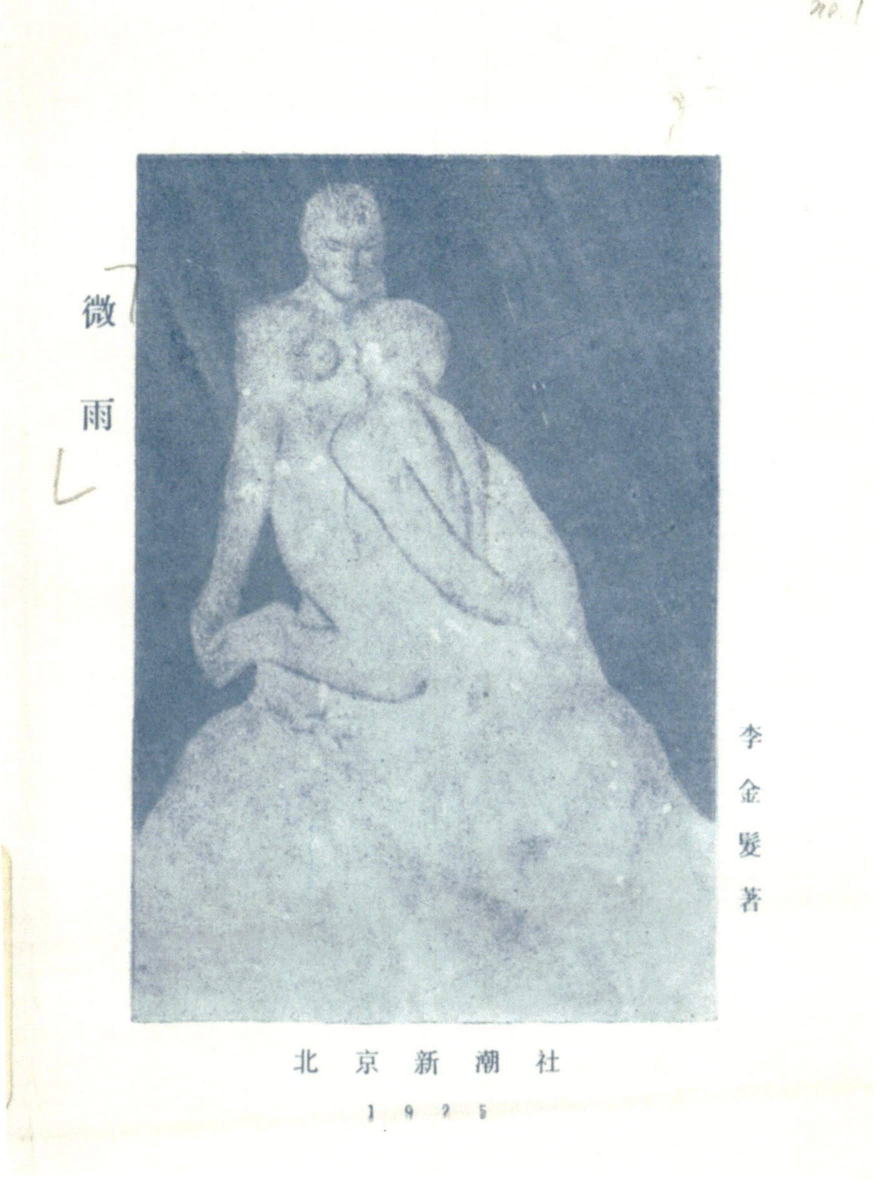

Figure 9. Cover image for *Light Rain* (*Wei yu* 微雨) by Li Jinfa 李金髪, 1925. Beijing xinchao she.

Another famous sculpture shows up in *Singing for Joy*, at the beginning of "Poet God" (Shi shen 詩神), the seventh poem in the volume. The poem starts with two bewildering lines of prose, indented and in smaller type font: "I completed a sculpture of the poetry god in July and loved it for its resemblance to the Venus de Milo, placing it on my desk like a Christian who just found a cross" (七月間成詩神像一具自喜酷似Venus de Milo 供之案頭猶教徒頓際之有十字架也, Li 1926, 20). The fragment introduces the first stanza, which continues its description of the poet god: "Not waiting to hold the pen, swiftly writing / Since the poet god incites the eye's tears on purpose: follow this glory to its chasms, / Forget the cruel leaves and light drizzle that the late autumn brings (不待扶筆疾寫，詩神既有心使眼兒流淚：追隨這光榮之尾閭，忘却深秋帶殘葉與細雨齊來。) In case any reader be mistaken that the poet god refers to Li Jinfa himself, the speaker begins the third stanza with a second-person address: "Hush, dear poet god, you want to be in my old heart" (吁，可愛的詩神，你欲在我老舊心田裏, Li 1926, 21). The image of the ancient Greek goddess, one of the most famous works of art on display at the Louvre, certainly resonates with the story of Li Jinfa's pen name and his golden-haired goddess. The poem does not resolve the mysterious figure's identity, even though the label "poet god" in Chinese literary history is often used to refer to Su Shi. Is the poet god a poet who has been inspired by a supernatural divinity, or does the term refer to the god who inspires poets? Either way the first poetic line negates the idea of the poetic muse as physically assisting in the writing process, since the poet god's power lies in its emotive evocation and its ability to penetrate the poet's heart.

The concept of artistic communion appears similarly in Li's treatment of Verlaine in the poem "Chat with Verlaine," also in *Singing for Joy*. "Chat with Verlaine" consists of an imaginary dialogue between two poets, the nineteenth-century French poet Verlaine and the author of the poem, Li Jinfa. Borrowing lines from "Ô mon Dieu, vous m'avez blessé d'amour," a poem that appears in the second of three sections in Verlaine's *Sagesse* (1881), the dialogue alternates between French-language lines directly taken from Verlaine's Catholic-themed poem and Chinese-language lines of Li's own creation, as "inspired" by Verlaine.

戲與魏崙 (Verlaine) 談

(自 Sagesse 二季) [3]

魏崙說: Mais ce que j'ai, mon dieu, je vous le donne.
——吁我以先執了理智的警告，怕來此生強之故里，造後偷偷眼兒，迷妄了，張手
　　向人走去，吁，我以先執了理智的警告。

魏崙說: Vous connaissez tout cela, tout cela.
——最喜歡肝膽相照，更願他聽我心拍的全部，—呵僅為他的拍，—縱為大道張皇
　　為青春興嘆，最喜歡肝膽相照。

魏崙說: Toutes mes peurs toutes mes ignorances.
——若能清理一下，也許尋出點潛力火焰與真理，夜兒多麼蕭索，山麓魑魅待人，
　　若能清理一下。

魏崙說: Voici mes mains qui n'ont pas travaillé, voici ma voix, bruit
　　maussade et menteur.
——攫取多少baisers之溫柔，摸索腰圍的輕瘦，吁，幾許細膩之工作。苦我的歌唱
　　無催眼之可能，則談說更成空泛既到海兒失却來源，我們情愛終如長城久峙，
　　吁從攫取多少baisers之溫柔。

魏崙說: Noyez mon ame aux flots de votre Vin fondez ma vie au Pain de votre
　　table.
——老舊的機能，新穎的情慾，縱不消愁亦漲煩充腸而去，吁，謝這老舊的機能。

Chat with Verlaine, from *Sagesse*, vol. 2

Verlaine says: But what I have, my God, I give it to you.
——Hush, had I first heeded reason's warning, feared that coming here
　　would strengthen home, 'til after stealing glances, lost and reckless, I
　　walked toward mankind with hands spread. Hush, had I first heeded
　　reason's warning.

Verlaine says: You know all this, all this.
——I most love sincerity's mutual reflection, more willing to have him hear
　　all of my heartbeat,——Ah merely for his beat,——Even for the Great
　　Way to get flustered, for spring's sighs, I most love sincerity's mutual
　　reflection.

Verlaine says: All of my fears, all of my ignorance.

——If it could be cleaned up a bit, maybe discover a spark of potential flame
and truth, the night is so dreary, at the mountain's foothill demons and
spirits await man, if it could be cleaned up a bit.

Verlaine says: Here are my hands that have not worked, here is my voice, a
sullen and lying noise.

——Seize however many tender baisers, grope the thin encircled waist,
Hush, how many exquisite tasks. Bitter, that my singing cannot possibly
be a lullaby, then chatter further becomes emptiness. Rushing to the
ocean without origin, our passion finally becomes as long-standing as
the Great Wall. Hush, seize [from] however many tender baisers.

Verlaine says: Drown my soul in the waves of your Wine, create my life from
the Bread of your table.

——Old-fashioned function, fresh passion, even though it doesn't dispel
worry still fills the body. Hush, thanks to this old-fashioned function.

"Chat with Verlaine" aptly illustrates how Li Jinfa confounded expectations associated with notions of comprehensibility, specialized expertise, and artistic inspiration raised in the negative reception of Li Jinfa's poetry at large. In terms of comprehensibility, the poem's structure immediately challenges the Chinese language reader, as the jarring and incongruous visual form of the poem features Verlaine's lines in French and Li Jinfa's responses in Chinese, undermining a basic assumption about dialogue or conversation (tan 談) as requiring one agreed upon language between its interlocutors. The poem forces the reader to forego one side of the dialogue and rely on the Chinese language responses, a strategy that fits with critiques of Li's poetic verse as "elliptical and idiosyncratic" (Lin 1972, 152). Even in the case when a Chinese-language reader can read French and is familiar with Verlaine's poem, the "responses" attributed to the second speaker, Li Jinfa, do not directly correspond in tone or content to Verlaine's in any obvious manner. The dialogue is structured in a way that implies a logical question and answer relationship between the two speaker's lines, and Li Jinfa's responses frustrate that relationship because ultimately it makes an indiscernible difference whether you can understand Verlaine's lines or not, which actually reproduces the one-sidedness of Verlaine's entreaty to God. In this sense, the bilingual composition of the poem also denies the French-language reader any substantive advantage in the meaning making process.

The inclusion of non-Chinese text in modern Chinese poetry is one of its most contentious features, and critics since the 1920s have argued about its merits, especially when it comes to the question of accessibility for Chinese readers, and the linguistic authenticity of the poet, who often is seen as blindly imitating Western poets. For example, Michelle Loi writes in her entry on Li Jinfa in *Modern Chinese Poetry Collections*: "It is true that sometimes the occidental accent is the result of an authentic meeting between the Chinese poet and Nerval, Apollinaire, Rimbaud or Rilke, but most often the use of French or German words is only a facile mannerism. Aside from numerous misprints and misspellings, the excerpts from Victor Hugo, Tristan Corbière, Tagore, D'Annunzio, Henri de Régnier, Verlaine and others lack true relevance to the content" (Malmqvist 1980, 158). But Loi's critique reveals the challenge of determining an exact definition of "authentic meeting" and similarly vague designations of "facile mannerism" and "true relevance." These labels may vary drastically from reader to reader, depending on each person's language and literary background.

Challenges to parsing "Chat with Verlaine" go beyond the initial visual shock of seeing the alternating lines in French and Chinese, and are closely linked to perceptions of Li Jinfa's linguistic and literary expertise or lack thereof. The poem begins by implicitly asking the reader to consider why Li has chosen these particular lines from "Ô mon Dieu, vous m'avez blessé d'amour," then continues to perplex with its Chinese lines of dialogue that, even when read as stand-alone text, exhibit the strangeness of scattered *wenyan*, including literary phrases and constructions such as 若, 之, 縱. These referents, which have been interpreted by critics as Li Jinfa's superficial attempts to imitate classical poetry, are juxtaposed with unfamiliar images of the body and emotions, resulting in a series of confusing associations, such as the metaphor comparing the durability of the iconic Great Wall to passionate love. The modern poet's use of repetition, usually a lyrical strategy that facilitates comprehension, further hinders Li's ability to demonstrate literary expertise. Verlaine's three-line stanzas with alternating rhyme schemes are partially preserved by Li Jinfa, who repeats the first phrase within each of his imagined "responses" as a concluding clause in each stanza. But in "Chat with Verlaine," the repetition of obscure phrases like "if it could be cleaned up a bit" (若能清理一下) in the third stanza, which awkwardly blend the literary *ruo* (若) with the casual "a bit" (一下), frustrate the reader's attempt to demystify the subject of the clause, emphasizing instead the out-of-placeness of each word.

Finally, Verlaine's poem about conversion provides the literary source of inspiration for Li Jinfa's celebration of "fresh passion" and "tender baisers [kisses]." In the aftermath of Verlaine's breakup with Arthur Rimbaud, including the former's arrest, trial, and imprisonment for shooting Rimbaud in 1873–75, the collection of poems in *Sagesse* were composed during Verlaine's reconversion to Catholicism. In his preface Verlaine emphasizes the book's role as a "confession solicited by the idea of religious duty and French hope" (Verlaine 1973, 21), and the *Sagesse* poems promote forsaking fleshly temptation for a faith-based, God-loving life. Ironically, Li Jinfa's poetry is presented as being driven by the opposite motivation. In his 1925 introduction to *Singing for Joy*, he recounts sending his two collections of poetry to Zhou Zuoren for publication two years earlier. Classifying his work as a volume of love poetry (情詩) Li admits that some readers may complain about its intimately loving nature (卿卿我我), but he hopes his poetry can improve "the desolate conditions between the two sexes in China" (補救中國人兩性間的冷淡), in order to pave the way for an open heart-to-heart discussion (公開的談心) between genders. Both poems, sharing a similar tone, can therefore be characterized as love poems. But where Verlaine's one-sided conversations in *Sagesse* are essentially the poetic speaker's monologues directed at a silent God, Li Jinfa in "Chat with Verlaine" inserts himself in a third role that is equally visible to Verlaine's speaker. If Li is simply responding to the French poet's entreaties, does he represent God's imagined voice, responding to Verlaine's mere human, or does Li Jinfa see himself as Verlaine's equal counterpart?

In either case, the third role is an example of the inspired and intoxicated artist who sings a song that defies understanding. Conventionally accepted forms of inspiration for the composition of classical Chinese poetry include existing works of painting and poetry, encounters with natural elements, or the commemoration of particularly meaningful events. In "Chat with Verlaine," poetic inspiration takes on a new form as the creative "spark" or flame in the night. Some critics have read Li Jinfa's liberal use of non-Chinese language as the modernist equivalent of inspiration; for instance, in reference to *Singing for Joy*, one critic observes, "Li Jinfa begins twenty-five of these poems with quotations from European poets, the majority of them French.

This is supposed to be a clear indication of his source of 'inspiration'" (Malmqvist 1980, 152). This implies that Li Jinfa's reader does not need to be able to read the content of the non-Chinese quotations in order to recognize them as potent symbols of connection with world literature. Shu-mei Shih points out in *The Lure of the Modern* that the May Fourth writer writing in *baihua* "was more of a double translator, translating Chinese vernacular into a more scientific and 'modern' language while translating Western and Japanese languages into Chinese. His or her heavily Europeanized and Japanized (i.e., translated) vernacular might in effect be as alien to the ordinary reader as wenyan" (Shih 2001, 71). However difficult to parse in meaning *wenyan* may have been for the average Chinese language reader, the visuality of Roman letters in a block of Chinese characters must have elicited a more forceful visceral impact, and as a shock tactic, did not win over many fans.

Even in the case of beloved poets like Dai Wangshu, positive connotations equating foreignness with literary modernism were usually outweighed by negative criticism, as a quick look at one of Dai's love poems demonstrates. Dai Wangshu was born in Hangzhou, and after graduating from high school in 1923, he enrolled first in Shanghai University then transferred to Shanghai's Aurore University because of his increasing interest in foreign, especially French, literature. The Jesuit institution offered a special one-year intensive course in French, called *le cours special*, which taught by rote learning and extensive reading of texts (Lee 1989, 2–3). In 1932, Dai Wangshu left for France and spent the next three years in Paris, Lyon, and Marseilles and traveling in Spain until his return to Shanghai in 1935. Along with fellow writers Shi Zhecun and Liu Na'ou (劉吶鷗 1905–40), Dai Wangshu cofounded the famous Shanghai publishing house Diyi shudian, and by the age of twenty-three his reputation was firmly established by his celebrated 1928 poem "Rainy alley" (Yu xiang 雨巷).

Dai Wangshu's straightforward poem titled "Change Your Mind!" (Huile xin'er ba 回了心兒吧, 1927) features three phrases in French.

回了心兒吧[4]

回了心兒吧，Ma chère ennemie,
我從今不更來無端地煩惱你。

你看我啊，你看我傷破的心，
我慘白的臉，我哭紅的眼睛！

回了心兒吧，來一撫我傷痕，
用盈盈的微笑或輕輕的一吻。

Aime un peu! 我把無主的靈魂付你：
這是我無上的願望和最大的冀希。
回了心兒吧，我這樣向你泣訴，
Un peu d'amour, pour moi; c'est déjà trop!

Change Your Mind!

Change your mind, my dear friend,
From now on, I will not bother you

Oh, look at me, look at my broken heart,
My pale face, my eyes red from crying!

Change your mind, come caress my scars,
With a winning smile or a soft kiss.

Love a little! I pay you with a soul that has no master:
This is my greatest wish and hope.
Change your mind, this is my cry to you,
A little love for me, it's already too much!

In "Change Your Mind!" the speaker directs his first line at "Ma chère ennemie" and begins the last stanza with the exclamatory command "Aime un peu!" concluding with "Un peu d'amour, pour moi; c'est déjà trop!" (Dai 2001, 20). According to Gregory Lee, after appearing in *My Memory* the poem was not republished again until it was published posthumously, because of its "overemployment" of French: "The use of French is overdone and without this artifice, an already weak poem becomes even weaker" (Lee 1989, 153–54). Judging Dai Wangshu's use of French, Lee distinguishes between phrases taken from French sources and those of Dai's own creation. Only one ("chère ennemie") comes from sixteenth-century French poet Pierre de Ronsard's love poem "Douce Maîtresse," and "the other phrases in French would seem to be the poet's own; certainly 'Aime un peu' (line 7) is not very good French" (Lee 1989, 154). Dai Wangshu's borrowed French is lacking in context, and

Lee judges his "original" French as equally ineffective. Thematically and stylistically, with the exception of the use of French interjections, "Change Your Mind!" and "A Chat with Verlaine" could not be more disparate, and "Change Your Mind!" was composed in 1927, before Dai ever set foot in France. Regardless of the poet's motivation or French language ability, the two poems ask when, if ever, are modern Chinese poets warranted to use French or any other non-Chinese language? In other words, if Dai Wangshu had personally known Ronsard, or if Li Jinfa had actually met Verlaine, would their incorporation of the French language be more legitimate or more literarily effective?

There are few instances of literary criticism on Chinese modernist poetry that offer a positive account of the appropriate usage of French language, yet the poems of Li Jinfa and Dai Wangshu illustrate the obvious desire of Chinese poets to experiment with writing in a second language. Li Jinfa's claim about poetry as personal record stands in proud defiance in the face of the 1930s growing leftist literary movement. In a strange way, his poetry is actually more accessible because it did not require any preexisting knowledge or expertise to appreciate it, as comprehensibility was not its desired end result. If comprehension is not crucial, it matters less that in many print versions of *Singing for Joy* (hard copy and ebook), *Sagesse* is spelled without the letter "a." This detail recalls the work of contemporary Japanese writer Yoko Tawada, who reclaims the label of "bad translation" commonly used to critique a writer's work as a way to highlight the transparency behind a text's foreign influence, arguing, "That's exactly what I love, I want to write like [a] bad translation" (Tawada 2020, 12:27). Picking up on Tawada's celebration of the bad translation as a creative expression of the strangeness of words and language, I want to return to Zhilin's observation that reading Li Jinfa's poetry gives one the impression that they are "reading a translation." Li Jinfa's poems render visible the fissures between Chinese and French without attempting to find any equivalence in translation, and the concepts of transposition and exophony ("outside mother tongue"), can serve as fruitful alternatives to translation in thinking about Li's experimentation. Exophonic writing, the "phenomenon where a writer adopts a literary language other than his or her native language as a vehicle of literary expression" (Tawada 2013, 2), is another form of artistic expression that permits and even celebrates the flexibility and freedom of moving between languages. Considering these alternative modes of linguistic play can provide readers and critics with new ways to appreciate Li Jinfa's poems and his status as "language criminal," and it forces writers and critics to revisit commonly held assumptions about comprehension and inspiration.

Explaining his motivation for translating the work of eight Western poets in *Light Rain*, Li Jinfa admits, "As I read, each translation just flowed from my pen [shunbi yixia 順筆譯下], and I've some abandoned errors [miuwu 謬誤] but others persist intentionally; there are plenty of mistakes and now I can't address them. In the future I won't do any more translations" (Li 1986, 1–2). This disclaimer views the translation process as a kind of subconsciously powered process rather than a meticulous academic discipline but also admits the challenges of translation (yi 譯), and Li Jinfa's frustration and resignation to not continue down this path. The translations may flow smoothly, but they are not works of perfection. Coincidentally, the verb he uses to describe what he has done with the mistakes, "abandoned" (qi 棄), is also used in the title of the first poem in the collection, his most famous poem "Abandoned Woman" (Qifu 棄婦), which appears on the page directly following the foreword. In fact the realm of poetic creation described in Li's foreword is not far from the desolate landscape where the abandoned woman of the poem finds herself, where despite prevalent images of decaying body matter (bones, blood), sensory expression persists (howling of the wild wind): "Since the reform of Chinese literature, the state of the poetic world has become incurable [wu zhi 無治] regarding all poetic form [ticai 體裁], causing the dissatisfaction of countless people, but this isn't vital, as long as everything can still be expressed" (Li 1986, 1). In the second stanza of "Abandoned Woman," the first-person speaker describes the ability to find ways of self-expression, whether it's the sorrow found in "the register in a flitting bee's brain" or in the back and forth with God (yu shangdi zhi ling wangfan 與上帝之靈往返) (Yeh 1992, 33; Li 1986, 3).

For all of the attention that Li Jinfa's poetry has received on the themes of degeneration, ruin, disillusionment, there is a void of commentary on the theme of travel, which undoubtedly played a crucial role in his creative process as a poet. In these self-proclaimed love poems, Li Jinfa employs the theme of travel to emphasize the despair of distance. As much a characteristic of his cosmopolitanism as the frequency with which he employs the French language, his references to travel and homesickness seem nonetheless ill fitting for his self-proclaimed project of sexual renewal, yet they reveal his complicated attitude toward his country during this formative time abroad. In his foreword, he clearly positions himself as an outsider, having gained the experience of studying abroad and familiarity with Western notions of romantic love. Li's pronounced political detachment, apparent from the poetry he feverishly produced in the years he was in Europe (1923–28), places him at the periphery of the Chinese literary canon. Unlike the work of contemporaries such as Guo Moruo, whose reputation as a national poet was firmly established with the publication of *The Goddesses* (*Nüshen* 女神, 1921) after the May Fourth Movement, or Li's symbolist successor Dai Wangshu, who was able to blend the musicality of traditional Chinese poetry with a modern sensibility, Li Jinfa's poetry remains an unsettling reminder that aesthetic revolution was insufficient in the face of national revolution. Lacking a coherent narrative, Li Jinfa's poetic project, and specifically his attempts to blend classical diction with unfamiliar images borrowed from French symbolist poetry and non-Chinese language, failed to find a wide readership. But reading Li Jinfa's "poetry of intoxication" as transpositions—a unique blend of classical poetic sensibility and linguistic experimentation—highlights the literary connections underlying artists' inspiration in the domain of poetic expression.

Li Jinfa's experiments with Chinese and French poetic markers, particularly as inspired by the experiences of being a Chinese artist in Paris, challenge readers to think about the role of language in transposition. By transposing the most recognizable markers of two prestigious literary traditions, he nonetheless encountered resistance, skepticism, and even outright accusations of crimes against the Chinese language and ignorance. At the same time, approaching Li Jinfa's work from the perspective of transposition unsettles the conventional understanding of the relationship between universal accessibility and poetic inspiration. In the context of 1920s Shanghai as his poetry collections were first published, Chinese readers had access to French symbolist poetry through the translations of poets like Li Jinfa and Dai Wangshu, and the "universal appeal" (Denton 1996, 390) that Li hoped for pointed to a global readership imagined beyond what he viewed as the limited revolutionary themed poetry in politically focused Chinese literature. Closely linked to his exposure to French art and literature in Paris, Li's poetic inspiration aspired to be both individual and universal, but the poor overall reception of his work, and its failure to make a celebrated mark in Chinese literary history, points out the inherent limitations of artistic claims to the universal label.

CHAPTER 5

Xu Xu and the Artist's Studio

Having lost the use of the traditional narrative, how is the modern
Chinese artist to express himself?

— WEN C. FONG, "WHY CHINESE PAINTING IS HISTORY"

In Xu Xu's travel story "Montparnasse Studio" (Mengbainasi de huashi 蒙擺
拿斯的畫室) the first-person narrator "Z," along with his female Chinese
friend "K," visit a Dutch artist at his studio in Paris to have her portrait
painted. Z is impressed by the paintings hung on the wall, amply adorned
with images of different models, and describes the space in detail, noting the
piles of painter's smocks and textiles scattered around the room. But he also
has a few reservations: "A couple of these were large compositions, and I
could discern from them the artist's lifestyle and his training; but despite the
lavish use of color that characterizes the work of Dutch masters and an obsession with transcending tradition, he still couldn't match their mastery" (Xu
1948, 120). Another casual observation turns out to have more serious implications, as Z continues to criticize: "There wasn't a single proper chair in the
entire place, so I sat next alongside an old chair piled high with broken
objects" (Xu 1948, 121). Initially, the comment fits with Z's general assessment of the Dutch artist as a disarming bohemian, and the space as a physical extension of his messy life.

After failing to produce a satisfactory likeness during their first visit to
the studio, the unnamed Dutch artist convinces K to come back and model
for him another time, by proposing to paint an oil portrait that could be
entered in the next year's spring salon. But Z is still busy thinking about the
studio: "I didn't pay much attention to K's reaction, because in my mind I
was too busy thinking about why there wasn't a single suitable chair to sit in.

Then I remembered reading somewhere—I couldn't remember where exactly—that in France, people were so sexually promiscuous because there were no proper chairs in any French rooms. Was there actually some truth to this?" (Xu 1948, 122). The subtle line of questioning, presented merely as a narrative aside earlier, resonates with the story's broader message about effective modes of artistic expression. The cultural stereotype of the hyper-sexualized Western artist and his depraved French art studio can be read as a continuation of the fascination with the image of the decadent artistic life-style circulated by writers like Xu Zhimo, as discussed earlier in chapter 2. Yet on another level, "Montparnasse Studio," which was published in Xu Xu's collection *Sentiments from Abroad*, reflects a shift in the imagining of the Montparnasse art studio as a site of sexual fantasy. The studio's sexually liberal atmosphere, and French culture in general, rather than being progressively admirable, prove to be a temporary illusion and ultimately less aesthetically successful.

The writer Xu Xu was born in 1908 in Cixi, Zhejiang Province, and graduated from Beijing University in 1931 with a degree in philosophy, then continued to study psychology until 1933, when he moved to Shanghai. In the early 1930s he was known mainly for his association with the then already-established Lin Yutang, the cultural critic for whom he worked as an editor at the Analects School publications *The Analects Fortnightly* (*Lunyu banyuekan* 論語半月刊) and *The Human World* (*Renjian shi* 人間世). By the fall of 1936, Xu Xu decided to travel abroad to Paris to study philosophy. He quickly returned to Shanghai in 1938 after the outbreak of the Second Sino-Japanese War, then lived in the U.S. and Singapore before settling down in Hong Kong. Although his time in Europe did not last long, the experience certainly played a role in the formative years leading up to the writing of his bestselling novels, during which time he published his work in literary journals like *Cosmic Wind* (*Yuzhou feng* 宇宙風), and often in serial form.

Most Chinese- and English-language literary studies have analyzed Xu Xu's popular longer works, in particular his two famous novels, *In Love with a Ghost* (*Gui lian* 鬼戀, 1939) and *The Rustling Wind* (*Feng xiaoxiao* 風蕭蕭, 1946). The essay form *xiaopin wen*, which translates literally to "little product" essays, refers to the genre of short familiar essays that became the chosen medium of the Analects group to promote their signature humorous (youmo 幽默) style of writing. In devoting their literary attention to seemingly mundane topics like smoking and other subjects that fit the hedonistic pursuit of pleasure and the glorification of sensual enjoyment, writers of the

Analects group, including Xu Xu, purposely distanced themselves from the mainstream agenda of literature that would mobilize the masses. Although the 1920s and 1930s have been called the "golden age of the essay" (Lau and Goldblatt 2007, xxvii), the familiar essay and its counterpart, the preferred medium of the revolutionaries, the topical essay (zawen 雜文), are two sub-genres of modern Chinese literature that have frequently been overlooked in literary studies, which tend to focus on fiction and poetry. Both *xiaopin wen* and *zawen* convey the author's personal reflections on a variety of subjects, but the topical essay, as represented most notably by Lu Xun, delivers a specific argument, whereas the familiar essay is used to showcase the writer's "wit, humor, insight, erudition, intimate sentiments, personal quirks, and prejudices" (Lau and Goldblatt 2007, xxvii).

Xu Xu's early *xiaopin wen* reflect a ceaseless fascination with human psychology, and furthermore reveal his pressing concern with the proper civic role of the modern individual, in particular the artist-traveler. Scholars have connected his interest in French philosophy and psychology to his time studying abroad, which is viewed as a major turning point in Xu Xu's life. For instance, Chen Xuanbo proposes that during his time in Paris, "Bergsonian philosophical concepts of continuity and heterogeneity replaced earlier notions of materialist dialectics and life impulse and became the core of Xu Xu's cultural belief" (Chen 2004, 13). But instead of applying these beliefs seriously to his literary messaging, Xu Xu focused his attentions on creating thinly veiled semiautobiographical narrators who dabbled in romance. In a comparative study of Xu Xu and his contemporary Wumingshi, Christopher Rosenmeier points out that despite both authors being extremely popular in the late 1930s, "they have now been largely forgotten" (Rosenmeier 2017, 1). The combination of Xu Xu's ambivalent tone and the entertaining subject matter of his essays can explain why the Chinese literary canon does not quite know how to recognize his role in the development of modern literature. One account points to his sense of humor as a possible reason for why he is not considered a May Fourth writer: "Despite his interest in psychology, Xu Xu does not indulge in the soul-searching or social analysis characteristic of May Fourth fiction. . . . Like his associate Lin Yutang, Xu Xu has never been regarded as a major actor in literary circles, since detachment, wit and lightness of spirit have always been his preferred tone" (McDougall and Louie 1999, 229–30). But as this chapter shows, Xu Xu's travel essays addressed a wide range of politically relevant topics in the 1930s and 1940s, including dating and intercultural marriage, and while his tone was not consistently moralistic, his semiautobiographical protagonists did not shy away from sharing their positions on pressing social issues.

Throughout his career Xu Xu's wavering position also explains why he was once named by Lin Yutang in his 1962 collection of essays *The Pleasures of a Nonconformist* as one of the best writers of short stories, alongside Lu Xun, Shen Congwen, and Feng Wenping, but is only now being slowly rediscovered in the first decades of the twenty-first century (Lin 1962, 313).[1] Lacking a literati upbringing and formal classical education, Xu Xu's adoption of the familiar essay as his primary genre plants his work squarely in the tradition of wenren literati aesthetics, outside the realm of politically engaged leftist (or leftist leaning) literature. Yet, like the blurry boundary separating the categories of *zawen* and *xiaopin wen*, his "apolitical" travel essays demonstrate an active concern with the need for intercultural exchange as a way to improve the world's (or at least the French public's) understanding of China.

Xu Xu's travel essays have been read by the literary scholar Wu Yiqin as examples of mysterious and romantic entertainment literature praising "the strange" and "Western flavor" (Wu 2008, 127), at the same time the *xiaopin wen* are also replete with allusions to classical poetry. For example, in "Autumn in Louvain," the narrator makes frequent references to the autumn poems (shi ci 詩詞) of Song official-poet Ouyang Xiu (歐陽脩 1007–72), and excuses his malaise by blaming his desolate surroundings, "In the midst of this kind of fall setting, for someone like me who has just gone abroad, naturally it is easy for me to feel homesick, moreover for someone who has this sensitivity toward neurosis?" (Xu 1940, 14–15). As the narrator refers to classical Chinese poetry, so does his travel account recall the genre of traditional travel literature, in which the protagonist's natural environment—in this case a fall season spent in the dreary university city of Louvain in Belgium— acts as a reflection of the traveler's inner spirit. Xu Xu's identity as a wenren affiliate is defined by his choice of genre and the literati sensibility espoused by the semifictional male characters in his stories, in particular "Montparnasse Studio" and "The Duel" (Juedou) from *Sentiments from Abroad*, which both address interracial and intercultural desire, and challenge the familiar trope of the Chinese male intellectual as sexually inferior.

This chapter analyzes Xu Xu's early familiar essays, which were written in the 1930s and subsequently compiled in *Fragments from Abroad* (*Haiwai de linzhao* 海外的鱗爪, 1940) and *Sentiments from Abroad*. Returning to Chang Yu's neighborhood of Montparnasse, I propose that the concept of transposition illustrates the recurring theme of intercultural romantic love in two of

Xu Xu's travel narratives set in Paris, where physical location plays a crucial narrative role. The studio, or the artist's creative space, is central both to Xu Xu's imagining of the creative process and to the fictionalized expression of the sentiment or mood (qingdiao 情調) embodied by the male protagonists and referred to in the title *Sentiments from Abroad*. In "Montparnasse Studio," Xu Xu's narrator finds himself at the center of a love triangle with a French woman and a Chinese student, both of whom end up choosing him over the Dutch artist. Similarly, the protagonist in "The Duel" seduces his female French love interest with his uniquely "oriental" poetic sensibility from his sickbed, which doubles as a secluded spot for aesthetic contemplation. For Xu Xu's characters, romantic and sexual victory indicate that Chinese aesthetic expertise is finally being desired and appreciated in Paris, where the space of the artist's studio becomes a microcosm of intercultural encounter, artistic education, and romance. Xu Xu's transposition of classical Chinese art and poetry in these fictional travel stories therefore proves that the modern wenren or literati offers specialized knowledge and skill over his western European male rival in the cultural sphere.

AN UNCERTAIN INTERPRETER

In his foreword to *Sentiments from Abroad*, Xu Xu confesses to readers,

> Me, I am but the son of a farmer,
> Who knows not how to raise his head toward the sky,
> And can only stand in the midst of the rice paddy fields
> Gazing at the moon's reflection.

> So, please listen quietly to my stories,
> As you lie on your sickbed or at night when you have insomnia.
> There may be some muddled truth in there,
> But it is definitely not a reliable, true account. (Xu 1940, 103)

In the first stanza, the first-person narrator speaks from the perspective of a simple farmer's son, who is inspired by the reflection of the moon, a mediated version of the iconic symbol of nostalgic longing in classical Chinese poetry. The lyrical depiction shifts abruptly in the second stanza, which introduces a pervasive element of uncertainty, both on the part of the reader, who is described as being in a state of restlessness and illness, as well as by the narrator, whose tales are only partial truths. The narrator's inability to return to the original source of inspiration is not the result of a conscious decision but due to a lack of expertise, and the subsequent essays, like the moon's reflection, should be read as creative interpretations of reality. Instead of taking up the conventional position of writer as a lofty authority figure, Xu Xu emphasizes the importance of a good story over personal expertise or reliability, and shatters the illusion of the proper social class, for even though the farmer's son is from humble origins, his account may still not be reliable.

The modest figure of the farmer's son in the foreword is a far cry from the confident cosmopolitan traveler usually associated with Xu Xu's writing, and resembles more closely the narrator of "turbulent times" used by literary scholar Nicole Huang to describe writers like Eileen Chang (Huang 2005, 5). By the time that Xu Xu's familiar essays appeared in Shanghai in the early 1940s, the city had emerged from the end of its "Orphan Island Era" while the rest of the country was under Japanese colonization. Chinese readers may have been tired of patriotic war stories by the end of 1941, when the Japanese army officially took control of Shanghai at the outbreak of the Pacific War, but this didn't mean they were necessarily ready to embrace Xu Xu's essays about the foibles of human nature or the uncertain fate of the world (Gunn 1980, 5). During the Civil War era, even though Xu Xu's works were widely read bestsellers, the author faced considerable criticism for producing literature that did not fit the mainstream political ideology. In a famous series of heated debates over the issue of the "War of Resistance Eight-Legged Essay" (Kangzhan bagu 抗战八股) in 1938–1939, literary critic Ba Ren (巴人 1901–72) complained about the contents of one of Xu Xu's essays: "Although they face a mighty era now, they cannot forget the individualism at their origins. Can we allow them to return to this old home? No, we must launch the battle!" (Wang 1995, 66). The derogatory label of individualism was used to attack any work that did not address issues related to the Sino-Japanese political conflict.

Because of its ambivalent tone, Xu Xu's work was categorized in the politically suspect category of "not pertaining to the War of [Anti-Japanese] Resistance" along with writers Liang Shiqiu (梁實秋 1903–1987) and Shen Congwen, who were accused of "individualism and aestheticism" and not fully devoting their literature to the immediate needs of the war (Wang 1995, 66). Ba Ren publicly derided the outdated self-centered authors in April 1939:

"Moreover in Shanghai, there have been those who treat War of Resistance commentaries or debates as 'using beautiful words to discuss life and death,' reading commentary essays as 'all private affairs'—this kind of reactionary writing, we have also seen. This is not a rare occurrence. The War of Resistance is a collective movement; today, these writers who detest the collective life have become—either consciously or unconsciously—responsive traitorous bugs" (Wang 1995, 66). As close readings of "The Duel" and "Montparnasse Studio" demonstrate, Xu Xu did not comment directly on the Second Sino-Japanese War in his travel essays in the same obvious way that Fu Lei included his reflections on the state of political affairs in his letters from France. Instead, Xu Xu focused on making casual observations about social interactions, and explored how everyday practices were shaped by differences in cultural beliefs. In his stories, Xu Xu transposed elements of classical Chinese art and literature, as embodied by his narrators, to prove the limitations of Western art and the cultural superiority of "oriental sentiment." The process of transposition takes place on the level of intercultural education through romance, as his fictional characters test out theories and practices of aesthetic technique, appreciation, and courtship.

MODES OF EXPRESSING LOVE AND ART IN "MONTPARNASSE STUDIO"

"Montparnasse Studio" opens with the narrator's explanation that the neighborhood's art studios, hotels, apartments, and cafés are appealing to artists, especially foreign students, and describes it to Chinese readers, who presumably have not been to Paris, as a cosmopolitan and artistic milieu where "strangers become familiar" (Xu 1948, 115). A young Chinese man, "Z," meets a Dutch painter and unnamed French woman after attending a Mozart concert with his Chinese female companion, a music student named "K." Initially, at a café, the Dutch artist introduces himself by sending to their table a remarkably accurate impromptu sketch (suxie 速寫) of the Chinese pair on the back of a notebook. The narrator is impressed, recounting, "I don't know why, but in the blink of an eye, I was drawn to that casual sketch; not only because it captured our likeness, but because it also expressed the kind of sentiment we brought coming out of the concert." The word "sentiment" (qingdiao) is used by the narrator to describe the effect of being under the influence of art, the indescribable effect of aesthetic experience—in this case, the physical effects of the music's spiritual influence, the kind of exhilaration felt after leaving a moving musical performance.

When the Dutch artist tries to re-create the drawing again, he is unable to because, as Z observes, "You're trying too hard. Actually when you just casually drew, that's when your genius could inadvertently be revealed—otherwise the entire image would be taken up your technique." Z and the painter disagree about the reasons for this failure, whether it can be explained by an excess of technique or skill (jishu 技術), which according to Z, accounts for how the second sketch inaccurately renders Z's pessimistic spirit into optimism: "No, no, my talent is my technique," the artist insists (Xu 1948, 118). After failing to re-create the genius of the original sketch and wasting ten sheets of paper, the painter warmly invites them to his art studio to pose: "He wrote his address on an eleventh sheet, insisting that we schedule a definitive time," and the narrator recalls, "And so our friendship began" (Xu 1948, 119). Intercultural relationships forged through artistic creation and criticism are linked to geographical place and used to support the narrator's claim that the neighborhood of Montparnasse is an international artistic community where strangers can get intimate.

But the Dutch artist's aesthetic mode ultimately proves to be flawed, confirming Z's innate aesthetic instinct that artistic skill is overrated. When Z and K visit the artist at his studio, the artist once again fails, leading Z to be confounded by the artist's attraction to K: "I don't know what about her could possibly have captured his 'inspiration' [transliterated in quotes as 因士披里純]." The narrator observes the unusual effect the studio space has on individuals: "The strangest thing was that in this art studio, K—normally so lively—suddenly looked like a country bumpkin caught on film who didn't even know where to place her hands and feet" (Xu 1948, 122). His astute observation overturns the sexual fantasy of the studio, which, instead of making K more attractive, actually decreases her sexual allure by making her overly self-conscious.

Near the story's conclusion, Z visits K's apartment and finds it transformed: "I barely recognized her room, which now was filled with new drawings. I could tell from just one glance that these had been given to her by that Dutch painter: there were some still-lifes, some landscapes, two were portraits of her, including the one in charcoal I had seen and an oil painting." He pretends to not know, however, asking innocently, "Oh, have you also been learning how to draw?" (Xu 1948, 133). K is forced to admit her relationship with the Dutch artist but then counters, "I haven't seen you in awhile—

rumor has it that you have a new girlfriend," citing the Chinese student gossip mill in the Latin Quarter. The story suggests that the café is a site of spontaneous artistic (more authentic) expression, in contrast to the studio space, which is associated with artificial and technical oppression that stifles true creativity, as shown by the solution Z offers, to return to the café. Although K confesses to Z that she never liked the Dutch artist and that she prefers to be with Z, she admits, "How could I love him? But his art studio did have some kind of magical power. After visiting twice, I always wanted to go back" (Xu 1948, 134). When pressed further by Z about whether she loves him or not, K is confused, "I don't know, I just feel that Westerners are better than Chinese at being attentive [xian yinqin 獻殷勤]," to which Z responds in typical blasé fashion, "Well go ahead and enjoy your 'attention' then" (Xu 1948, 135). The studio becomes a space of danger, so that when K concludes that she needs to move in order to escape the artist's romantic pursuit, she appears uninvited at Z's doorstep, explaining that if she stays in Paris, she runs the danger of running into the Dutch artist, "maybe to end up back at her place or even back at his studio" (Xu 1948, 138).

The Dutch artist's failure to recapture the authentic spirit of his Chinese subject is connected to the story's underlying message about romantic expression and the difference between Chinese sentiment and Western sentiment. The female French love interest is confused about Z's attraction to her, asking him, "How come you never expressed [biaoshi 表示] any interest toward me?," even though he pays for their numerous outings and meals, to which he responds, "Because I'm an oriental [dongfanren 東方人]" (Xu 1948, 129). In "Montparnasse Studio," Chinese sexual-romantic desire is less demonstrative but more authentic and effective in achieving its objectives. Unlike Fu Lei's narrator in chapter 3, who is never acknowledged and barely registered by white women, in Xu Xu's story the French woman is the one who is portrayed as being insecure, and has doubts as to whether Z is even attracted to her in the beginning. Z's ingenious romantic strategy of maintaining indifference while highlighting his cultural difference is remarkably effective in heightening the Frenchwoman's desire for and attraction to him. This process of self-exoticization succeeds in emphasizing the narrator's difference from the typical western European male as represented by the Dutch artist. Z is also depicted as an art connoisseur, as demonstrated at the beginning of the narrative when he notices the artist's initial skill in not only sketching their physical likeness but in accurately capturing the spirit of Z and K arriving at the café, as well as discerning that the artist's later works no longer live up to this aesthetic standard.

By the conclusion of "Montparnasse Studio," Z emerges as the clear sexual victor; he manages to "steal" the French woman from her Dutch artist partner, and Z's Chinese classmate, after also being momentarily seduced by the artist, decides to leave France for England with Z and his French lover. Upon closer examination, however, Xu Xu's story is about the plight of the modern woman, as Z is revealed to be morally superior to his Western male rival in his treatment of women. The issue of marriage appears repeatedly throughout the essay as a point of debate between the narrator and the two female characters. While K and Z are both under the impression that the French woman and the Dutch artist are married, the French woman tells Z that it would not help her financial situation to marry a foreigner. When he responds sarcastically, "Then you think your current situation is so fortunate?" (Xu 1948, 127), he implies that their cohabitation outside of marriage is somehow immoral. She explains that the alternative, to be a shopgirl, would be even worse, and that she is trying to pass her exams in order to have a real career. Upon hearing her lofty goals, Z automatically assumes, "So that means you won't plan on marrying?" (Xu 1948, 128), to which she replies, "One day, of course I'll marry, as long as I find a suitable French man." The topic of marriage is structured as a point of intercultural debate, as Z and K debate the question of how to express one's love: Is it through physical demonstration of affection in the "Western" style, or in the less demonstrative "eastern" way? And, as the French woman asks Z, must love necessarily lead to marriage? Clearly, the motivation for marriage, and the question of intercultural marriage, were pertinent social issues that Xu Xu himself found perplexing, as another *xiaopin wen* in the same collection is titled "Reasons for Marriage."

The narrator of "Montparnasse Studio," indignant that the Dutch artist has exploited his French partner to play three roles as "wife" (albeit not legally), "model," and "French language tutor," nonetheless rationalizes that his relationship with the French woman is entirely different. The woman affirms this, as she tells Z repeatedly that she finds herself unable to part from him, explaining that "I think I can't leave you, when I'm with you I experience an especially liberating feeling." Z tells her this is because he doesn't pursue (*zhuiqiu*) her, presumably in the manner of the aggressive Dutch artist. The narrative logic demonstrates how the strangeness and exoticness of the oriental man, and what could be mistakenly perceived as passivity—a weakness and failure of masculinity—can actually be sexually desirable, even morally upstanding qualities. Overly aggressive pursuit of art or love does not guarantee success and can even be an obstacle to achieving one's goal.

Z's romantic victory over both the French model and the Chinese student show that "oriental" signs of Chinese cultural identity, when transposed to the bohemian and cosmopolitan setting of Montparnasse, become desirable and superior in the new context. In the case of "Montparnasse Studio" the setting of Paris may seem progressive, with its international public sphere, but Xu Xu's protagonist teaches readers that the artistic community still has a lot of learn from its Chinese visitors. To return to the narrator's skepticism about whether sexual promiscuity is linked to the peculiar arrangement of furniture in French homes, Z's romantic victory over the Dutch artist at the story's conclusion shows how the artist's effusive trying is no match for Z's less demonstrative version of courtship, just as the artist tries too hard to recapture the authentic expression of an impromptu sketch. The effusiveness of French (Western) culture as overly open and aggressive does not bring about a more successful result in either pursuing women or in aesthetic expression; artistic and courtship practices that may be critiqued as outdated at home in China are shown in the context of Montparnasse to be effective and more importantly, superior, at achieving their desired outcomes.

EMBODYING ORIENTAL SENTIMENT IN "THE DUEL"

The trope of a white woman choosing Xu Xu's intellectual Chinese male narrator over his western European male rival reappears in "The Duel," a story about the protagonist Z's struggle with a French man "F" over the affections of a French woman named Kaisaling (most likely a transliteration of the name Catherine), who is referred to simply as "C." "The Duel" begins with a letter invitation from F addressed to the first-person narrator, challenging him to a duel at the Lac Ingerieur [*sic*, Inférieur] at the famed Bois de Boulogne, the second largest public park in Paris after the Bois de Vincennes. The narrator reflects, "You could say that on the usage of weapons, I was completely ignorant. Fencing I'd seen before, but only in costume drama movies; I had never fired a gun either, not to mention learned boxing. This kind of duel, although very familiar to me in movies, on the theater stage, in history, in records or novels, but I'd never encountered such a thing among friends nor did any elders have this experience that now I faced firsthand. I didn't wish to appear a weakling, especially since I was known as [bei renwei 被認為] a citizen of that feeble old country [shuailao guguo de renmin 衰老古國的人民]" (Xu 1948, 141). By introducing the story through multiple layers of mediation—first, the letter written by F to his Chinese rival Z; then Z's own self-consciousness that everything he knows about fighting has been gleaned through popular media and not real lived-experience—the passage drives home the main message that Z's persona as a Chinese intellectual in Paris is based wholly on his association with "that feeble old country," a trait he is passively and involuntarily assigned by others.

"The Duel" is centered around the labels "oriental" and "outdated," whose binary oppositions are presumably "Western" and "modern." However, in the story, the boundaries of these categories are not strictly defined. To begin with, Z introduces the male French character F by describing his seemingly excellent qualifications as a well-rounded modern man: "He was a lively journalist, fulfilled every kind of amazing requirement, excelled at hunting, fishing, skiing, swimming, traveled frequently, was a fantastic photographer, could even do a little sketching and play the piano" (Xu 1948, 141). But these qualifications do not impress Z and are not enough to sustain Catherine's affections. He then proceeds to point out F's inadequacies: "But I felt that he did not truly understand art, he did not enjoy listening to classical music, he didn't love watching formal theater, nor did he love attending famous art exhibits" (Xu 1948, 141). In the hierarchy of attractive male qualities, Z tries to distinguish the ideal modern man as someone who is closer to embodying traditional *wen* characteristics in the modern context: music appreciation is qualified as (Western) classical music, theater must be "formal" (zhengshi 正式) as opposed to popular or vernacular drama, and the art exhibits must be those of well-known artists. F on the other hand is portrayed as embodying *wu* or martial qualities, as even his more intellectual pursuits are described offhandedly as casual occurrences rather than any kind of true appreciation.

Chapter 2 flashes back to the initiation of Z and Catherine's romantic relationship, setting up their first meeting on a Sunday morning when the quintessential wenren narrator is in the process of composing "a poem expressing the kind of nostalgia [xiangchou 鄉愁] one feels at night" (Xu 1948, 144). Recounting how they initially become friends, after Catherine is sick and absent from class for days, she returns and asks to borrow Z's notes. Z demurs, "My notes aren't very good because my French ability is only mediocre" (Xu 1948, 143). Catherine assures him, "Don't worry, what I want to see isn't your French." Their friendship is based on interactions related to language, translation, and cultural exchange. When Catherine arrives at Z's apartment to return his classroom notes, she reassures him, "They're good, but there are many instances of Sinicized French [Zhongguohua de fawen 中國化的法文], which I took the liberty of correcting a bit since I was able to guess your meaning" (Xu 1948, 145). Flattered by Catherine's familiarity with him, Z can't help but also feel a bit shy.

As in "Montparnasse Studio," Z is not immediately drawn to the object of desire, and Catherine is first described simply as having a "still beauty" (Xu 1948, 141). Like the French woman in "Montparnasse Studio," Catherine is depicted as exceptional for her type: "It is truly rare for a twenty-year-old girl with such a healthy young body to have such a quietly beautiful soul" (Xu 1948, 141). Catherine's redemption comes in the form of her inquisitive nature, for unlike the women in Fu Lei's travel writings who display no interest in the male traveler's intellectual prowess, Catherine's curiosity is piqued upon discovering a pile of writings on his desk. When Z tells her they are poems, she asks for clarification, "What do you mean 'poems'?" He responds by telling her the genre, "homesickness" (xiangchou 鄉愁) (Xu 1948, 146), instigating her demand for him to translate the poems for her to hear.

In "The Duel," the cultural differences between East and West as perceived by Z do not lead to immediate intellectual exchange but manifest in gradual romantic exchange, as he explains to Catherine that discrepancies in cultural practices and preferences are what triggers his feelings of homesickness and the reason for missing friends from home. The classical motif of nostalgia and homesickness resurfaces in chapter 3, as the narrator begins with a description of the rainy winter season in Paris and its harmful impact on his health: "I hadn't been in Paris long and didn't have many friends; being lonely and bored intensified my homesickness. Lying on my sickbed, I felt especially miserable, and couldn't help but dream of home in my sleep and compose a few lines of poetry when I awoke" (Xu 1948, 147). Explaining the reasons for his *xiangchou* to Catherine becomes a potent mode of communication and exchange that cements their relationship, which was initiated by the exchange of notes, language, correcting, linguistic discrepancies, and translation.

Poetry triggers an ensuing discussion about the feelings between China and the West during this encounter, the intercultural sentiment that Z locates as the source of his homesickness. Z pinpoints this exchange as the start of their friendship, and as time passes, Catherine's desire for Z grows deeper in relationship to his identity as a poet. In chapter 3, the homesick and lonely Z falls sick with delirium, waking only to scrawl a quatrain of poetry on his wall: "The wutong tree shows a new bit of green. Green, like the jade on your ears. Hence, that is the rain at dusk. Rain, like a teardrop at the eye's corner" (梧桐上新露一點綠，／綠，那是你耳葉上的翠；／於是那黃昏時候的雨，／雨，那是我眼角的淚。 Xu 1948, 147). Evoking the literary trope of the *wutong* or parasol tree, Z links his personal experience of being in Paris during a miserable and rainy winter with the familiar symbol of rain and sadness in the classical poetic tradition. Catherine's appearance at his bedside during his illness is reminiscent of the blonde-haired goddess that rescued Li Jinfa from his supposed deathbed, and her healing power rests in her obsession with Z's poetic ability, which, with his guidance, she seizes upon as an essential part of his oriental identity.

Seeing his poems on the wall she asks him to read and translate them for her. He is reluctant to do so: "She asked me to translate them, I reluctantly [mianqiang 勉強] told her the original meaning [yuanyi 原意]" (Xu 1948, 147). This leads her to ask (even though she has already seen him writing poetry the previous time) why he never told her he is a poet, and Z blames her not being able to read Chinese, denying the label. But then she argues that his poems are "exceptionally rich in poetic flavor" (tebie you shiyi 特別有詩意 Xu 1948, 148), presumably a quality she has inferred from his translation, to which he replies, "The Chinese are a poetic race, for if we call them poets, then everyone in China would be considered a poet." Three implications of note here are first, that Z has a poetic sensibility simply due to his Chinese ethnicity; second, that this poetic sentiment or *shiyi* is translatable into French; and third, that, as a non-Chinese reader, Catherine is qualified to evaluate the quality of *shiyi* in translation. Regardless of the credibility of overcoming language barriers, Xu Xu's narrator reveals how the act of relaying nostalgia and homesickness by way of translated classical-style poetry is an aphrodisiac. Catherine is attracted to Z for his poetic skills and in turn Z is attracted to her appreciation of his literary skill, as from that day on, after learning of the Chinese cultural trait of poetic ability, her romantic feelings for him begin to blossom.

His feverishly inscribed poem inspires Catherine to return the next day, adorned with a pair of green earrings, hoping to "cure" him of his homesickness with her new look. On Catherine's part, this act of transposition does not bring about its intended result, since Z interprets her look as taking inspiration from his wall poetry's image of emerald green. Their interaction is characterized by mistranslation and failure when Catherine corrects him and explains that she was merely hoping to cure him of homesickness and aid his physical recovery from medical illness. Z counters, "But your outfit has no oriental sentiment" (dongfang de qingdiao 東方的情調) (Xu 1948, 149), a quality he informs her can only be acquired from studying Chinese landscape painting. After dutifully studying the Chinese paintings in his collection, mementoes given by his friends upon his departure from China, Catherine "fell in love with oriental sentiment, and thus fell in love with me" (Xu 1948, 149). As the embodiment of *qingdiao*, demonstrated by his affinity for the most easily recognizable and identifiable *wen* practices of poetry and painting, Z equates himself with oriental sentiment, but only through careful studying can nonexpert outsiders recognize, understand, and truly appreciate his cultural identity.

Chinese literary tradition is further evoked in "The Duel" when Z contemplates the dreaded duel invitation by considering his numerous options and possible coping strategies, especially how to avoid looking weak (nuoruo 懦弱) (Xu 1948, 151), including consulting and asking advice from various Chinese friends in Paris: "In China, there were many who had claimed for love of money or love of a woman, to commit suicide as a way to avoid punishment, or for the record they claimed to do it for their love of the country; the first time I was motivated to write [dongbi 動筆] I also followed this formula" (Xu 1948, 152). The literary art is presented as a worthy weapon of self-defense, and Z decides to compose personalized letters to his parents, Catherine, and the consulate in order to respectively "honor" his family name, love, and nation. Even the letter writing process is couched in traditional cultural context, as he cites the Confucian Analects about a dying man's last words: "When a man is about to die, his words come from the heart" (人之將死，其言也善 Xu 1948, 152). In the domestic interior space of his apartment, even though Z feels like a phony and keeps trying to rewrite the letters, the act of literary creation is empowering, in contrast to the Bois de Boulogne, whose external public facing world of a park presents uncertainty and shakes his confidence.

One main parallel with "Montparnasse Studio" is that Z predictably ends up the romantic victor over his western European rival. Z's reluctance to fight, which he self-consciously attributes to his cowardice, is interpreted by

Catherine as further evidence of his oriental sentiment and cultural identity of "a poet, not a butcher" (Xu 1948, 158), which is romantically desirable and superior, in contrast to F, the experienced fighter (but inferior lover). "The Duel" concludes with a letter from Catherine to the French rival F: "Dear F, This matter of letting God choose between two men who cannot coexist is a story from an outdated novel. So I put the choice in my own hands; the spirit of 20th century France is fraternity, peace and liberty [liberté, égalité, fraternité]; I actually put it into practice, F. I will accompany Z on X day and X month and will have already arrived in England by the afternoon. C" (Xu 1948, 161–62). By choosing her lover, Catherine is depicted as the ideal modern woman, and like the unnamed French woman in "Montparnasse Studio," her act of leaving with Xu Xu's narrator Z is described as one that ironically grants her the ultimate freedom. It is important to point out that Z, like F, represents different outdated notions of chivalry, romance, and honor. Z's willingness to die for Catherine for example is criticized by her as "a relic of the Middle Ages" (Xu 1948, 161–62). The exoticism of Xu Xu's white female characters lies then not in their physical appearance, or in their brazen sexual behavior or demeanor, but rather in their sexual attraction to the exoticism of oriental sentiment, typically indicated by markers of wenren culture. Sexual potency in Xu Xu's stories can be traced back to the narrators' insider knowledge of Chinese culture, such as their perceived connection to traditional art and poetry. Their cultural capital conveniently acts as an aphrodisiac to their white female love interests, who possess both a strong desire to understand Chinese culture and recognize the intrinsic value of the modern wenren's specialized know-how over his white western European male counterpart.

The stories also reveal both narrators' heightened awareness of how they are perceived in the foreign setting of Paris, as they imagine the burden that they must overturn social perceptions about Chinese culture, which is often conflated with the Asian race at large. Elements of Chinese artistic and literary culture—customarily seen as partially responsible for China's national crisis—are transposed to the creative space of the studio where intercultural encounters instigate new acts of artistic expression and romantic desire. In these semifictional reimaginings, Chinese aesthetic practices are proven to be sexually advantageous, rather than obstacles to artistic and romantic success. In both "The Duel" and "Montparnasse Studio," Paris plays such a prominent role in the forging of friendships and romance that each time the narrator stops to formally announce that "this is when our friendship began [dingjiao 訂交]" (Xu 1948, 146), thereby establishing the reputation of Paris as a city where people from different cultural backgrounds come together. However, there are also subtle differences between the way the city space is depicted in the stories. While the Dutch artist's studio in Montparnasse is presented as a sexually alluring location with transformative power on its artistic subjects, the studio's aesthetic and romantic potential is eventually proven to be illusory. "The Duel" presents a more effective alternative to the bohemian studio in the narrator's apartment, which is described as an even more alluring space of artistic education, appreciation, and expression that is superior in every way to the French version.

Close readings of these two travel stories offer additional layers of meaning and complexity to what has been interpreted as fantastical (apolitical) exoticism in Xu Xu's writing told from the perspective of an over-confident cosmopolitan womanizer. Christopher Rosenmeier suggests in *On the Margins of Modernism* that foreign settings take a backseat to the protagonist: "In Xu Xu's writings, it is the settings rather than the language that mark a departure from realism. His romances are mostly set in exotic and alluring locales, from cruise yachts and opulent mansions to secret island hideouts. Many of his stories take place in Europe, although the foreign settings are rarely developed and mostly serve as abstract, fantastic backgrounds highlighting the cosmopolitan nature of the male Chinese protagonist" (Rosenmeier 2017, 4). But in "Montparnasse Studio" and "The Duel" the male narrators seem to revel in their Chineseness, drawing on wenren traits to attract women from all cultural backgrounds. Rosenmeier argues that in some of Xu Xu's other stories, which feature mystical or supernatural woman characters, "the female characters appear as exotic and unattainable supernatural beauties steeped in tradition, legend and myth. This is tradition as a source of storytelling material and entertainment, rather than as a source of pride, nationalism or exhorting the masses to action" (Rosenmeier 2017, 4). While the women love interests in "Montparnasse Studio" and "The Duel" belong very much to the mundane world, the literary references to Chinese cultural tradition in the stories are certainly a source of national, racial, and ethnic pride, as recounted or shared with the women by the male narrators.

Xu Xu's English translator Frederik H. Green summarizes Xu Xu's trademark "lyrical exoticism" in his commentary on *Bird Talk and Other Stories: Modern Tales of a Chinese Romantic*: "In fact, most of Xu Xu's fiction of those years, especially the short stories produced during his sojourn in Europe, is characterized by an exoticism that remains in large part aloof from politics and concerns itself more with questions of aesthetics and literary style" (Xu 2020, 17). The process of exoticism extends beyond the white women love interests, to include Chinese women, imagined to be exoticized by their Western counterparts, as well as the semiautobiographical Chinese narrators, who capitalize on their perceived exoticism in a foreign setting in order to emerge as victorious in their romantic conquests. But even though they win by the stories' resolution, the journey is not without its challenges, contrary to Rosenmeier's claim that "Xu Xu playfully juxtaposes tradition and modernity, but the results are quite different as the cosmopolitan outlook is rarely challenged. Instead, it is reaffirmed as the protagonists self-assuredly navigate between various foreign and enticing women who court them" (Rosenmeier 2017, 117). As the protagonists in "Montparnasse Studio" and "The Duel" illustrate respectively, navigating art and love in Paris requires grappling with self-doubt and self-consciousness, particularly with respect to how Europeans view the Chinese visitors.

The stories may provide entertainment in the form of male fantasy, but the images of Chinese masculinity are closely tied to perceptions of cultural identity and difference, preventing the reader from labeling them as purely "escapist entertainment" (Rosenmeier 2017, 73). In these semifictional travel narratives, Paris plays a crucial role, not so much in its foreignness, which Rosenmeier has suggested, "highlights the unfamiliar nature of the characters and events" (Rosenmeier 2017, 74), as in its unique position as the ideal meeting place for artistically minded individuals to encounter people from different cultural backgrounds, and even more importantly, for those who appreciate art to give Chinese artistic identity the respect and admiration it deserves. The "Montparnasse Studio" and "The Duel" narrators do not fit with Xu Xu's typical male traveler, as described by Rosenmeier:

The narrator is an intellectual Chinese man who lives abroad . . . modern sophisticated, well educated and frequently interested in philosophy. Economically well off, he can afford to gamble and pay for entertainment wherever he wants. Culturally, he considers himself a knowledgeable insider. He speaks the local language, French or English, perfectly and is able to engage with people at all levels of society without hesitation or misunderstanding. By being Chinese, his foreignness is made distinct, but nationality is rarely an issue that is foregrounded. On the contrary, his national identity is downplayed in favour of international cosmopolitanism. His cultural fluency and knowledge reveal his sophistication. He is a world traveller whose self-confidence lets him feel at home in any setting. (Rosenmeier 2017, 80)

Instead, the stories from *Sentiments from Abroad* are full of cultural misunderstandings and doubts, and by transposing elements of a wenren sensibility to the bohemian setting of interwar Paris, Xu Xu allows his characters to navigate intercultural relationships that are based on mutual assumptions and perceptions of desire and appreciation, even though they are always hyperaware of their outsider status as oriental.

DISILLUSIONMENT AND HOMECOMING

Strolling through a Parisian alleyway one evening, Xu Xu wryly observed the intimate relationship between a place and its inhabitants: "Homes are like people—both get old. The districts that were so prosperous in the 17th and 18th centuries have now become dilapidated little neighborhoods. No matter how many times the appearance changes, we can still discern something of its existence" (Xu 1940, 45). The verb "changing look" (gaiguan 改觀) that Xu Xu uses poses its subject as ambiguous: who is changing the look—is it the viewing subject, the inclusive "we," including Xu Xu's first person narrator? Or is it the physical space of the Parisian neighborhood and the rundown homes, whose owners, Xu Xu notes, have used "floor wax to shine the worn out floor boards and a flowered cloth to hide the ragged windows" (Xu 1940, 45)? Away from the bustling crowds of the city center, the space transforms in the dark night, revealing its true nature. The narrator is overcome with an "indescribable melancholy," and responds by singing spontaneously:

In the middle of the night, under the lamplight in a deserted alley,
without a single person wandering around,
only a small curly haired dog wagging its tail,
shuddering in this cold air,
So I rest here and kick this pathetic animal,
I don't mind if it bites me
or howls wildly at me,
On this street in the middle of the night, I get a little angry,
it brings out the deathly silence of this cold and stillness.

This solitary figure from Xu Xu's essay "Paris Chitchat" (Manhua Bali 漫話巴黎) may seem hard to place in his larger oeuvre, characterized by what Green has called "transnational romanticism" (Xu 2020, 200). Green argues persuasively that Xu Xu's later fiction "constitutes a creative engagement with romantic aesthetics that links modern Chinese literature to a global literary modernity" (Xu 2020, 198). But the narrator's pessimistic view of Paris, which arises from the stark contrast between the image of Parisian splendor of the past and its dismal reality in the present day, echoes a similarly dissatisfied, disappointed sentiment in Xu Xu's semiautobiographical travel writings set in Paris in the 1930s, which shatter the modern myth of Paris as the ultimate example of a progressive, more advanced society as merely an illusion.

In "Paris Chitchat," which was first published in September 1940 in *Western Wind* (*Xifeng* 西風), Xu Xu begins the essay with a lengthy passage of his own loose translation of historian Émile Saillens's (1878–1970) *Toute la France* (1925). But rather than admiring and confirming the French author's boastful claims of his nation's countless accomplishments that warrant its position at the center of the world, Xu Xu skips to a quote from author André Gide (1869–1951) that commends the industry of French workers, then immediately points out that the accounts written by Saillens and Gide belong to an outdated past that no longer exists. Instead, Xu Xu turns to a more telling, accurate representation of the current state of affairs in the nation's capital: the 1937 World Exposition. "We can see how sloppy and careless the French people [*mingzu*] have already become" (Xu 1940, 37), he laments. Taking turns on each country's exhibit at the fair, Xu Xu contrasts, for instance, Germany's emphasis on its workers and engineering projects and the Soviet Union's promotion of its advances in manufacturing, with France's exhibit, which lacked a main objective and instead "bragged vaguely about everything . . . its beauty and its prosperity" (Xu 1940, 37). In the span of fourteen pages, Xu Xu cites three French writers—Saillens, writing in the 1920s; André Gide; and Nicolas Boileau (1636–1711), a seventeenth-century poet and critic—placing himself in critical dialogue with some of the most prominent French intellectuals of the twentieth century.

Near the end of the essay, when Xu Xu repeats his translation of Saillens's quote that "in the span of a few centuries, all of the artwork that has been created in the country, this most noble society can only have been produced by the loftiest spirit, the greatest drama" (Xu 1940, 46–47), it's not to confirm Saillens's assessment, but rather to demonstrate that the French spirit of hard work and sacrifice has been lost, rendering the statement outdated and bemoaning the decline of a city long past its prime. Then by switching the point of view to first person and recounting the depressing but enlightening experience of walking through the dilapidated neighborhood, Xu Xu subtly shifts the commentary from one of specific political urgency to a broader criticism of human psychology.

Like the illusion of a well-to-do city of Paris, the artist's studio becomes a stand-in for the larger cultural and social discrepancies between China and the West under Xu Xu's imagining. Xu Xu's narrators express their disillusionment with the decline of France and China, and an underlying uncertainty about the escalating war. Unlike Fu Lei, who consciously tried to distance himself from thinking about the crisis in China without much success, Xu Xu's narrators reveled in their feelings of homesickness and nostalgia, using them as creative inspiration. Green correctly situates Xu Xu's concern with "metaphysical homelessness" in the context of modernity and the twentieth-century phenomenon of artists rejecting "a purely scientific depiction of reality and instead seek[ing] alternative realities within dreams or the fantastic" (Xu 2020, 23), and locates this sense "at the root of the nostalgic longing expressed by Xu Xu's fictional protagonists" (Xu 2020, 198). Wavering in their disillusionment, Xu Xu's characters could not easily adopt the position of the knowing critic promoted by Fu Lei, or the confident "interpreter" as idealistically described by Lin Yutang in *My Country and My People*: "He explores the beauties and glories of the West, but he comes back to the East, his Oriental blood overcoming him when he is approaching forty" (Lin 1939, 14). They may have been able to pass for the ideal native Chinese espoused by Lin Yutang—"the modern cosmopolitan Chinese who has re-discovered his Chinese-ness" (Qian 2011, 181)—but their travels did not guarantee an enlightened return home.

In contrast to Fu Lei's "turned back" artist who uses travel purely as a conduit for self-cultivation, Xu Xu's narrators treat Paris as a site of intercultural encounter to educate others in addition to themselves. They use their time abroad to affirm their cultural superiority as expressed in the poetic flavor (*shiyi*) and sentiment (*qingdiao*) associated with their Chinese artistic heritage. These uniquely lyrical traits, transposed to the setting of Paris on the brink of German occupation during World War II, do not offer any explicit, moralistic lessons to Chinese readers about individual social responsibility to mobilize the masses, nor do the stories promise to inspire readers to transform society. Xu Xu's familiar essays show how the process of transposition, as a form of creative engagement, can be used as an effective way to assuage anxieties about cultural prestige. Depicting his characters in intercultural romantic relationships, Xu Xu deliberately endows them with an outdated wenren sensibility that conveniently overtakes local dating and artistic practices in Paris that *seem* progressive and enlightened, but are actually proven to be even more outdated and ill-suited for the uncertain future. Reading his stories in terms of transposition shows that although Xu Xu's writing was not interpreted as politically relevant, he was certainly engaged with global perceptions of Chinese art as outdated in comparison to Western art practices, and sought to recuperate elements of Chinese aesthetic identity by transporting them to Paris. His semiautobiographical, semifictional depictions of the modern Chinese artist in search of the best mode of self-expression failed, however, to address the intersectional complexities associated with being a Chinese woman artist in France, as Pan Yuliang's life and work illustrate in the next chapter.

CHAPTER 6

Speculating Pan Yuliang

Given their invisibility, the act of female self-portraiture—a woman
declaring that her existence is something worth recording—is one of
radical defiance: "Look at me," she is saying, "I exist. I have something
to say."

—JENNIFER HIGGIE, THE MIRROR AND THE PALETTE

In a special issue to celebrate the 1929 National Art Exhibition, the Shanghai-based *Ladies' Journal* (*Funü zazhi* 婦女雜誌) featured a photographic spread of nine modern woman artists, including Pan Yuliang (潘玉良 1895–1977), Fang Junbi (方君璧 1898–1986), Cai Weilian (蔡威廉 1904–39), and Li Qiujun (李秋君 1899–1973). Each artist's image was accompanied by a biographical description, and Pan Yuliang's profile emphasized her years of studying in Italy and France. The photograph of Pan Yuliang, featured prominently at the center of the spread, presents a serious and determined young woman, dressed in a collared housecoat and sporting a bobbed haircut, looking off to the camera's right. The photographic image was immediately confirmed by the corresponding text: "Do not let the great artists like Manet have the monopoly on beauty, she has painted in the scorching sun for days without rest, and even became ill from this. Nonetheless, she continues to hold a paintbrush, wear an artist's smock and work at her easel. Rumor has it that Rodin worked sixteen-hour days, Edison went without sleep for seven days at a time when he was inventing the lightbulb—Ms. Pan Yuliang's spirit is simi-lar" (Qi, *Funü zazhi* 1929, 6).

The artist Pan Yuliang (born Zhang Shixiu) was born in Yangzhou, Jiangsu Province in 1895 and studied briefly under Liu Haisu at the Shanghai Academy of Art in 1920. A year later, in 1921, with the encouragement of her government official husband, Pan Zanhua, Pan Yuliang traveled to the Insti-

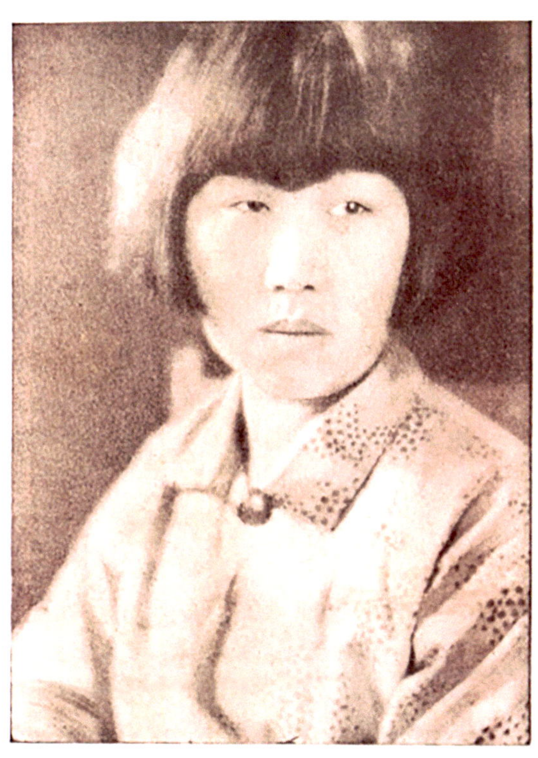

侶貫無華之潘女士，其究研藝術，有瞿啓甄先生所謂之「慢性」，及吳遵所謂「君子自彊不息」之其精神。遊學於意大利法蘭四諸國，昌四畫不輟者八年。回國後任上海美專，中央大學，上海藝大等教職；然仍日處於藝苑始盡研究所中製作，努力於發之精神，不讓大藝術家孟耐Manet等專美於前，曾在到日中作畫修目不少息，受日小助熱兩得病，然聯日執畫筆，按畫衣，與畫架相周旋。吾閒羅丹氏每日之工作十六小時，潘女士之精神別無貺價之。其作品之精妙，會已有定評，茲結不贅。狀觀本刊篇首附置之「顧影」一圖，亦足以見其才藝矣。

Figure 10. Photograph and profile of Pan Yuliang 潘玉良 from *Ladies' Journal* (*Funü zazhi* 婦女雜誌) 15, no. 7 (1929): 6.

tut franco-chinois in Lyon, France, ending up in Paris in 1923 at the École Nationale des Beaux-Arts under the instruction of Lucien Simon. In the nine-year period from her return from studying in Europe in 1928 to leaving China permanently in 1937, Pan was an active participant in the Shanghai art world, exhibiting her work in five solo shows and fourteen group exhibits (Wong 2017a, 17). Her photographic image was widely circulated in Chinese-language journal publications during this "golden era," and her career was held up as representing the most successful example of a modern woman artist (Dong 2013, 7).

This chapter begins by briefly introducing ideas about the Chinese woman artist that circulated in popular media in the 1920s, including Pan Yuliang's contributions to discourse attempting to define a national art, women's potential role in this dynamic field, and how her association with the city of Paris fits into the image of the woman artist. Then I discuss the significance of Pan Yuliang's nude works, which were widely perceived, and continue to be interpreted as, her primary contribution as the "by far best-known female artist of the Republican era" (Wangwright 2021, 60). Finally, the chapter turns to Pan Yuliang's self-portraits produced in both Shanghai and Paris, and situates these works alongside existing art historical scholarship on Pan in dialogue with the themes of speculating versus spectating.

Pan Yuliang's reputation in China was built around two biographical elements: first, the "bootstrapping" story of her association with being raised in a brothel after her parents' death before being taken on as a concubine by her husband; and secondly, her worldly experiences traveling back and forth from China to Europe. The first narrative remains unshakeable in accounts of Pan Yuliang's work today, as countless works of art historiography have emphasized her salacious origin story even as they simultaneously acknowledge its tenuous relevance to her artistic contributions. Art historian Ralph Croizier writes that during Pan's life, "one of her paintings in an exhibition was defaced with the scrawled graffiti: 'a prostitute's tribute to her patron'" (Croizier 2003, 418), and this record of how her marginalized social status negatively impacted the reception of her work in 1920s and 1930s China is helpful in revealing the social stigma Pan Yuliang faced throughout her life. But critics have continued to cling to the sexually illicit details of her early life as crucially linked to her artistic production and its success; for instance, the title of Xie Lifa's 1984 article in the Taiwan-based art journal *Lion Art* (*Xiongshi yishu* 雄獅藝術), "A Painter's Soul in the Brothel: Pan Yuliang's

Artistic Career," draws on the title of Pan Yuliang's biography written by Shi Nan 石楠 and alludes to the duality of her two careers, prostitute and artist. In the contemporary anglophone literary sphere, Jennifer Cody Epstein, American author of the 2008 novel *The Painter from Shanghai*, was inspired by viewing one of Pan's self-portraits at a Guggenheim exhibit alongside a biographical note: "My husband Michael—a filmmaker with a good eye for plot and image—took Pan's image and her stunning lifeline (prostitute-turned-concubine-turned-post-Impressionist-icon) in. Then he turned to me. 'This,' he announced, with characteristic certainty, 'is your first novel'" (Vartanian 2008).

The sensationalist approach to pairing Pan Yuliang's sexualized identity with her oeuvre was firmly established with the 1983 publication of Shi Nan's biography *Soul of a Painter: Zhang Yuliang, A Biography* (*Hua hun: Zhang Yuliang zhuan* 畫魂：張玉良傳). In the original introduction, Shi asked readers to imagine the "ordinary woman" who "struggled from a muddy swamp," emerging to undergo countless transformations, from orphan to child prostitute, from concubine to artist, from professor of China's most prestigious art school, finally to globally renowned painter: "Hers is an exceptional case: nearly mythical, she is nevertheless definitely real! She is a miracle, a nearly mythical type of miracle!" (Shi 1983, 2). The mythical view of Pan Yuliang's meteoric rise in the art world is inseparable from popular perceptions of her global prestige and expertise, particularly her education in Paris. The "Three No's" referred to in her nickname "The Woman of Three No's"—"no foreign citizenship, no love affairs, and no contracts with art dealers"—pointed to her cosmopolitan savvy, as well as to the challenges she faced as a doubly marginalized (foreign) Chinese woman in Europe. That Pan Yuliang successfully exhibited her work in France, then still chose to return to China in 1928, moreover indicated to Chinese audiences that women in China had finally learned to express themselves freely and were being accepted as equals in mainstream society. My reexamination of Pan Yuliang's work is driven by this underlying tension in existing research on her paintings and their place in the development of modern Chinese art. While art historical accounts of Pan Yuliang insist that her art "achieved self-expression" (獲得了'自我' Chen 2018, 74), general interest in her artistic life has continued to rely on speculations about her biography.[1] The author of *Forgotten Histories: The History of Chinese Women's Painting* astutely observes, "Due to her extraordinary life, Pan Yuliang became a household name; yet as much as people are drawn to her status as a former prostitute, or interested in her legendary experiences as a concubine, they know very little about her as a prominent woman artist in China's early Western art movement" (Tao and Li 1999, 189).

The word "speculating" in this chapter's title therefore refers to the intimate connection between speculation and spectatorship, and the chapter explores Pan Yuliang's practice of self-portraiture in Shanghai and Paris, which became the site for her transpositions of the photographic and textual images of the modern Chinese woman artist. As seen in the 1929 *Ladies' Journal* blurb, the vivid description of a Chinese woman painter hard at work, on the one hand, elevated her status to the level of world fame among renowned nineteenth-century white male geniuses such as Manet and Rodin. On the other, as one of a number of equally qualified women artists, Pan Yuliang's reputation demanded visual verification from skeptical readers. In the 1931 oil painting *My Family* (Wo de jiating 我的家庭) the artist wears a colorful dress and glasses, with a painter's palette propped precariously in her lap. Pan Yuliang, depicted mid-brushstroke, gazes forlornly at the viewer, while her husband and stepson on either side carefully inspect the family portrait she paints and poses for. While some analyses of the unusual family portrait emphasize the centrality of Pan's position in the composition (Yao 2011, 102), I situate the painting as an illuminating example of how Pan Yuliang adopted the practice of self-portraiture as a mode of transposition.

In self-portraits such as *My Family*, Pan Yuliang consistently pointed to the look-at-ness of women, actively engaging with widely circulated images of modern women artists in Chinese media, by presenting a personal private realist view that challenged both established and new ways of depicting the woman's body. Although the visual persona of Pan Yuliang the artist breaks the conventional fourth wall by looking squarely at her imagined viewer in *My Family*, her two male companions in the painting stare at the metapainting, as Pan Yuliang's mirror image is transposed to the depicted canvas. This intriguing painting-of-a-painting, a mediated painted surface where Pan Zanhua's image is not replicated, offers the artist a moment of pause from her creative process.

The painting as a whole serves as a reflective mirror for self-depiction and self-creation, while the metapainting draws the audience—her family members—away from her painterly subjectivity and toward her actual artistic output. Transposition in Pan's case means taking the woman's body to the public sphere—not as a nude or photo to be publicly critiqued and consumed—but as a way of documenting everyday life and the mediating

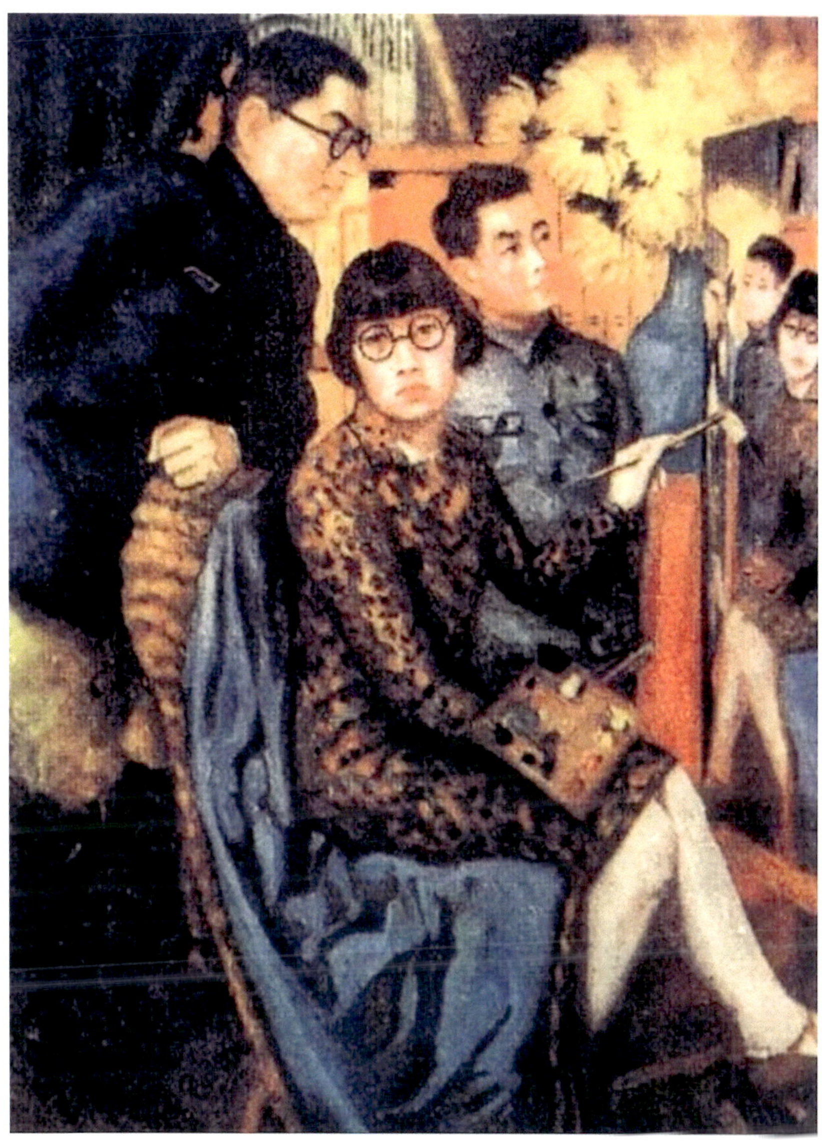

Figure 11. *My Family* (*Wo de jiating* 我的家庭), oil on canvas by Pan Yuliang 潘玉良, 1931.

role of art, the act of making public the woman artist's status as visual spec-tacle in alternative ways other than as a nude or an abstraction. In her paint-ings, and especially in her self-portraits, Pan Yuliang recognized and con-fronted head on the phenomenon of Chinese woman artist as public spectacle. I argue that Pan Yuliang's self-portraits occupy an experimental space in between Chinese intellectual speculations about the modern woman artist on the one hand, and the significance assigned to her nude paintings based on her identity as a Chinese woman artist in Paris on the other. While both mutually affirming discourses promoted Pan Yuliang's career trajectory as the ultimate evidence of a successful art education in France, a closer look at her self-portraits in the context of popular media reveals the persistent obsession with speculating about the modern Chinese woman artist rather than paying attention to her creative expressions of self-hood and subjectivity that appeared to be at odds with perceptions of cos-mopolitan audiences in Shanghai and Paris.

DEFINING WOMEN'S ART

Upon Pan Yuliang's return to China in 1928, she became known as the face of the modern Chinese woman artist, and her work was used to determine what women's art should do, and its ideal relationship to life and society. Viewing Pan's solo exhibit in December 1928 at the Ningbo Hometown Asso-ciation in Shanghai, women's art advocate Jin Qijing (金啓靜 1902–82) first published her impressions in the Shanghai newspaper *Shen Bao*, arguing that Pan's works confirmed the innate relationship between women and art: "Art is women's mission, since women possess extreme feelings and have strong intuition, they are full of flowing sensations. The creation of art relies on emotion" (Jin 1928, 12). The following year, after witnessing the warm recep-tion of Pan Yuliang's work at the National Art Exhibition, along with por-traits by fellow woman artists Cai Weilian and Wang Jingyuan (王靜遠 1893–1968), Jin Qijing was even more convinced of the infinite possibilities for women's artistic development: "Now is the time for the women's art move-ment, its joyful sounds are already calling in the air! The god of beauty is already standing in front of us! The world's weakest most incompetent thing is when 'the tortoise shell and jade are ruined in the case' [gui yu hui yu du zhong 龜玉毀於櫝中]. I hope people don't overlook us women who love art, a social movement surely isn't something that the power of two or three people can carry out. And I hope that women comrades studying the arts work hard quickly, rid themselves of their inner vanity, truly make a real effort to develop women's talent, instead of quietly waiting to see, and letting men struggle to establish the path to art on their own. We need to take advantage of our natural talents to seize the golden key to art" (Jin 1929, 33).

Of course the relationship between women's allegedly "natural" talents and the social project of developing women's art or the "golden key" (jin yao 金鑰) was not clearly defined or agreed upon. Nearly a decade later, the writer Su Xuelin reviewed Pan Yuliang's work on display at a show on Shanghai's Xizang Road in 1938, and characterized its exceptional qualities as distinctly masculine: "Most of women's art[work] is delicate, gentle, serene, graceful, musical, barely ever daring. Even though this is the unique beauty of women's art, there's no need to pretend and be forced to follow men. Though women's art barely reveals women, we must admit this is hard to do yet valuable. Yuliang's paintings, with their deep tones and vigorous spirit, express strength; her large paintings pulsate with life and unrestrained passionate feeling, not once resembling a woman's weak, slender strokes" (Su 1938, 207). Art should be inspired by life, but as Su Xuelin's review highlights, "passionate feeling" should ideally surpass the timid qualities of feminine art. As Lesley W. Ma points out, contemporary critics like Jin Qijing and Su Xuelin were equally interested in Pan's artwork as they were in her cultural cachet: "The fact that Republican women artists had the liberty to show their Western-style or traditional Chinese paintings in public exhibitions and to participate openly in the national dialogue on art and culture is a powerful sign of a modern female identity. Yet their worth was as much measured by the artworks they produced as by their social identities and femininity" (Ma 2013, 203).

In Pan Yuliang's case, her social identity as a Western-educated woman artist was the product of frequent appearances in news media beginning in the late 1920s, which promoted her international reputation as a sign of China's progressive modern art movement. Periodical captions proudly called out the artist's return to China, and her photo was often accompanied by two sets of captions, one in English and another in Chinese. An English language caption in the *Eastern Times Photo Supplement* on August 24, 1927, for example, announced her as the "Famous Chinese Painter in Europe.—Miss Pan Yuen-liang," whereas its Chinese language counterpart (潘玉良女士為旅歐有數之女畫家) emphasized both her gender and overseas experience as states of exceptionalism (youshu 有數) by the title of address "Ms." (nüshi

女士) combined with "woman artist" (nü huajia 女畫家). Although studying abroad was perceived as being essential to the image of the ideal modern artist, Pan herself was careful to not sugarcoat her experience in Europe, especially when weighing the pros and cons of staying in China.

And while Pan's life story was used repeatedly to glorify overseas art education, in moments when given the opportunity to share personal reflections on her career, she chose to convey a more balanced tone, and candidly shared her feelings of failure and disappointment. When *Shanghai Sketch* (*Shanghai manhua* 上海漫畫) heralded her return by promoting an exhibit at Xizang Road of more than eighty pieces produced in Europe, an article including a photo of an oil painting of Pan by her former instructor Umberto Coromaldi contained an excerpt from her 1928 essay "A Minor Impression" (Cun gan 寸感): "In our country's heavy and silent art world, studying Western art has not been easy, especially for us women. On the one hand we have been trapped in the middle of this horrible environment, yet once we escaped into the cruel atmosphere, to locate the correct research path, the obstacles we encountered naturally were countlessly more difficult than for the average person. . . . Even though I think fondly of not only Rome but all of Europe, there was no way I could have stayed there, which is why this spring I returned to my home country" ("Ms. Pan Yuliang's Art Exhibit" 1928).

Years later, she shared her experiences in the essay "My Views on an Artistic Life" as she prepared to return to France from China for the last time as a forty-year-old woman artist. Summing up her life as a city dweller who benefitted from early art education in *xiesheng* painting in Shanghai, then having studied overseas in Lyon, Paris, and Rome before returning to teach in Beijing and Shanghai, Pan declared, "Internationally and domestically, I've had four solo shows and participated in more than twenty group exhibits; this is the summary of my artistic life. Now over forty [years old], with not much to my name, I must ask myself what little I have accomplished. I often say, time has neither past nor present, people are neither great nor weak, without art there is no life, which is to say, all of life is for art, and art is for life" (Pan 1936, 178). Reconsidering the frequently invoked intellectual debate between art for art's sake and art for life's sake, Pan Yuliang structured her reflections in terms of the tension between the content of her words and those of her thoughts: "I often think, among our nation's women, those in the countryside are self-sufficient with mulberry cultivation, weaving, needlework, homecrafts are forms of self-sustenance. But what about women in the city, what about those who don't do well in school or in the trades, just studying for a doctorate in vain, or studying singing and dancing? The knowledge of our new era is not practical, the old household tasks no longer pay off; neither [option] makes use of the world's abilities nor improves family management. Isn't this just too pathetic?" (Pan 1936, 179).

Advocating for a more expansive category of "art" (yi 藝), Pan concluded her essay in *Dangdai funü* by addressing her fellow countrywomen: "Art is a basic principle of life, each should do their best according to their abilities. Not everything learned overseas is necessarily art, and everything old from our country is not; or everything learned in school is necessarily art, and everything passed down in the family is not. As long as we are frugal and hardworking, everyone can have art and life. Why worry about cultivating moral character or ruling the nation?" (Pan 1936, 179). According to Pan, art and life should be mutually inclusive, and be able to transcend national and institutional boundaries. Overseas studies did not guarantee a successful artistic career, nor did new forms of domestic education in China ensure the improvement of women's everyday lives. Pan Yuliang's reflections on the role of women's art overlap with those of Jin Qijing and Su Xuelin in agreeing that if women's art should serve any social purpose, that objective should build on women's natural abilities and talent.

THE CONVENIENCE OF WOMEN PAINTERS

One mode of figurative art that was particularly associated with women's art and cultivating moral character in the face of Western-style art was the controversial practice of painting from nude models, which was discussed in chapter 2 in the context of Chang Yu. To return to Guo Jianying's *Introduction* cartoon of the artist in his studio at the beginning of this book, I turn in this last chapter to another cartoon image of the modern artist that circulated during the same time. Popular conceptions of the woman artist were linked specifically to the nude female body, and the topic has been well researched in edited volumes like Jason C. Kuo's 2007 *Visual Culture in Shanghai, 1850s–1930s*, which examines the "limits of feminine modernity" in the cosmopolitan consumerist mediascape of 1920s–1930s Shanghai (Kuo 2007, 7). Pan Yuliang has long been associated with the nude female form, which she identified to Vadime Elisseeff, the museum director at the Musée Cernuschi, as the "most suitable to account for the evolution of her art" in preparation for a 1977 group exhibition that was the last show of Pan's career (Lefebvre 2018, 47). My reading of Pan Yuliang's work suggests that while she actively experimented with the nude form, she simultaneously challenged popular conceptions of what women's art should look like in her self-portraits, which consciously rejected the image of modern women as necessarily constituted by Westernized notions of sexuality.

In a reenvisioning of the artist's studio, the private space of the woman's boudoir becomes conflated with the public space of exhibition and artistic creation in *The Convenience of Female Painters* (Nü huajia de bianli 女畫家的便利), a cartoon published in the Shanghai art journal *Arts and Life* (*Meishu shenghuo* 美術生活) that appeared on the illustrated page's bottom-righthand corner (Zhang 1934). Its tongue-in-cheek title implies that women artists are at an advantage compared to their male counterparts, since now that nude female paintings are in vogue, how convenient it is for a woman artist to model for herself! Here, one woman artist's body becomes the source of three repeated, nearly identical nude images, and the voyeuristic pleasure of looking gets cleverly reproduced, as the viewer simultaneously confronts three naked women for the price of one. Strangely, while the act of painting is seen twice (once in the image of the actual woman artist, plus a second time indicated by her reflection in the oversized mirror), the painting she produces removes the signs of the woman's painterly identity, as symbolized by the palette, canvas, and brush.

Like in Pan Yuliang's *My Family*, the woman artist, portrayed holding a brushstroke, occupies the compositional center, but here the visual device of the mirror is even more obvious, as the viewer is invited to stare at the mirror reflection, in a parallel viewing relationship to the woman painter and her artistic creation on the easel she faces. Incidentally, on the same page as *The Convenience of Female Painters*, another cartoon about women, mirrors, and self-image appears adjacent on the left. *Haha, Women in Front of the Mirror* shows a series of three women facing their mirror reflections. The thinnest woman sees her overweight reflection and exclaims, "Who says I'm skinny, that's just nonsense!" The woman in the middle sees a tall thin reflection, and complains, "Who says I'm short and plump, that's just nonsense!" The last one in the sequence stares at her wavy reflection, and says, "Who says I don't have any curves, that's just nonsense!" (Han 1934).

The two cartoons, when considered alongside each other, reflect a shared anxiety about women's agency, and highlight the mirror's potential as an unfair tool of empowerment. No matter what social discourse dictates, the

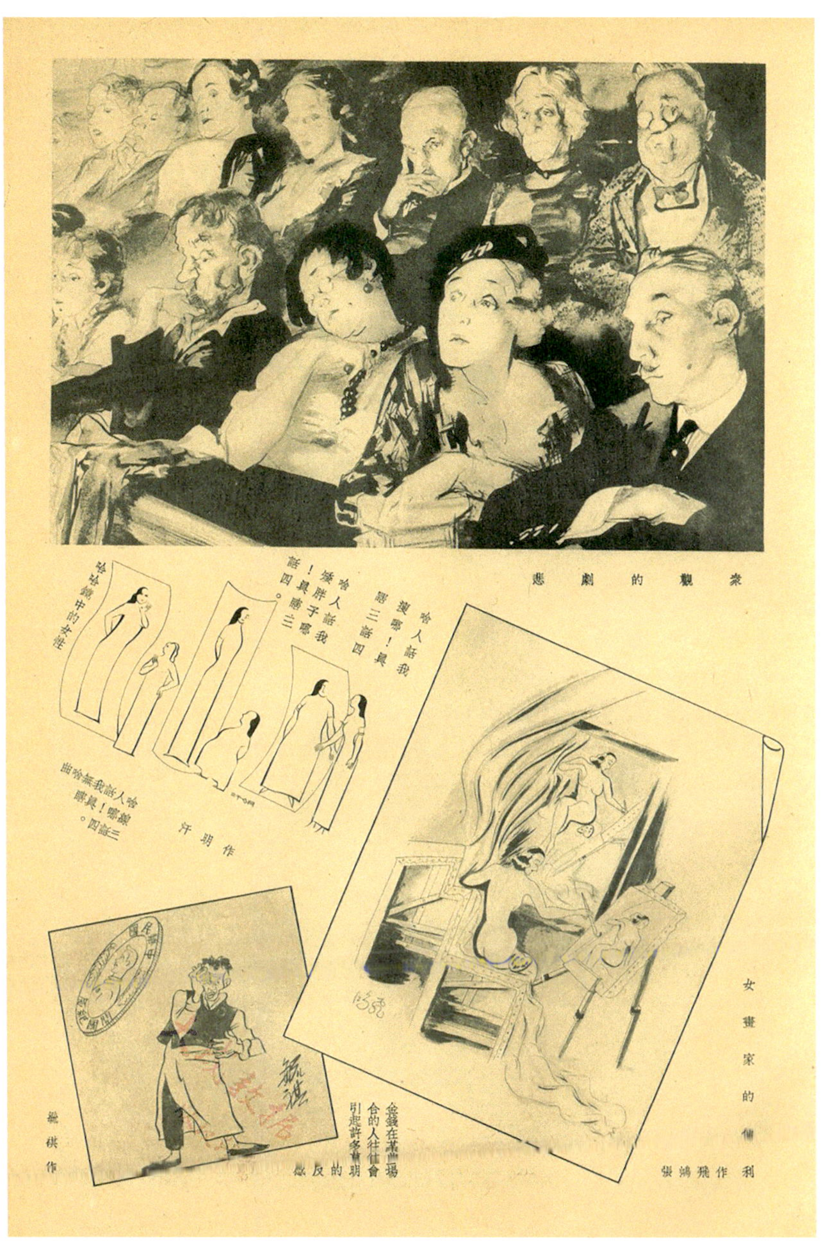

Figure 12. *The Convenience of Female Painters* (Nü huajia de bianli 女畫家的便利), cartoon illustration by Zhang Hongfei 張鴻飛 from *Arts and Life* (*Meishu shenghuo* 美術生活), no. 5 (August 1934).

two cartoons suggest the possibility that the determination of a woman's image and her self-identity may lie within the visual domain of the subject herself. Given the popular perception shown in the cartoon that women artists had it easier, especially if they chose to paint nude self-portraits, we can only imagine what readers imagined to be the implicit connection between the image of the modern woman artist and her work of art. In the case of Pan Yuliang's biographical description in the 1929 *Ladies' Journal* photographic spread, the accompanying caption pointed readers to immediate proof of Pan Yuliang's undeniable talent, as shown in her nude pastel drawing *Solitude* (Guying 顧影), a full-color photo reproduction of which graced the same issue's inside cover.

The drawing, which was one of Pan Yuliang's submissions to the 1929 National Art Exhibition, depicts a young woman fixated on her reflection in the mirror. Lips pursed in a half-smile, she fits the trope of the narcissistic modern girl that circulated in Chinese literature by Republican-era writers such as Ding Ling (丁玲 1904–86) and Eileen Chang. In Ding Ling's 1927 short story "Miss Sophia's Diary" (Shafei nüshi de riji 莎菲女士的日記) the first-person protagonist Miss Sophia describes the frustration of viewing oneself in the mirror: "Glancing from one side you've got a face a foot long; tilt your head slightly to the side and suddenly it gets so flat your startle yourself. . . . It all infuriates me" (Ding 1989, 51). The mediated effect of the mirror's distortion also appears in Eileen Chang's 1943 novella *Love in a Fallen City* (*Qingcheng zhi lian* 傾城之戀), when divorcée Bai Liusu studies herself to determine her sexual desirability, eventually succumbing to the soundtrack of a *huqin* playing outside on the balcony to dance: "As she performed in the mirror, the *huqin* no longer sounded like a *huqin*, but like strings and flutes playing a solemn court dance. She took a few paces to the right, then a few to the left. Her steps seemed to trace the lost rhythms of an ancient melody. Suddenly, she smiled—a private, malevolent smile; the music came to discordant halt. The *huqin* went on playing outside, but it was telling tales of fealty and filial piety, chastity and righteousness: distant tales that had nothing to do with her" (Chang 2006, 121–22). Both fictional examples describe the narcissistic and gendered act of viewing oneself that results in a sudden jolt of misrecognition and subsequent feelings of disillusionment.

The characters' realizations are not motivated by unfettered self-expression and jubilant self-definition, but rather emphasize the gendered social conventions that compel modern women's reluctance to reconcile and identify with their mirror images. Tani Barlow traces the "gazing girl"

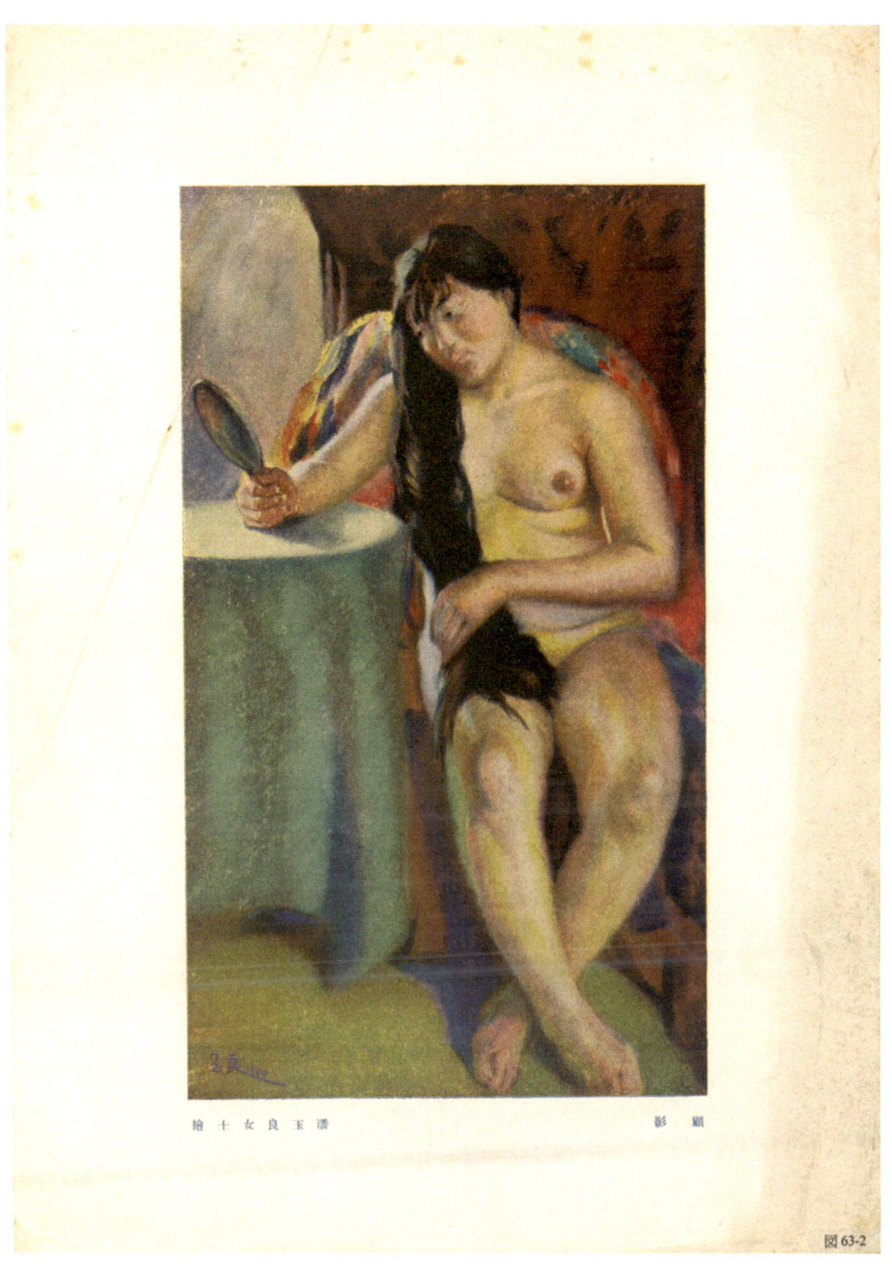

Figure 13. *Solitude* (Guying 顧影), color pastel drawing by Pan Yuliang 潘玉良, 1929, 27.5 x 19.9 cm. Courtesy of Chen Cheng-po Cultural Foundation.

prevalent in 1920s commercial advertising to seventeenth-century art, showing that the *"mise-en-scène* of the artfully mirror-gazing female figure proliferates as genre and technologically alters what can be thought about the present moment, the now" (Barlow 2016, 442). Rather than providing an indulgent space for escapism, the mirror in Eileen Chang's and Ding Ling's stories emphasizes the transitory passing of time and wakes them from self-delusion. Returning to Pan Yuliang's pastel drawing, its title is adapted from the first half of the idiom about self-pity, "Feeling sorry for one's own shadow" (guying zilian 顧影自憐), a trope from boudoir lament (guiyuan 閨怨) poetry. The corresponding caption in *Ladies' Journal* states, "This illustration expresses woman's state of self-pity; the outline is extremely correct. The hues are full of emotion, intentionally showing many variations. The strokes convey oriental symbolism and flavor, showing a simple elegance" (Chen W. 2018, 75). The issue's coeditor Li Yuyi 李寓一 (n.d.) added a quote to contextualize Pan's artistic contribution: "Others do not cherish me, I cherish myself" (Renjia bu aixi wo, wo aixi wo ziji 人家不愛惜我，我愛惜我自己！ Yao 2010, 132). The mirror as visual device enables both self-appreciation and self-pity, and conflicting layers of meaning, as conveyed by the drawing's visual content, its title, and the accompanying critical texts, are further complicated by the drawing's implicit relationship to the artist's biography and photographic image.

The image of a long-haired young woman sitting with her ankles crossed and head tilted, holding a hand mirror may have been familiar to viewers, but to gaze at oneself in the nude, as the woman subject of *Solitude*, was another matter. The young woman's ambivalent facial expression refuses interpretation, yet as Li Yuyi's commentary reveals, this refusal nevertheless invited critical interpretations quick to confirm the connection between women's art and feminine emotion. *Ladies' Journal* promotion of *Solitude* also indicated the critical insistence on reading Pan Yuliang's nudes as proof of combining "oriental flavor" with Western content, which offered significant implications for both Pan's individual career as well as the development of Chinese modern art. On one level, the drawing affirms Amanda Wangwright's claim that "Pan Yuliang's female nude turns accountability back onto woman herself, asking her to value herself and determine her own fate," operating to "promote progress within the art community and [as] a vehicle for individual female artists' ascent from professional obscurity (Wangwright 2021, 73). On a broader scale, nude works like *Solitude* could potentially be perceived to "elevate the nation's women as a whole" (Wangwright 2021, 73), and accordingly, most discussions of Pan Yuliang's oeuvre have focused on her nude paintings, engravings, and prints.

Francesca Dal Lago argues that instead of "objectifying and sexualizing the bodies of women" during a time of intense social and political battles for gender inequality, Pan's early interest in the nude subject amounted to her mastery of "a genre that symbolized the highest technical achievement in the system of artistic education in which she had chosen to train" (Lefebvre 2018, 55). Dal Lago continues, "As a woman artist of Chinese origins in the 1920s Paris, painting the nude amounted then to a double challenge: for a woman, it represented a hard-won success obtained after long years of rejections and exclusions exclusively based on gender inequality; for a *Chinese* person, it symbolized mastering the highest form of academic practice in the very form that most definitely signified the difference between the Chinese and Western artistic traditions" (italics in original, Lefebvre 2018, 55). In China, Pan Yuliang's nudes signaled the fruits of a successful overseas art education while allowing Chinese viewers to pat themselves on the back for being open-minded enough to appreciate a woman artist's sexual liberation.

After Pan Yuliang returned to France in 1937, she continued to produce work featuring nude women. In her catalogue of Pan Yuliang's prints, Rita Wong identifies the nude form as the most important genre that Pan "was singularly engaged in" during the 1940s and 1950s, speculating that the artist's turn to printmaking in the 1940s was motivated by financial factors, specifically cost-cutting materials and the ease of selling prints during World War II (Wong 2017a, 21). The poster for a 1953 exhibit of 114 works by Pan, which was held at the Galérie D'Orsay for instance, features one of the artist's representative nude prints, *Solitary Beauty* (Beauté solitaire, 1952), made from an etching then hand painted and highlighted in watercolor (Wong 2017a, 80–81; zinc plate Wong 2017a, 150 pp20).

The print depicts a nude woman's profile view; with her hair pulled back in a low bun at the base of her neck, her face is turned to the side, and she sits half-crouched on an embroidered cushion, one hand resting on the cushion, the other resting pensively at her throat. In the poster version designed for the show, the model's nude flesh is strategically framed by two words, "Orient" and "Occident," as if contained by these two polar categories. Compared to Pan's earlier pastel drawing *Solitude*, the print, due to its medium, relies less on detailing and the use of color and shading. The Chinese woman's body nonetheless retains its centrality, whose image is a silent and beautiful spectacle to be seen, appreciated, and consumed. In France, the depic-

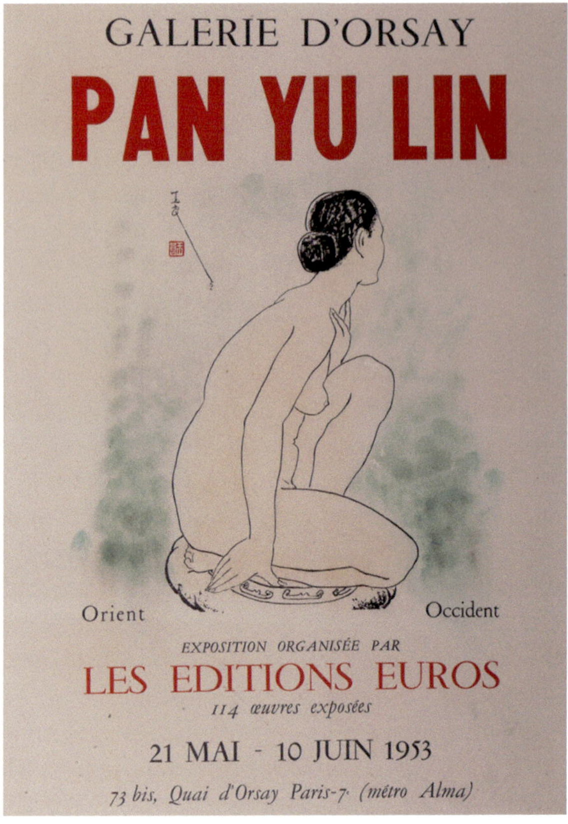

Figure 14. 1953 Galerie d'Orsay exhibition poster based on *Solitary Beauty*, relief print by Pan Yuliang 潘玉良, 1952. Courtesy of Anhui Museum Collection.

tion of a Chinese nude by a Chinese woman artist could be an indication that Western art education had finally overcome the sexual and aesthetic oppression inflicted for centuries by traditional Chinese culture. According to art historian Phyllis Teo, these nude works serve as proof that Pan Yuliang "achieved a new way of being modern": "Given the prescribed notions of femininity and artistic vocabularies available to women of her era, there was neither an easy nor obvious strategy to follow in the representation of the nude. The approach of shuffling between East and West allowed her to gain new insights into both traditional and Western art, while she differentiated, filtered, and naturalized elements that were relevant to her" (Teo 2010a, 46). A press release for a recent exhibit at the Musée Cernuschi corroborates this reading: "During this period, she transposed certain methods of Chinese painting to adapt them to Western subjects. Her nude representations in ink are at the heart of these experiments" (Pendant cette période, elle transpose certaines méthodes de la peinture chinoise afin de les adapter à des sujets occidentaux. Ses représentations de nu à l'encre sont au coeur de ces experimentations) (Musée Cernuschi 2011, 12).

Instead of viewing these nudes as transpositions in terms of the approach of Chinese aesthetic methods meet Western subjects, I suggest that thinking about Pan Yuliang's self-portraits in terms of transposition can better illuminate how Pan elevated the facetious notion of "woman has become her own muse" (Wangwright 2021, 73) to a new meaning, creating new ways of how the woman artist could do this *outside* of the nude form or the photographic image, especially since visual forms of proof of the woman painter's artistic ability were a necessary and direct response to the popular sentiment conveyed in Zhang Hongfei's cartoon about the convenience of women artists. In a review of Pan Yuliang's exhibit, Su Xuelin recounted two instances demonstrating the stupidity of Pan's work ethic and diligence (ben gongfu 笨功夫), once during her time in Lyon, when she borrowed a plaster mannequin to practice: "She sat there in the studio all day, squinting at the mannequin with her head tilted, measuring the length and height with her brush, reciting over and over, 'The ratio of head to chest is X, the ratio of arm to leg is Y'" (Su 1938, 212). Complaining that a rough draft took days for the artist to complete in order to guarantee perfection, Su Xuelin shared with readers another occasion, during which Pan Yuliang was sketching a chrysanthemum: "Because she painted it during the first light of dawn, she had to wait every day for that same time to paint a little. She couldn't finish it in one day, and it took days to complete. Worried the chrysanthemum would wither before the painting's completion, she even got up at midnight to spray it with cold water to make sure the lighting was correct" (Su 1938, 212–13). While published accounts by Su Xuelin attested to Pan Yuliang's reputation as a diligent worker—one as hardworking as her artistic French forefathers Rodin and Édouard Manet—they also had the potential to make Pan Yuliang look ridiculous, as if in her steadfast pursuit of verisimilitude, she lost sight of any poetic flavor.

In the same review published in 1938, Su Xuelin argued that the ideal of figurative drawing should follow Chinese poetic philosophy, an inherent cultural trait that set Chinese artistic practice apart from that of the rest of the world: "Chinese people are the smartest in the world, others walk step by step on earth, we must fly toward the sky, and we should adopt this same attitude toward art, as [Su] Shi already said long ago, 'Anyone who judges painting by resemblance to life / Has the understanding of a child. Anyone who insists on writing the poem assigned, / Is certainly not a man who knows poetry" (Su 1938, 208; English translation of Su Shi's poem in Egan 1983, 426). Pan Yuliang's self-portraits can be seen as a creative response to Su Xuelin's push for the mode of "poet's painting" (shiren de hua 詩人的畫) that "rejects and overturns formal likeness" in service of developing Chinese artistic talent (Su 1938, 208).

RETURNING THE GAZE IN SELF-PORTRAITURE

Like Chang Yu, Pan Yuliang produced numerous paintings featuring nude figures and still-lifes, but departing from Chang Yu's oeuvre, Pan Yuliang turned occasionally to self-portraiture. In a 2018 article on Pan Yuliang's self-portraits for *Art Marketplace* magazine, Chen Weiqi contended, "If we view Pan Yuliang's self-portraits as a confessional vehicle [zibai zaiti 自白載體], then we discern from beginning to end Pan Yuliang's dignified expression, always containing within it her inferior status" (Chen W. 2018, 77). Pan Yuliang produced the bulk of her self-portraits in the period from 1924 to 1949, totaling at least nineteen works according to one account (Chen W. 2018, 76), and indeed her contemporaries such as Zhang Daofan (張道藩 1897–1968), insisted on interpreting her self-portraits in particular as a mode of deciphering, announcing in a review of Pan Yuliang's 1937 show, "After seeing her 'Self-portrait,' and her portraits of 'Barbarian Girl' and Mr. Chen Yu, we must admire Ms. Pan's self-knowledge, otherwise she would not be able to evoke herself and the spirit of those others so realistically into painting" (Zhang 1937). Art historians have consistently read Pan Yuliang's self-portraits in the confessionary mode of Chinese women's social liberation in the early twentieth century, but as Chen Weiqi's proposal illustrates, references to Pan's unconventional and illegitimate upbringing persist, even as critics agree that her career constituted a definitive step toward women's equality and social progress.

Art historian Yao Daimei argues that self-portraits in general represent a symbol of early twentieth-century individualism: "This mode of artistic and spiritual expression asked who am 'I' and how am 'I,' as a narrative form, including women authors' self-awakening, self-examination, self-naming and self-positioning during this period" (Yao 2011, 107). Reading Pan Yuliang's work in terms of the broader trend of women's self-narration (zishu

自述) writing, Yao asserts, "No matter the medium, Pan Yuliang's work shared a distinctive trait: in her world she always spoke for herself [zishuo zihua 自說自話]" (Yao 2010, 133). More recently, curator Eric Lefebvre argues that Chinese women's practice of self-portraiture amounts to an act of reappropriation of Western art practice: "The image of a woman being the author of her own portrait conveyed by contemporary press is rightly perceived as a sign of social emancipation. It was also the consequence of the opening of China to the outside world, and of the re-appropriation of Western pictorial traditions by Chinese artists who have chosen to train in Europe" (Lefebvre 2018, 25). These interpretations of Pan Yuliang's art align conveniently with the national narrative of women's liberation and a global feminist agenda, but also overlook the discourse of silence and invisibility that underpins scholarly work on Pan.

My discussion and analysis of Pan Yuliang's portraits take a more balanced approach; by considering her self-portraits as works of transposition, I examine how Pan's exhibition strategies served in the construction of woman artist as visual subject. In her self-portraits, Pan Yuliang invited viewers in China and France to reconsider their expectations of what a modern Chinese woman artist should look like by transposing photographic images and critical narratives of this new figure. Pan Yuliang presented curious viewers with one version of her artistic identity in Paris in the 1943 work *Garden Party* (Tingyuan juhui 庭院聚會). The painting depicts six women and two dogs gathered in a private garden, encircling Pan Yuliang, who sits at the center in a vibrant *qipao* dress with her canvas on her lap. Self-portraits of the woman artist painting such as Pan Yuliang's *Garden Party* and *My Family* are commonplace in the history of portraiture, and these kinds of images act as visual corroboration, dovetailing with anecdotes of women's suitability for the artistic profession.

While Lefebvre reads one version of the painting symbolically as "an image of a dialogue between Chinese and Western cultures" that conveys "female fraternity, an image of solidarity and peace in a world at war" of French women gathered around a Chinese artist, my interpretation emphasizes the act of painting as spectacle (Lefebvre 2018, 35). In the garden image, Pan Yuliang documents her centrality as the focus in compositional terms, while she is conscious that her racialized presence is significant as a vehicle for conversation and artistic exchange, as her friends (youren 友人) look at everything except her. In this gendered, contained space of cultivated nature, Pan appears in her brightly colored qipao,[2] eyes downcast at her can-

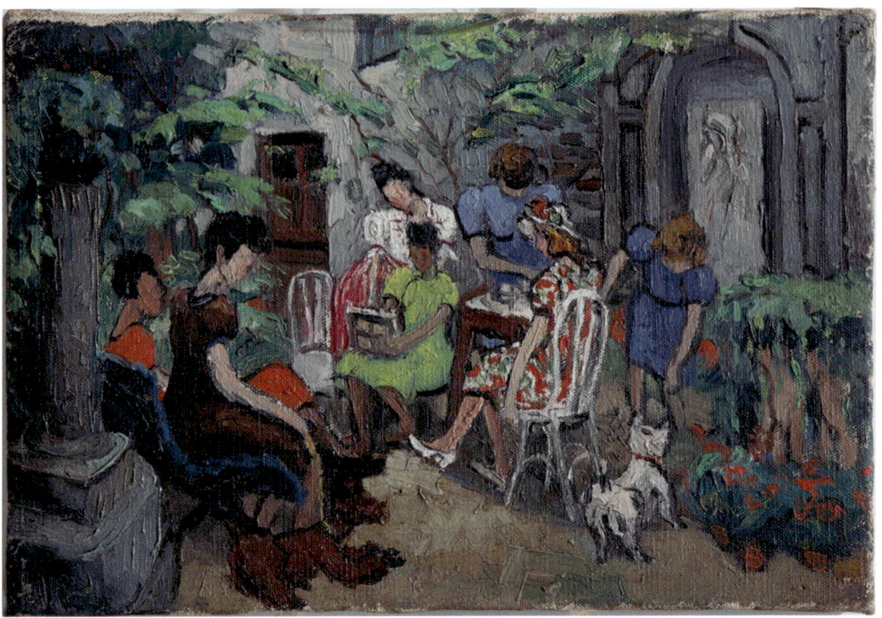

Figure 15. *Garden Party* (Tingyuan juhui 庭院聚會), oil on canvas by Pan Yuliang 潘玉良, 1943, 27 x 41 cm. Courtesy of Anhui Museum Collection.

vas, which is situated as a starting point for conversation among women about art.

In Pan Yuliang's solo self-portraits, the visual subject—the artist herself—pointedly challenges two tropes: that of the woman artist and also that of the gazing girl. Refusing to depict the act of looking at herself, the subject in her self-portraits looks directly at the viewer. Existing Chinese-language scholarship on Pan Yuliang points to her self-portraits as the ultimate example of modern women's self-expression (ziwo biaoda 自我表達), but rather than reading her self-portraits as free declarations of self-expression, they need to be considered in the context of discussions of the modern Chinese artist in Paris, and also gendered conversations about the modern woman artist. Pan Yuliang's self-portraits fulfill in fact Su Xuelin's call for young Chinese artists to create "decadent and weird" (tuifang guaipi 頹放，怪癖) poetry (art), based on Yuan Zicai's (袁子才 1716–97) poetic theory (Su 1938, 213). As outliers in modern Chinese art history, Pan Yuliang's self-portraits serve multiple functions, as Sandy Ng observes: "She documented herself as an artist, however, through self portrayal, making her artistic skills, personhood, and professional choices manifest in painted form. Her portrayals revealed fundamental qualities of the artist's body and self. Pan lived in an era when a woman's grace and beauty were paramount, when images were a crucial avenue to understanding a dynamic culture. Through her compositions, she constructs her story and her own sense of identity. In her photographs, she gazes into the distance, a typical demeanor required of women to appear modest, or she is seen as a working artist, sculpting intensely. Her self portrayal affirms her professional prowess. Rather than depicting herself in a flattering manner, she regains the subjectivity of the female model" (Ng 2019, 26). As visual forms of self-construction, Pan's self-portraits reflect Lesley Ma's analysis of similar works in this genre by women artists that appeared in modern periodicals such as *Liangyou*: "Self-portraits present artists from their own point of view and are essentially performances that offer visual clues into the artists' self-perception" (Ma 2013, 211). By performing the contradictory part of a direct and straightforward yet somehow still inscrutable artist, Pan Yuliang invited, even required, the viewer's speculation in her paintings.

Although Pan Yuliang's self-portraits did not end up on any magazine or journal covers, many were submitted to be exhibited in group shows in France in the 1940s. Compared to the self-portrait on the cover of *Liangyou* by women artists such as Liang Xueqing (梁雪清 1890-?) in June 1926, Ma suggests, "A female artist's self-portrait on a magazine cover signified an endorsement of both her progressive art and her sellable looks. . . . it seems that the female bodily image holds significant value, sometimes more than her artistry, in terms of popular appeal" (Ma 2013, 213), Pan Yuliang's exhibition strategy in Paris in the 1930s and 1940s was for a markedly different audience than the intended urban Chinese female reader-consumers in Shanghai. By putting herself on display, she could not avoid being objectified, but she certainly had agency over *how* to present herself to viewers in France, China, and potentially elsewhere.

In two oil paintings from 1939, Pan Yuliang sits on a chair and faces the viewer, arms folded in her lap, recognizable in her stylish bangs and short bobbed haircut. *Self-Portrait with Fan* (執扇自畫像 1939) was submitted to the fifty-third official exhibition of the Société nationale des Beaux Arts, Salon de 1939, held at the French National Fine Arts Palace. The austerity of her unadorned black qipao is offset by the subject's eye contact with the viewer; head slightly tilted, her questioning gaze is highlighted in contrast to the light coming in from a sunlit window behind Pan. The coat rack in the back-

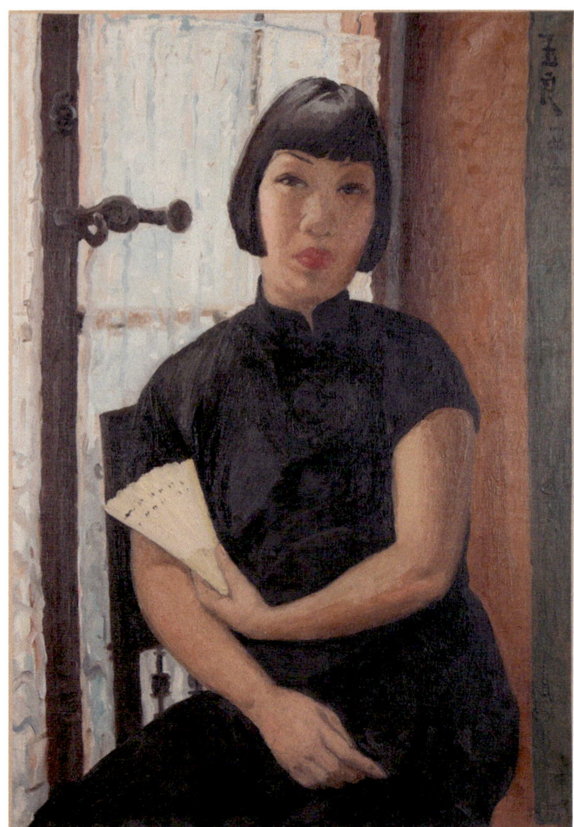

Figure 16. *Self-Portrait with Fan* (Zhi shan zihuaxiang 執扇自畫像), oil on canvas by Pan Yuliang 潘玉良, 1939, 91 cm x 64 cm. Courtesy of Anhui Museum Collection.

ground, the wavy lines of the hanging curtain, along with orangish wall with green painted framing that holds her signature in its bottom left corner in the background, emphasize the painting's vertical orientation. Other than the white folded fan held loosely in her left hand, the wooden coat rack, and the simple chair whose back is barely shown, there are no other props that adorn the room to give us clues into her private life.

In *Self-Portrait in a Green Dress*, another oil on canvas from 1939, Pan Yuliang does not look directly at the viewer, and holds her head rigidly straight, right arm cradled at her waist. Pan's left arm rests in her lap and holds a red book (not *the* red book!). With her nails painted light pink, and with a white powdered face and blush on her cheeks, Pan Yuliang presents another perfectly coiffed version of herself, complete with her signature red lipstick and black eyeliner. She wears a light green qipao dress patterned in

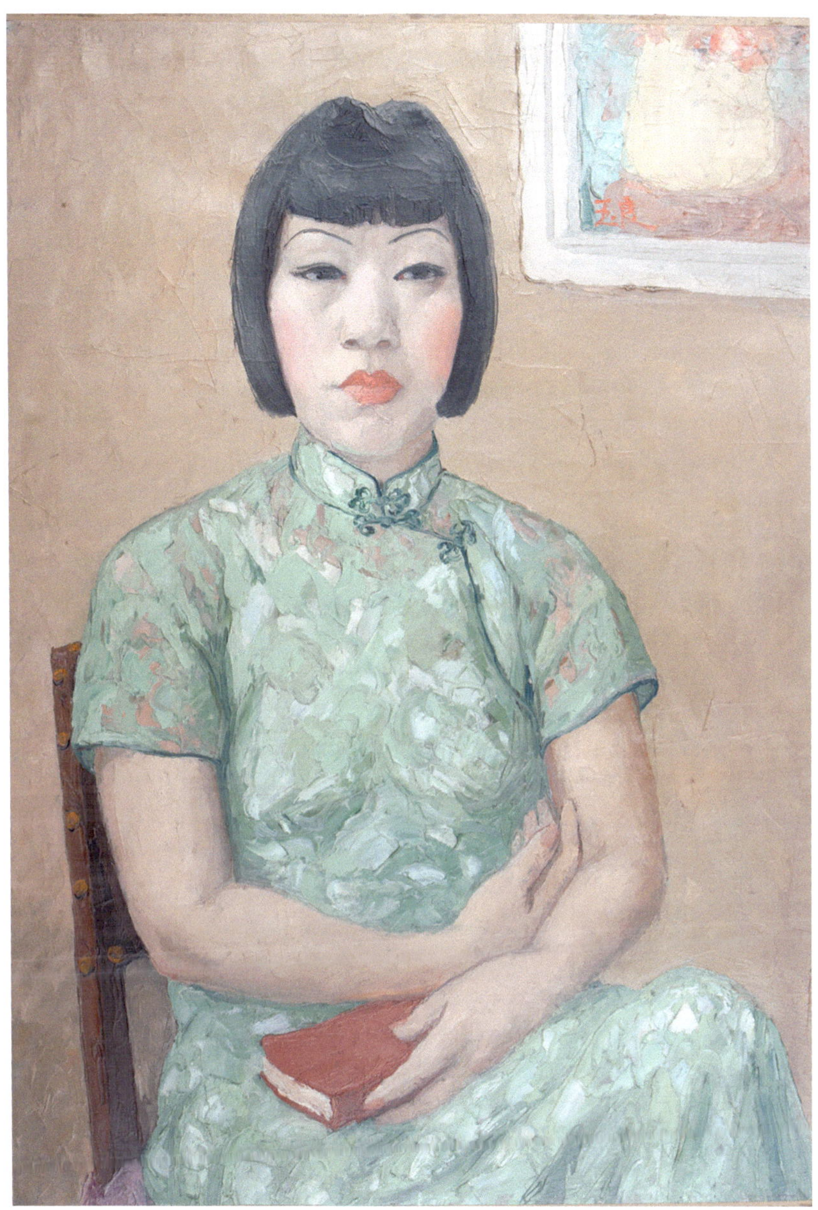

Figure 17. *Self-Portrait in a Green Dress* (Zihuaxiang lüqun 自画像绿裙), oil on canvas by Pan Yuliang 潘玉良, 1939, 91 cm x 64 cm. Courtesy of Anhui Museum Collection.

impressionist colors, featuring a detail of dark green knotted *pankou* 盤扣 buttons. The painting, which was shown at Salon des Indépendants that year, features a simple and plain background, except for the bottom left corner of a framed painting in the upper right corner. Like the window in *Self-Portrait with Fan*, this part of a frame, along with the book, alludes to a mediated world, another layer of separation that distinguishes Pan's interior state from what lies beyond. In *Self-Portrait in a Green Dress*, the partial-painting reveals only a peek at the bright colors set against its white frame, and the painting is also a clever holder for Pan Yuliang's signature. In these two self-portraits, Pan Yuliang retains recognizable markers of Asian identity, such as a folding fan, her qipao, and the two characters denoting her Chinese name (versus Sanyu's romanized signature). At the same time that Pan refuses to evoke the sexually alluring, narcissistic modern girl, the viewer is reminded of the implication in all self-portraiture—the work's creation is only possible logistically through repeated gazing at one's image, reproduced either in the mirror reflection or in a photograph.

Although there is no scholarly consensus on the historical origins of the iconic qipao dress, its popularity in 1920s-1940s Shanghai is undeniable (Barlow 2021, 216). The word, used interchangeably with its Cantonese romanization *cheongsam*, suggests both gender and ethnic definitions at its origins (Ng 2015, 55). In "A Chronicle of Changing Clothes" (Gengyi ji 更衣記, 1943), Eileen Chang reflected that early twentieth-century versions of the dress were motivated by women's desire to dress like men, but by the Republican period, its outward form had clearly evolved: "What remained was a tight sleeveless sheath, showing the neck, the arms, and the part of the leg below the knee. What is important now is the person: the *qipao* became nothing more than a foil faithfully setting off the contours of the figure" (Chang 2005, 72). In her analysis of the qipao, Antonia Finnane contends that gradually shortened hem lines and sleeves, and body-skimming seams, along with its defining feature of side splits, indicated recognition that "clothes created a perception of exposure much more powerful than was achieved by actual nakedness" (Finnane 2008, 156). In this context, even though Pan Yuliang's modest self-portraits seem like a far call from her nude prints and paintings, the subject's gently sloping, bare arms, which intimately frame the curves of her body, invite the viewer to visualize the sensual flesh obscured by the qipao.

A similar composition appears with noticeable variations in the two self-portraits painted in France in the 1940s, as Pan Yuliang faces her viewer

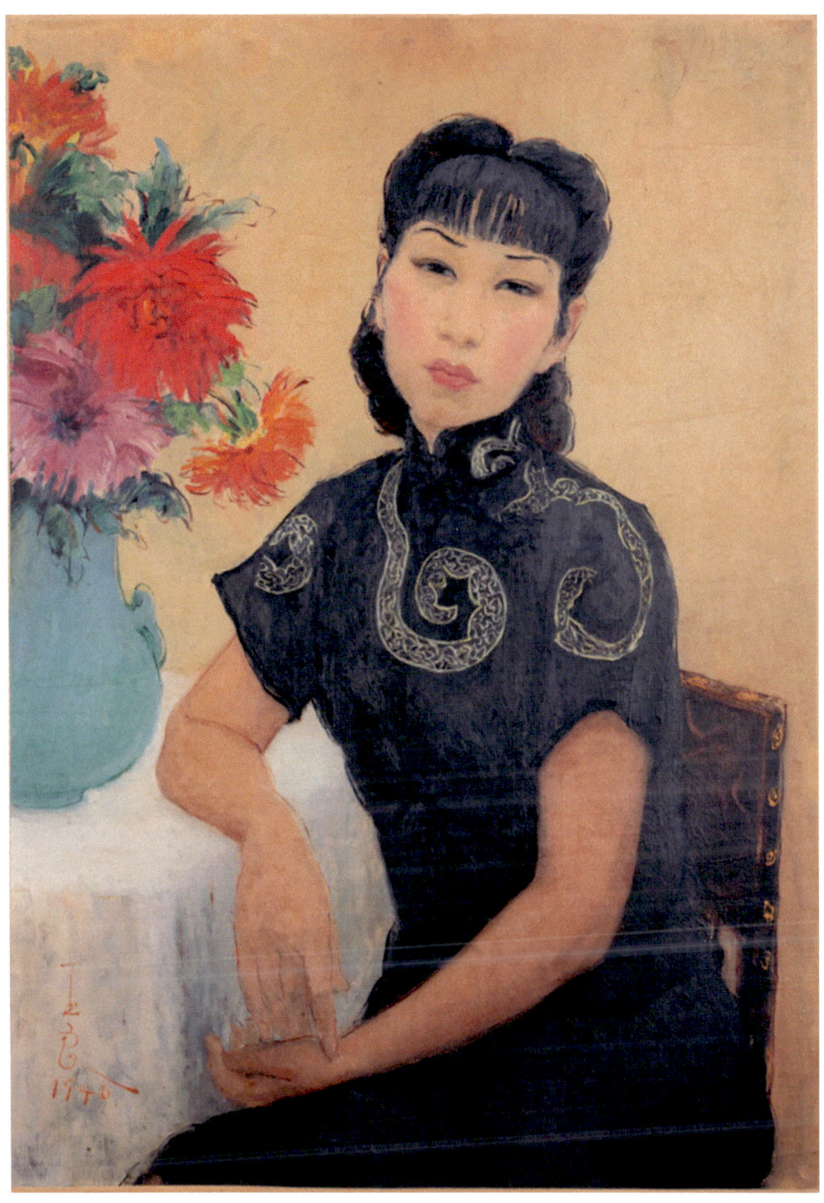

Figure 18. *Self-Portrait* (Zihuaxiang 自畫像), oil on canvas by Pan Yuliang 潘玉良, 1940, 90 cm x 64 cm. Courtesy of Anhui Museum Collection.

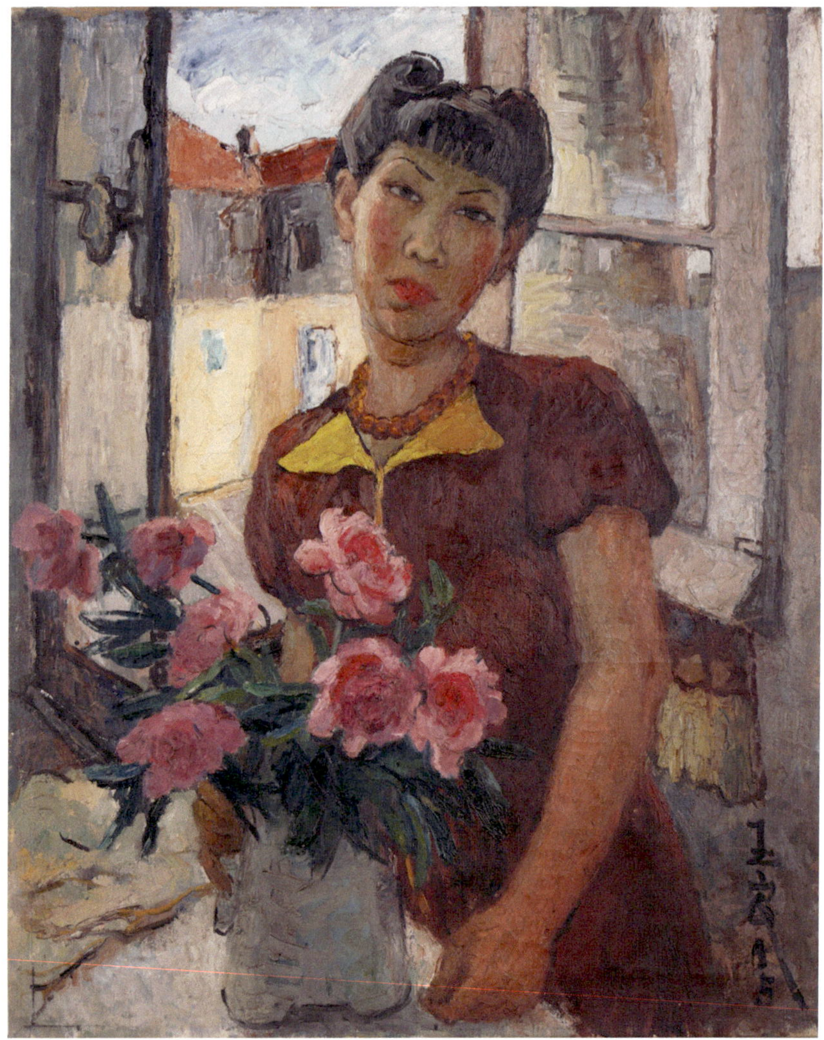

Figure 19. *Self-Portrait* (Zihuaxiang 自畫像), oil on canvas by Pan Yuliang 潘玉良, 1945, 73 cm x 59 cm. Courtesy of Anhui Museum Collection.

with head tilted and eyebrows carefully arched, accompanied in each piece by a floral arrangement. *Self-Portrait* from 1940 depicts Pan Yuliang sitting in a chair with her right elbow propped on a table. Part of a bouquet of multicolored chrysanthemums in a blue vase has been placed on a white tablecloth, but other than the chair, a table, and the vase, nothing else in the room is illustrated.

Pan wears a black qipao with swirling, white embroidered detailing at the neck, chest, and shoulders, and she gazes at the viewer, eyes slightly narrowed. Her trademark bangs are the focus of her nearly shoulder-length, slightly wavy black hair. Hands empty, Pan points her right index finger down into her left palm. Except for the brilliant vibrance of magenta and red blossoms, the tone of the painting is wistfully subdued, contemplative, and understated.

In the 1945 *Self-Portrait*, the viewer finally gains a better sense of the apartment's exterior setting, as Pan Yuliang poses in front of an open window. Neighboring rooftops in the city are visible against the blue sky spotted with clouds. Wearing a dark red dress with a contrasting yellow collar and an orange necklace, Pan appears in her short hair and trademark bangs, with a slightly downturned mouth. She stands, lightly leaning on a table that holds a vase of bright pink peonies. The bouquet is displayed nearly in its entirety, and its unwieldy size and striking color draw the viewer's eye away from Pan. Her impressionistic use of contrasting dabs of color makes this the least realistic painting out of the four self-portraits here but still we sense that she is documenting and memorializing a particular moment in time and specific place, even if we know that practically she must have fastidiously worked on these self-portraits obsessively, as Su Xuelin documented the issue with the chrysanthemum sketch.

In addition to the shifting gendered implications of the qipao, the article of clothing also became a visual symbol of Chinese cultural identity during a time of cross-cultural encounters. Finnane cites the memoir of former first lady of the Republic of China, Madame Wellington Koo (née Oei Hui-lan 黃慧蘭 1889–1992), who moved to Shanghai in the 1920s before going to Paris in 1932 to accompany her husband, V. K. Wellington Koo, the Chinese ambassador to France until 1940. In her autobiography *No Feast Lasts Forever*, Oei Hui-lan attested to how her identity as an Indonesian-Chinese socialite was largely shaped by sartorial preferences: "When I first arrived in China, I wore Western clothes, dresses and coat I had brought from Paris and London. . . . The so-called chic Chinese women often wore smartly cut jackets and trousers, but they looked down on the beautiful Chinese silks, preferring French fabrics, and they wore their hair Western fashion, going to the French beauty shops" (Koo 1975, 181). According to Oei Hui-lan, the "smart Chinese ladies in Shanghai" did not appreciate local Chinese fashion: "It was all as ridiculous and phony—if I may use that modern word again—as their British accents. They never understood the importance and value of their own beautiful silk and the exquisite workmanship that was so typically Chinese" (Koo 1975, 182). As a foreign outsider in Shanghai, Oei Hui-lan attained trendsetter status simply by recognizing what local women overlooked when they chose to wear foreign fashion.

Rejecting the trend of following Western styles, Oei Hui-lan could conveniently challenge mainstream practices, while also publicly demonstrating her appreciation of Chinese culture. For Pan Yuliang, as a Chinese woman artist in Paris, to portray herself dressed in the qipao would similarly convey a multiplicity of messages. Wearing a qipao could be read as subverting the widely accepted practice in Shanghai of appropriating Western fashion, at the same time recalling the wearer's cultural heritage. In the 1940s, due to the shifting political landscape and the growing leftist movement in mainland China, wearing a qipao acquired further connotations, as Sandy Ng points out: "Qipao continued to be worn by Chinese women after the 1940s, but largely outside mainland China because a feminized appearance was criticized as a sign of gender oppression; androgynous and plain colour clothing such as grey cotton tops and trousers were favoured" (Ng 2015, 72). Pan Yuliang's deliberate and repeated depictions of the qipao in Paris reflect Eileen Chang's shrewd observation that "in a time of political chaos, people were powerless to improve the external conditions governing their lives. But they could influence the environment immediately surrounding them, that is, their clothes" (Chang 2005, 71).

Analyzing Pan's 1940 and 1945 self-portraits in the context of her return to Paris, art historian Yao Daimei writes, "In the period right after her return she must have felt a sense of rebirth, having finally escaped that gossipy [renyan kewei 人言可畏] Chinese society, cast off her illegitimate, polygamous family and messy status, and could now fully immerse herself into her art in order to truly liberate her body and soul" (Yao 2010, 132). Yet her self-portraits do not openly convey an exuberant sense of liberated body and soul; instead, the mood is still controlled, and the result is a closely regulated image especially in terms of framing and composition. Building on Eric Lefebvre's assessment that Pan's self-portraits "were at the heart of the exhibition strategy of an artist who would only consider her work through a regular confrontation with her audience, whether in China or in France" (Lefebvre 2018, 35), I would argue that Pan Yuliang employed the practice of transposition as an exhibition strategy in order to challenge the popular image of the Chinese woman artist. Surely the nude prints and paintings were easier to find a receptive audience for, but self-portraiture, according to Lefebvre, was "closely linked to two Western techniques that were at the core of her training, namely painting and sculpture" (Lefebvre 2018, 35).

Pan's self-portraits are carefully composed, featuring serious facial expressions that give very little away, save for a pair of carefully groomed and arched eyebrows, pursed lips, and eyes looking straight at the viewer. Playing with the trope of the gazing girl, Pan's subject forsakes the mirror to break the fourth wall and invites the viewer to stare back. This mirror reflection also forces the viewer into the perspective of the subject, to participate in the act of looking at oneself. With an emphasis on propriety, Pan Yuliang does not invite intimacy but holds the viewer at a distance. The self-portraits share a deliberate mood of antiemotion, and a refusal to hint at emotion or feelings. To view these self-portraits through the lens of transposition forces us to question what the woman artist's self-construction looks like: What kind of performance does she put on, and what purpose can the portraits serve that is different from photographs or paintings of Pan proving her artistic mettle for the viewer's visual verification and gratification? These self-portraits frustrate the photographic images of the artist performing the role of woman artist in China or in France, and in a series of significant moves that depart markedly from mainstream media in the 1920s-1940s, Pan Yuliang rejected the label of the emotional woman artist, and provided another way to perform the identities of woman, modern, and Chinese. What was revealed? Not her painterly identity through detailed clues like clothing, props, and setting, and while it's not exactly a documentation of everyday life either, the mise-en-scène is still carefully arranged, very intentional and not casual. These self-portraits engage with the image of the nude female body, creating a deliberate misreading of "women's art"—a woman who is clothed, gazing not at herself, but at the viewer. She is not painting or dressed like a painter, but wears a qipao, a modern and fashionable Chinese dress. Although the paintings certainly emphasize Pan Yuliang's physical appearance and highlight a version of feminine beauty, they do so not in the socially prescribed ways.

Writing for *Zhongyang ribao* in 1935, Li Jinfa praised Pan Yuliang after seeing an exhibition of her work: "Her work is placed among those of the first wave of artists who studied in France, and I dare say it's not inferior there. In our country there are plenty of opportunistic [touji quqiao 投機取巧] male artists, so let's not even try to compare. Her success isn't by chance. Watching her navigate between figurative drawing and oil painting, we can tell that she has painstakingly devoted at least ten years of hard work" (Fan 2015,

108). The image of the toiling woman artist circulated in 1930s and 1940s China in mainstream media in photos and journalistic accounts, which were then corroborated by autobiographical accounts and visual art by women artists like Pan Yuliang. In order for a woman artist to gain social acceptance in China, she needed to have the proper credentials of global recognition and international prestige in the art world beyond. Still, even a prolific celebrity like Pan Yuliang could end up in relative obscurity decades later. Tani Barlow cites Pan Yuliang's "marginal existence" in Paris as a case where discourse about women's self-awareness in China collided with the visual motif of the gazing woman in modern art: "A former concubine from the demimonde, she promoted a truth about women's erotic pleasure in being gazed at, at a time when Chinese critics and viewers generally had trouble countenancing pictures of naked women at all, not to mention images who stared back at them" (Barlow 2021, 163). Ironically, by centering the woman subject's interiority and experience in visual form, Pan Yuliang did not succeed in making herself more visible on the global stage.

Commemorating the thirtieth anniversary of the biography's publication, Shi Nan recounted, "Before writing *Huahun—Zhang Yuliang's Biography*, I had never seen her paintings or prints. Only when I interviewed Pan Zanhua's daughter-in-law Peng Dexiu did I first encounter Pan Yuliang's painting 'Self-Portrait' and three postcards featuring photos of her bust sculptures, including the gracefully bearded 'Head of Zhang Daqian'" (Shi 2014, 1). Despite only having access to these images Shi was nevertheless deeply affected by the encounter with Pan's "poems cast in bronze." Pan Yuliang's legacy tells the transmedial success story of how literature moves artwork: readers of Shi's biography serialized in *Qingming* journal wrote to the Ministry of Culture asking for the repatriation of Pan's works to China, which led to the shipment of 2,000 of her oil and ink paintings, sketches, and sculptures from France to Shanghai, and eventually, Shi was finally able to see Pan's original works at the Anhui Museum (Shi 2014, 1). It eventually moved money and auction sales, and in 2014 Pan Yuliang's oil painting 1946 *Nude by Window* sold for a record $4.45 million USD.

In October 2010, when I met with Eric Lefèbvre at the Musée Cernuschi in Paris, he brought me downstairs to the facility's basement where I felt a strange combination of dismay and privilege to see a number of Pan Yuliang's paintings put away in storage. The experience has remained with me, and I experienced a jolt of déjà vu when hearing the voiceover narration by curator Mia Yu in her 2017 experimental video essay *Pan Yuliang: A Journey from*

Silence, a documentary film about the experience of a group of curators and artists traveling to the Anhui Provincial Museum in Hefei to prepare for an art exhibit inspired by Pan Yuliang: "Even though there are plenty of research materials about you, I can barely find any of your own comments on art. You remain illegible" (Yu 2017, 000:05:49). Yu questions what brought about Pan's silence, and these self-portraits in their forceful nonsilence may help to recuperate her voice.

Conclusion

Challenging the Universality of Paris

They were beautiful, Paris was beautiful, life was beautiful, and I and them, I and Paris, my life felt so dear. We were Les Enfants du paradis, without nationality or student credentials, far from home, each abandoned by her beloved.

—QIU MIAOJIN 邱妙津, LAST WORDS FROM MONTMARTRE

REPRODUCING FRANCOPHILIA AND PARIS WORLD-MAKING

On July 15, 2022, the Taiwanese pop star Jay Chou (周杰倫 b. 1979) released the music video for a new song titled "Greatest Works of Art" (Zui weida de zuopin 最偉大的作品) from his eponymous album. The video, which depicts Chou dressed as a magician at the La Samaritaine luxury department store in Paris, was viewed almost ten million times on YouTube in the first two days after its initial release. References to surrealist heavyweights René Magritte and Salvador Dalí in the first minute are not too surprising, as Chou travels back in time to the 1920s with his friend Funky Tu (Du Kuo-Chang), but I had to pause the video before the two-minute mark to make sure I was not imagining Chang Yu's colored sketches plastered on the walls of an artist's studio. Rapping that "decadence is the freest ink in worldly art," Chou refers to Paris by its nickname, the "flower capital" (huadu 花都), as the camera pans over Chang Yu's illustrations of women: "Elegant legs are a smear of this universe's brush" (Chou 2022, 1:47). He continues, "The nostalgia that floats across the ocean's waves is a gentle nothing, only from lonely branches can Chang Yu's flowers bloom" (Chou 2022, 1:51). In addition to Chang Yu's drawings, the video for "Greatest Works of Art" cites a steady stream of artistic greats, namely Henri Matisse, Vincent Van Gogh, Edvard Munch, and Claude Monet, punctuated by Chou's climactic duet with the renowned pianist Lang Lang. The story concludes in a café where Chou meets Xu Zhimo, as the song's conclusion refers to the latter's *Fragments of Paris* and the power of music to "read" through the pages of the past (巴黎的鱗爪/ 感傷的文法/ 要用音樂翻閱).

"Greatest Works of Art" certainly increases the visibility of Chang Yu's work in the context of twentieth-century modern art, while it further reinforces the mythology of 1920s Paris, albeit by the inclusion of Chinese figures into the historical narrative. As I researched modern Chinese art and Paris over the last decade, a quote incorrectly attributed to Chang Yu about the city's appeal kept resurfacing; sometimes in English translation but most often in Chinese-language (with some omitted words) online posts related to Chang Yu's late-founded success on the art auction circuit, the repeated reference was even linked to Ni Yide in one occurrence (Qin and Lin 2016, 369).

> There's one advantage to living in Paris—they're not snobby! The Chinese are way worse in this area—the poor have their poor snobbery, the rich have their rich snobbery, those half-in-decline have their half-in-decline snobbery—that's what you call semi-civilized, barbaric! Take someone like myself, with hair like a hedgehog, a scruffy beard that hasn't been shaved in eight or nine days, dirty rags that haven't been changed in half a year, and unbuckled leather shoes—in China who wouldn't call me a foreign beggar, how would I ever be allowed into a stuck-up place like the Beijing Hotel? But in Paris, looking like this, I can just go and ask any beautifully-dressed perfumed young woman to dance, and nine out of ten will say yes—can you believe it?[1]

The oft-cited passage actually originates from Xu Zhimo's essay "Sir, Have You Ever Seen Such Gorgeous Flesh Before?" from the aforementioned 1927 *Fragments of Paris*. In the essay, the Chinese artist continues, informing his curious friend, the narrator, "When it comes to models, It's even more ridiculous—those art students in Paris, no matter how poor they are, they can get more than ten or more sparkly-eyed models to pose in one year, who cares how shabby their house is? This is the bohemian lifestyle! According to what you say, that models shouldn't have to sit on a broken sofa, you would prepare a satin-embroidered palatial armchair to invite her over—that'd be the only way you could feel at ease, right?" (Xu 1927, 23–24). The comically exaggerated passage resonates most obviously with Xu Xu's story about the art studio in Montparnasse in chapter 5, but it also reflects broader social and cultural attitudes toward the modern artist's life in Paris, and the figure's relationship with those less experienced, less enlightened individuals, as imagined by contemporary writers of the period. Echoing the sentiment expressed in Guo Jianying's cartoon *Introduction*, which was discussed in chapter 1, Xu Zhimo's rant posits the superiority of Parisian culture at the cost of the woman model, who is imagined to be no more than a sexualized quintessential accessory in the bohemian lifestyle. The fact that the passage has become associated with the popular image of Chang Yu's identity as a Chinese artist navigating cultural expectations and social customs in 1920s Paris speaks to the pervasive attitude about Sino-French encounters at this historical juncture. Furthermore, all three examples project a sense of critical irony toward the seemingly more civilized Parisian society as being far less refined than commonly believed.

This book has highlighted how the city of Paris in the Chinese cultural imaginary played a significant role in facilitating the development of new ways of viewing from the 1920s through the 1940s. Long celebrated as the center of Western art, the city's location and its related mythologies, especially for travelers from China, stimulated a range of modes of artistic expression and experimentation. In some cases, the period of exchange inspired ambivalent feelings of pride and resentment. André Warnod shrewdly anticipated the potential benefits of what he described as a parasitic relationship between the host country and foreign students: "Should we be upset that they bring with them nothing more than the desire to enrich their art with what they find here [in France]? They create, if nothing else, a very useful climate. . . . They pay for the others, the followers, the imitators, the junk sellers, the others who know to stay in their place and happily to come to France to study the Beaux-arts, then [they] just go home to use what they came here to acquire and loyally spread the sovereignty of French art around the world" (Warnod 1925, 8). He was not referring specifically to Chinese students, and for the five figures discussed in this book, the opportunity to go to France provided lived experiences that far surpassed what reading translated works at home could offer. But their experiences as Chinese youth traveling in Paris—the last generation allowed to study abroad until the reopening of China during the Reform period in the 1980s—reveal more disillusionment than enchantment, and they were subsequently marginalized by national literary and art canons. An in-depth examination of their visual art and literature and its lackluster reception shows that Warnod's hope of spreading "the sovereignty of French art around the world" did not come to fruition as he predicted.

My analysis complements claims about the universality of Paris in the development of global literary history, such as Pascale Casanova's assertion that "descriptions of Paris are hardly the privilege of French writers—belief in the special supremacy of Paris quickly spread throughout the world. The accounts of Paris composed by foreigners and brought back to their own countries became remote vehicles for belief in its literary power" (Casanova 2007, 26–27). Casanova's reading fits with the studies on participatory cultures in new consumer media, and the concept of transmedia storytelling, which Henry Jenkins defines as "the art of world making" (Jenkins 2008, 21). In his conceptualization, transmedia storytelling is "a new aesthetic that emerged in response to media convergence—one that places new demands on consumers and depends on the active participation of knowledge communities." Yet as my project shows, convergence (both top down from state institutions and industries, and bottom up from the individual or grassroots level) has long participated in actively spreading stories across media platforms. Jenkins's emphasis in the digital age is on connectivity but even this earlier predigital period in the early twentieth century—less connected in technological ways—contributed in meaningful ways to the world-making of Paris that has persisted in the subsequent decades and has spanned geographical regions. The epigraph in this chapter from the Taiwanese novelist Qiu Miaojin (1969–95), which references the 1943 film classic *Les Enfants du paradis*, directed by Michel Carné, attests to the far reach of the city's cultural cachet, and to its lasting power to elicit strong emotions of love, romance, and beauty, especially in association with student life.

Not only did Chinese artists and writers bring home less than flattering stories about their time abroad that challenged the "special supremacy of Paris," their experiments to find the most effective or creative modes of enriching "Chinese" art reflect a diversity of approaches and strategies. Transposition, which I use as an expansive term that defies a singular definition, helps us identify and think more critically about the kinds of negotiations that Chinese writers and artists encountered in trying to make Chinese identity comprehensible and attractive to their audiences, in particular revealing how artists adapt or borrow cultural markers and make them recognizable in a new context. The visual-verbal dynamic is especially pertinent to this concept, which, in the Chinese context, is most obviously reflected in the interconnectedness between poetry and its visuality, "a verbal and visual art that, particularly when coupled with landscape painting, amounted to the highest form of cultural expression in China" (Manfredi 2014, xxi), but extends to other art forms, such as music and sculpture. David Der-wei Wang states that for Chinese intellectuals seeking national strength in the early twentieth century "the question of how to read and write China ranked high on their agendas" (Wang 1992, 2). My approach builds on the flexible relationship between media by expanding the "search for a new narrative paradigm" and addressing literature and art together as two forces that are at times mutually reinforcing, at other times conflicting, constitutive modes of representation.

Eric Hayot has pointed out that "to imitate a modernist is to fail the test of modernism. What possibilities for 'Chinese modernism' in such a framework?" (Wollaeger and Eatough 2013, 158). Rather than be resigned to Hayot's response, "Not many," this book has revealed some of the forgotten interstices of early twentieth-century Sino-French intercultural exchange, as an attempt to shed light on the role of Paris in the development of modern Chinese literature and art, and to provide some possible alternative models of thinking beyond the impossible binds set in place by claims of imitation. The trope of imitation is a version of Johann Wolfgang von Goethe's mirroring concept, upon which the category of world literature was initially construed: "Left to itself every literature will exhaust its vitality, if it is not refreshed by the interest and contributions of a foreign one. What naturalist does not take pleasure in the wonderful things that he sees produced by a reflection in a mirror?" (Damrosch 2003, 7). When Goethe first wrote about world literature in the early nineteenth century, he conceived of world literature as a network of ideas, especially the circulation of his writing and its international (European) reception.

The five Chinese travelers discussed in this book looked to France, hoping that they too could see something of themselves in the French culture they studied, and potentially return home using their experiences abroad to affect change in China. But unlike Goethe, Chinese writers and painters could not necessarily count on their own writing to circulate in Europe. Fu Lei and Chang Yu contributed articles to French publications, but these were rare exceptions, and for the most part, the circulation of their literary work was limited to China, although Chang Yu's and Pan Yuliang's artwork received exposure in the European art circuit via exhibitions and art publications. David Damrosch contends in *What Is World Literature?* that "world literature is not an infinite, ungraspable canon of works but rather a mode of circulation and of reading, a mode that is as applicable to individual works as to bodies of material, available for reading established classics and new discoveries alike" (Damrosch 2003, 5). New discoveries such as the ones explored here can enrich our understanding of artistic movements, challenge our perceptions of cultural identities, and encourage new areas of scholarship.

It is no coincidence either that Chang Yu's and Pan Yuliang's paintings have circulated more widely than the literary works discussed here—the difficulty of translating Li Jinfa's French-inflected Chinese poetry makes the neither-nor label assigned to visual artists seem over simplistic. Damrosch suggests that "works of world literature take on a new life as they move into the world at large, and to understand this new life we need to look closely at the ways the work becomes reframed in its translations and in its new cultural contexts" (Damrosch 2003, 24). For many Chinese travelers to Paris in the first half of the twentieth century, being associated with France did not guarantee being translated or any other form of global recognition, nor was Paris the revolutionary haven they envisioned, in either the aesthetic or political sense. As marginalized figures working outside of the mainstream political ideology, none remained in mainland China other than Fu Lei, the sole figure to return permanently to China, who committed suicide during the Cultural Revolution. After traveling in Europe and Singapore, Li Jinfa worked in the 1940s as a diplomat for the Kuomintang in Iraq and Iran, and eventually immigrated to the U.S., where he resided until his death in New York; Chang Yu traveled to Japan, Europe, and the U.S. Xu Xu studied in Europe and Japan before moving to Hong Kong after the war, and Pan Yuliang stayed in Paris until her death in 1977.

To return to the questions this book started with, what was the role of modern art in promoting intercultural understanding in the early twentieth century? More specifically, what kinds of images of the modern Chinese artist circulated in cultural production, and what kinds of expectations did Chinese writers and artists face in Paris? The visual-verbal dynamic has shown how the modern artist was in a unique position to identify and appreciate cultural diversity and difference, through the negotiation of various kinds of expectations placed on Chinese artists in Paris in the 1920s. Transposition provided a range of experimental modes of artistic expression used to make Chinese identity comprehensible and attractive to a more global audience, including viewers, readers, and consumers in France, as well as those at home in China.

Chang Yu's culturally synthetic paintings in the 1920s and 1930s, unlike those of his more successful (renowned) colleagues, not only disengaged from the prevailing national discourse of realism in China, but his adaptation of nonrealist technique as inspired by the literati tradition and Western modernism did not claim any allegiance with the popular national movements of the time. His unique position as a Chinese painter residing in Paris gave him the freedom and flexibility to work outside the state institutions, to reconfigure modern Chinese visual language from afar as he wished, exhibited most strikingly in his etchings for Liang Zongdai's translations of Tao Qian's poetry. Chang Yu's experiences as a male expatriate artist—and more importantly, his persona as a Chinese bohemian—were connected to the new visual language he created, which withdrew from a celebration of Western modernity, and instead favored an imaginary dreamscape that conveyed the sense of a private, inner world. Rather than relying on gimmicky cultural referents, his work relies on a paring down. His oil paintings of female nudes and chrysanthemums—one the quintessential marker of Western modernity, the other extending back to traditional culture in Chinese art history—emphasize the acts of contemplation and imagination, on both the part of the artist and the viewer of art.

The artist Xu Beihong, Chang Yu's colleague and fellow compatriot in Paris, proposed a recipe for reform in 1920: "As far as the ancient methods are concerned, maintain the good ones, revive the interrupted ones, improve those that are not good, strengthen the weak ones, and assimilate the appropriate elements from Western painting" (Yao 1932, 109). The prescriptive language of synthesis, representing the larger goal of China's harmonious assimilation into the international art scene, was simply not Chang Yu's top priority, and his friend, the collector Johan Franco observed, "His present work is therefore completely Chinese with a minor European influence" (Wong 2011, 57). Chang Yu's affinity for literati themes and techniques may have charmed his French contemporaries, it but did little for his reputation back in China, despite the irony of *guohua*'s connection with the nation.[2] For artists who studied abroad in the West, their return to China was supposed to precipitate a reexamination of traditional art with a newfound perspective, which in turn would lead back to the inevitable question of national salvation, as Fu Lei's essays on Liu Haisu and Pang Xunqin in chapter 3 confirm. Chang Yu did not return to China, and his work occupies a much trickier position, as his themes, techniques, and style all defy clear categorization of local versus foreign, traditional versus modern, East versus West. Rather than try to integrate disparate elements organically, Chang Yu's paintings show how the art of transposition depends on the accentuation and appreciation of cultural differences. Like Pablo Picasso, Chang Yu created a new form of visual art that depicted or allowed for the creation of an alternative reality through the juxtaposition of unlike elements, working with the belief that the relationship between discordant things could reveal new meanings.

But although Chang Yu explicitly acknowledged Western conventions of composition, his unusual choice of color and space results in a very different finished product than those of both his Western and Chinese counterparts. Compared to the vibrant and nearly dizzying still-life compositions of an artist like Matisse, Chang Yu's chrysanthemums appear subdued and muted. Similarly, compared to the still-life paintings of his Chinese contemporary Lin Fengmian, Chang Yu's paintings are much more contemplative and expressionistic. The growing popularity of Chang Yu's expatriate successors, such as Gao Xingjian and Zao Wou-Ki (趙無極 b. 1921), both much better known in the West than Chang Yu, as well as more recent contemporary Chinese artists such as Zhang Xiaogang (張曉剛 b. 1958), Ai Weiwei (艾未未 b. 1957), and Cai Guo-Qiang (蔡國強 b. 1957)—all favored by Western collectors—have led to a revival of earlier-era Chinese painting, including the rediscovery of forgotten painters with international cachet such as Chang Yu.

While Chang Yu incorporated traditional literati aesthetic into Western modernism for art's sake, Fu Lei did so in the name of national salvation, believing that China could recapture its glorious past by incorporating elements of Western modernism. Writing as an art critic, a role he carved out for himself, Fu Lei believed that the ideal position for the artist was to stay physically removed or at a distance from reality; yet his experiences as a student abroad reveal that travel as a mode of physical detachment did not guarantee spiritual or emotional detachment. Despite Fu Lei's repeated attempts to distance himself from guilty thoughts of the crisis in China, the turning back to one's "national soul," in his own words, is necessary in the work of a true artist. In Fu Lei's social commentary on France his unshakable sense of civic responsibility is never far away, causing him to feel incessantly guilty about leaving China. As a traveler to the West, he took seriously the responsibility to educate his readers, to address "real" concerns from a seemingly outside, detached viewpoint.

In his numerous acts of transposition—promoting the avant-garde work of artist Pang Xunqin, theorizing the crisis of modern Chinese art, sharing the experiences of a young Chinese student abroad for the very first time in Paris—Fu Lei remained all but detached. While his anxiety about Western colonialism is apparent in some of his travel accounts, and he questions the inherent contradiction between the cosmopolitanism of Paris and its inability to accommodate outsiders such as himself, he stops short of trying to propose any kind of societal solution. His ideal of being outside reality in order to better view reality, or being a dreamer, can never be truly realized. In his youth, Fu Lei believed that his idealism, his refusal to compromise aesthetic integrity, was for the good of the people. But by the time he realized that the political tide had turned and he was caught on the other side, he realized both that the dream of idealism was over and that it was time to detach himself even more from the mundane matters of everyday life.

His colleague for over thirty years, the Chinese film theorist, literary critic, and playwright Ke Ling (柯靈 1909–2000), wrote after Fu Lei's untimely death, "He was stubborn to a fault; being a bookworm his whole life caused him to be seriously out of touch with reality. Regarding his views on political issues and societal problems, he believed that he was being fair [中正] but in reality he could not avoid being biased" (Jin 1996, 5). Comparing Fu Lei to "a red-crowned crane from heaven, holding his head up high, never lowering his head to glance at the mud at his feet," Ke Ling's rather harsh criticism explains why Fu Lei's concerns for China did not successfully translate into the revolutionary zeal prescribed by the Chinese Communist Party.

The poetic contribution of Li Jinfa did not outwardly demonstrate any obvious concern for the fate of the nation, and his work was remembered even less favorably. In his experimental poetry, Li Jinfa challenged Chinese readers to reconsider what could be considered modern Chinese poetry, and his attempts to blend classical diction with unfamiliar images and non-Chinese language failed to find a wide readership. Aided by the symbolist philosophy that symbols alone—not descriptions or allegories—have the power to evoke feelings, Li Jinfa's enigmatic and bizarre images coexist like the elements in a classical Chinese painting or poem, not linearly but side by side. Unlike Hu Shih's belief that poetry, like dreams, must first be experienced in order to have some kind of legitimacy or authenticity at its foundation, Li Jinfa's poetic philosophy did not make any claims outside of the purely personal; for him, poetry was something that could best be expressed in a dreamlike drunken state; and "inspiration," triggered by the visitation of an artistic muse, could be transformed through an undiluted expression of individuality.

That so many critics were and continue to be frustrated by his "poetry of intoxication" reveals the literary anxiety surrounding questions of nationalism and cultural legitimacy, namely how a Chinese writer could express himself using non-Chinese language and still be perceived as a modern Chinese writer. Leo Ou-fan Lee's argument about Chinese modernity highlights the inescapable tension between Western modernism and Chinese nationalism: "It was the Chinese writers' fervent espousal of Occidental exoticism that turned Western culture itself into an 'other' in the process of constructing their own modern imaginary. This process of appropriation was crucial to their own quest for modernity—a quest conducted with full confidence in their identity as Chinese nationalists. In fact, in their minds modernity itself was in the service of nationalism" (Lee 2001, 308–9). For Li Jinfa, however, the causal relationship between nationalism and modernity was not so clear-cut, and his poetic project in both linguistic and thematic terms signals a moment of disruption in the narrative of Chinese modern literature, during which the poet's sacred role in modern society was called into question.

For Xu Xu, traveling to France, the beloved birthplace of the revolution, served as a wake-up call that a rich cultural heritage was not infallible. His essays express a disconcerting level of cynicism about the uncertain political future of China and France during the war period, as well as toward the limitations of literary representation. Xu Xu's semifictional stories challenge the conventional discourses of Chinese modernity that push for the "haste to modernize" and the self as champion of individualism and free will. Unlike Fu Lei, who consciously tried to distance himself from thinking about the crisis in China (without much success), Xu Xu's narrators revel in their feelings of homesickness and nostalgia, using them as creative inspiration. Nor could his characters adopt the position of the confident "interpreter" as represented by his colleague Lin Yutang. The subtle humor that comes across in Xu Xu's writing is subtler than Lin Yutang's obvious satire; in fact, it often appears as pointed social criticism, and almost always eventually calls into question the narrator's own shortcomings.

As a storyteller, Xu Xu believed in the writer's responsibility to advertise his unreliability and dismantle the modern myth of individual subjectivity as a self-contained vehicle of free will. His acute self-awareness became a constant acknowledgment that a person's mood and emotions, his mental state of being, had a significant impact on his subjectivity and, ultimately, his writing. In Xu Xu's travels, this self-awareness manifests most frequently in fantasies concerning artistic spaces of creation, transformation, and appreciation, such as the art studio, and their role in inciting romantic desire. For Xu Xu's disillusioned protagonists, the longing for home and female desire are connected to feelings of alienation and loneliness. As an outsider in the West, Xu Xu never tried to give his readers at home the impression of any particularly patriotic allegiance to "his" China, nor that he had any insider information about the way things are outside of China. Travel was a practice best used to reexamine social reality from a distance, and it facilitated ways of reflecting on everyday cultural practices from a new perspective. Reading Xu Xu's *xiaopin wen* written on the eve of the second Sino-Japanese War (1937–45), we can better empathize with the disappointment and corresponding relief that the writer felt during his stay in interwar Paris, and surmise the reasons why his informal essays, in contrast to his novels, did not attract a wide readership among his contemporaries.

Lastly, Pan Yuliang's artistic contributions encourage reflection on the changing relationship between gender and aesthetic concepts of poetic flavor and oriental sentiment circulated on an imagined global stage. Women artists in China had to prove that they were at least as skilled as their male counterparts, and even then, were still criticized for having an unfair advantage. Caught between two convergent national discourses celebrating the newly liberated and educated modern woman in China, and the influence of a Western art education in France, Pan Yuliang's life and work were long held up as evidence that both China and France fostered the artist's development from her socially illegitimate origins to gaining an internationally renowned reputation. But a closer look at Pan Yuliang's transpositions of the image of the modern Chinese woman artist in the form of self-portraits reveals that despite repeated efforts to assert herself and circulate her self-constructed image for a world viewership, critics and audiences preferred reading her work through speculation and mythology.

Due to—and not despite—the transpositional elements of their work, Li Jinfa's poetry, Chang Yu's and Pan Yuliang's painting, and Fu Lei and Xu Xu's prose pieces need to be included in discussions about Chinese and French art and literature, not just as curiosities or aberrations, but as examples of transcultural modes of artistic expression in the larger context of the political upheaval and social and aesthetic movements of the twentieth century. Yu Dafu described the imaginary musings of his protagonist in his best-known story "Sinking" (Chenlun 沈淪, 1921): "Sometimes, when the mood struck him, he would translate his own stories into some foreign language, employing the simple vocabulary at his command. In a word, he was more and more enveloped in a world of fantasy, and it was probably during this time that the seeds of his hypochondria were sown" (Goldblatt and Lau 2007, 38). Research on the May Fourth Movement and the widespread practice of translation in the Republican period have typically emphasized how voraciously Chinese intellectuals were consuming Western culture, especially Western literature and philosophy by way of translation, either directly from French or German, for example, into Chinese, or through the middleman of Japan. Yu Dafu's protagonist, however, is a reminder that there was always a desire to translate from Chinese to a wider audience, as well as a self-consciousness of the difficulty of achieving global recognition.

For Chinese writers, the act of writing in French has been beset with its own set of controversies. In 2007, forty-four writers, including Chinese-born author and filmmaker Dai Sijie, signed a manifesto titled "Pour une 'littérature-monde' en français" (Towards a world literature in French), which was published in *Le Monde*. Written after five out of France's seven major book award wins were dominated by foreign-born writers in the 2006 literary awards season (Jonathan Littell of New York; Alain Mabanckou of Congo; Nancy Huston of Canada; and Léonora Miano of Cameroon), the manifesto called for an end of "francophone" literature and the birth of world literature in French (Rivais et al. 2007).[3] Calling francophone literature "a light from a dying star," the writers asserted, "Let's be clear: the emergence of a consciously affirmed, transnational world literature in the French language, open to the world, signs the death certificate of so-called Francophone literature." The manifesto's primary concern was with the racist inequality in distinguishing between French literature as written by white writers born in France versus Francophone literature by those born for the most part in France's former colonies, but it's unclear where and how ethnic Chinese writers writing in non-Chinese languages fit into either Sinophone or Francophone categories.

The myth of Paris has barely diminished in the twenty-first century, and the legacy of traveling abroad to Paris for creative freedom continues to this day for Chinese writers and artists, with the lives of cultural figures like the expatriate writer and Nobel Prize laureate Gao Xingjian and the writer-filmmaker Dai Sijie as prime examples. Julia Lovell has pointed out the influence of literary prestige on contemporary Chinese writers and artists. Writing about Gao Xingjian's contentious 2000 Nobel Prize in Literature win, Lovell argues that "French literary culture still carries a prestige to which foreign writers can actively subscribe to bolster their own artistic stature"

(Tsu and Wang 2010, 208). In his Nobel lecture, Gao expressed gratitude to his country of citizenship: "I should also thank France for accepting me. In France where literature and art are revered I have won the conditions to write with freedom and I also have readers and audiences" (Gao 2000). He subsequently revealed to an interviewer, "I had to pick a place to exile myself, and Paris is the ideal place for artists, writers and painters" (Rekdal 2000), affirming a sentiment expressed even earlier in *Le Monde* in 1998: "The only works of mine that have a true value have been written or finished in this country. . . . Where is my country? In this spirit of freedom that unites humanity, that is the soul of France, and that I will embrace forever" (Tsu and Wang 2010, 209).

Similarly, Dai Sijie was born in China and permanently relocated to France in 1984 after being forbidden by Chinese authorities to make his films in China. His novel *Balzac and the Little Chinese Seamstress* (*Balzac et la petite tailleuse*, 2000) was originally written in French and translated into English in 2001, then adapted into an award-winning Chinese-language film in 2002, directed by Dai. Both the novel and its film version were celebrated and criticized for their portrayal of Western literature, particularly the rosy depiction of the transformative power of French literature.[4] In the novel, contraband copies of Fu Lei's translations of French classics forever alter the lives of two sent-down youths in the countryside and their fellow villagers. Near the end of the book, the protagonist exchanges handwritten copies of Balzac's *Ursule Mirouët* and Rolland's *Jean-Christophe* for a medical favor; upon reading the text, written on the leather of a sheepskin jacket, the doctor murmurs, "The translation is obviously by Fu Lei. . . . I can tell from the style. He's suffered the same fate as your father, poor man: he's been labeled a class enemy" (Dai 2001, 172). The protagonist is reduced to tears by the doctor's observation: "It was not the Little Seamstress's predicament that was making me weep, I think, nor was it relief at having come this far in my efforts to save her. It was hearing the name of Fu Lei, Balzac's translator—someone I had never even met. It is hard to imagine a more moving tribute to the gift bestowed by an intellectual on mankind." Albeit a fictional account of the impact that Fu Lei's translation had during the Cultural Revolution, the passage, the work as a whole, speaks to perception of the lasting power of literature, especially in the darkest moments, and its concrete effect of further contributing to the continuation of cycles of artistic creation.[5] Cynical critics would agree with James English's complaint about the category of world literature as a signpost for accepted social values: "Most world literature is valued as such not on the basis of any specifically literary excellence, but because those who control the global status hierarchy (the well-positioned literature professors and book reviewers, and, overlapping with these, the judges and administrators of the major literary prizes) systematically conflate literary value with social values, literary greatness with presumed political heroism, a more multicultural canon with a more democratic or socialistic or egalitarian world. 'World literature,' from the standpoint of this critique, is all 'world' and no 'literature'" (English 2005, 308). As my work proposes, more "world" and less "literature" may not be such a bad thing in the present moment.

THE INTERCULTURAL TRANSMEDIAL TURN

In 1953, at the beginning of the Cold War, when James Robert Hightower published "Chinese Literature in the Context of World Literature" in an effort to convince readers of Chinese literature's "literary value" (Hightower 1953, 121), few could have predicted that China would become a global economic superpower in the twenty-first century, and as such, Chinese literature is no longer the "by-product" of a "special interest" particular only to sinologists (Hightower 1953, 117). Fast forward to a decade ago in 2011, when Haun Saussy observed that people seemed to believe "Chinese literature is valuable, interesting and important because China is important" (Saussy 2011). A correlated consequence of China's position in the globalized economy extends from the literary sphere to the soaring prices in the Chinese contemporary art marketplace, which in turn have revived critical and consumer (the two often converging or at the very least interrelated) interest in Chinese modern art. Only a few years ago, as I sat at a Starbucks in Tempe, Arizona working on a journal article about the contemporary Chinese artist Cao Fei, I was approached by two men at the banquette where I was typing on my laptop. "What are you working on?," one asked me, unsolicited. "An article on Chinese art," I replied tersely, not especially pleased about being interrupted. "Is there even such a thing, Chinese art?" his friend added disdainfully, or maybe, he imagined, humorously.

The potential for art to create space for cross-cultural empathy and dialogue remains as necessary as it is difficult to carry out in practice, and *Paris and the Art of Transposition* has presented one possible way of striking a "third area" of comparative literature, in line with Zhang Longxi's concern about the paucity of East-West comparative studies: "The kind of study we try to envision cannot be simply the confrontation or juxtaposition of sinology or Asian studies on the one hand and a Eurocentric comparative literature or Western literary theory on the other, it must be established in a third area, a mediating ground on which East-West comparative literature will acquire its own identity as different from either of the specialist branches mentioned above" (Zhang 1998, 35). In my investigation, I have adopted, to the best of my ability, Eugene Eoyang's proposed comparative methodology of seeing "multisubjectively" and cross-culturally (Eoyang 2005, ix). Modern Chinese literature is a particularly rich source of investigative material, and it provides the comparative scholar an endless number of nooks and crannies for overturning and rediscovering new and old artists, writers, filmmakers, musicians, playwrights—fascinating figures that have been left behind in the brutal and oftentimes violent process of nation-building and canon-writing.

Transposition, as a range of diverse modes of artistic expression from this historical period, allows us think more creatively and inclusively about theoretical binds such as "what in Chinese modernism belongs to 'modernism,' and what in it is 'Chinese'" (Wollaeger and Eatough 2013, 149). If modern literary history is in fact the result of (northern) European economic and cultural prestige, as Casanova and others have claimed, my project uses the work of Chinese artists and writers to explore more in-depth the "kinds of recognition that emerge from Paris," as proposed by comparatists (Wollaeger and Eatough 2013, 152). By encompassing a broader range of modes of expression that transcends linguistic, national, and media borders, transposition also allows for ways of construing difference that do not depend on expertise limited to or based strictly on geographic or cultural region. The dynamic field of Chinese studies has greatly benefited from the theoretical contributions of scholars working in sinophone studies as pioneered by Shu-mei Shih (Tsu and Wang 2010, 29–48), but as a language-centric paradigm, its comparative and transnational attentiveness to Chineseness on the margins cannot fully account for practices like Fu Lei's or Li Jinfa's exophonic writing, even though in theory the sinophone is "polyphonic and multilingual" (Shih, Tsai, and Bernards 2013, 10).

In 1988, historian Ralph Croizier complained about the discrepancy in attention given to literature and art: "Modern Chinese literature, mostly fiction, has achieved recognition for its relevance to the dynamics of modern social, political, and intellectual change. But art, apparently one step further removed from social and political issues, has not received the same attention. The art historians are in Ming; the historians are into Mao. Meanwhile, modern Chinese art—the art of the twentieth-century revolution and of the period of East-West cultural confrontation—has awaited serious and integrated historical study" (Croizier 1988, 3). The East-West encounter continues to be inadequately studied outside the influence model, and literary studies can greatly benefit from being studied alongside visual art and vice-versa, given the fact that the fields of visual art and literature were (and remain) in constantly fluctuating states of overlap and intersection throughout Chinese history. During the period of the 1920s through the 1940s, both poetry and art took a backseat to prose, and the creative output of the central figures of this study reveal many more diverse modes of transmedial expression than those for which they have been given credit: Li Jinfa went to Paris to study sculpture and returned a poet. Chang Yu studied painting but also composed poetry; Fu Lei was an avid art and music critic. Xu Xu was both a poet and novelist who wrote stories about the bohemian art scene in Paris, and Pan Yuliang worked in sculpture and printmaking. My work is a reminder of the importance of intercultural transmedial encounters, by showing how transposition in its various forms is and has always been an integral part of the creative process, and encourages further studies that take into account other forms of artistic expression such as fashion, film, and music, which remain underresearched in the fields of Chinese and French cultural studies.

Notes

Chapter 1

1. The Four Wangs tradition refers to the School of Four Wangs consisting of Qing-dynasty literati painters Wang Shimin, Wang Jian, Wang Hui, and Wang Yuanqi. All four were influenced by the Ming painter Dong Qichang and heavily criticized for merely imitating the works of traditional painters without exhibiting any creativity of their own. They are usually discussed in contrast to the "monk painters" of the same period such as Shi Tao 石濤 who famously rebelled against imitation.

2. Institut franco-chinois, BML, Lu Spa box, pieces #20–21, letter dated Dec. 9, 1930. Original in French, "Avons-nous besoin de vous dire que Paris, capitale de la France, où de célèbres musées attirent les regard des visiteurs de tous les pays, où, les maîtres du monde entier se donnent rendez-vous, où des salons, des expositions et toutes manifestations artistiques ont lieu presque tous les jours, que Paris est vraiment une terre de choix pour ceux qui étudient les beaux-arts? De plus, en France, n'y a t-il un professeur de l'école des Beaux-arts qui n'ait fait ses études à Paris? Nous sommes venus en France specialement pour étudier l'art européen, n'est il pas une grande lacune pour nous de ne pouvoir faire nos études à Paris—capitale des beaux-arts?"

3. In a related article, I define wenren sensibility as a "fluctuating set of cultural connotations specific to an elite, intellectual social class that extend beyond the conventional designation of politically active scholar-officials trained to pass the imperial examinations through the practice of calligraphy and study of Confucian classics" (Chau 2017, 2–3).

4. The original passage in French reads as follows: "Les moins modifiés, et je crois les plus anodins, sont ceux qui reviennent du Boul'Mich' ou de la place Bellecour. Un léger débraillé très 'franco-chinois', de flottantes lavallières, des pantalons tire-bouchonnants qui s'obstinent à charlestonner les désignent autant que leur douce flemme, leur sens de la combine, leur scepticisme narquois, leur goût des phrases creuses et des discours pompeux et les opinions rosées qu'ils empruntent, sans les avoir beaucoup lus, à des auteurs fameux mais tant soit peu 'passés': Proudhon, Auguste Comte, Émile Zola."

Chapter 2

1. Originally published in English as "A Chinese Artist Who Has Lived in Paris a Long Time—Sanyu," *Arts and Entertainment* 2, nos. 7–8 (November 20, 1948): 9.

2. On the purported distinction between art and literature, art historian Kuiyi Shen writes, "Our understanding of that art, however, and in particular the oil paintings, necessarily differs from our understanding of the literature, because of basic differences in the nature of the two arts. Whereas the survival of a single copy of a literary work may be enough to ensure its place in the body of world literature, destruction of an original oil painting effectively removes it from the history of art. Even if it has been published and its importance in its time is well documented, the impossibility of experiencing the painting at first hand precludes the necessary immediacy of experience that might have been possible were the work extant. When paintings are lost, we find ourselves left with only traces, as though a summary of a great novel had survived as evidence of its importance" ("The Lure of the West: Modern Chinese Oil Painting" in Andrews and Shen, *A Century in Crisis*, 172). The case of Chang Yu demonstrates that despite the survival of the countless "traces" in Chang Yu's case, art historiography can still remove the artist at will.

3. See Liu Haisu 1925. Translated in Desroches and Chioetto 2004, 80. For more on this debate, see Andrews (An Yalan) 2001.

4. In poem 5 of the "Drinking Wine" 飲酒 series Tao Qian writes his immortal lines, "Picking chrysanthemums at my east fence, I see South Mountain / far off: air lovely at dusk, birds in flight / going home. All this means something, / something absolute: whenever I start / to explain it, I forget words altogether." Translated by David Hinton in *Classical Chinese Poetry* (New York: Farrar, Straus and Giroux, 2008), 117.

Chapter 3

1. The essay "Wo zaishuo yi bian: Wang he chu qu? . . . Wang shen chu qu!" 我再说一遍：往何处去? . . . 往深处去! was first published in *Yishu xunkan* 2 (1) (1932) and is reprinted in Fu Lei, *Lectures on Twenty Masterpieces of World Art* (2017): 188–90.

2. See, for example, Claire Roberts who quotes this line in *Friendship in Art*: "Later in life, Fou Lei would admit that his appreciation of Chinese art arose from his study of Western culture" (Roberts 2010, 25), and also Chen Guangchen's essay "Fu Lei and Fou Ts'ong: Cultural Cosmopolitanism and Its Price" (Wang 2017, 654).

3. My English translation; another English translation is available by Claire Roberts in *Friendship in Art*, 40–44. Chinese version published in *Yishi xunkan* 1 (4) (1932). Original French version, Fou-Nou En, "La crise de l'art chinois moderne," *L'Art Vivant: En Chine*, no. 152 (1931): 467–68. Mingyuan Hu has observed that in Fu Lei's Chinese translation of the 1931 essay, which was later published in his journal *L'Art* (*Yishu xunkan*) the following year, the word "crise" in the title has

been translated as "panic" (恐慌 konghuang) in the Chinese context, an apt example of what Hu calls cultural translation (Hu 2017, 45): "when it came to communicating with a specific audience, be it French or Chinese, he concerned himself with employing apt connotations" (Hu 2017, 45–46). In a footnote, Hu adds, "Fou Lei was legitimately liberal in translating his own text" (Hu 2017, 45).

4. In the original French: "Il fault donc attendre les événements qui se précipitèrent vers la fin du XIXe siècle, pour que la civilisation occidentale pénétra chez nous à la manière d'une invasion" (Hu 2017, 50 note 76).

Chapter 4

1. Li Jinfa's prose writings, including his memoirs, are collected in Chen Houcheng 陳厚誠, *The Memoirs of Li Jinfa* (*Li Jinfa huiyi lu* 李金髮回憶錄) (Shanghai: Dongfang chubanshe, 1996). Details about his trip to France were first published as a serial "Fu shen zhongji" in the Malaysian periodical *Banana wind* (*Jiaofeng* 蕉風) (October 1964–April 1966), 144–62.

2. Originally appeared in *Xin qingnian* 8, no. 5 (January 1, 1921); reprinted in Hu Shi 胡适, *Hu Shi shi cun: Zeng bu ben* 胡适詩存：增補本 (Beijing: Renmin wenxue chubanshe: Xinhua shudian, 1989), 230, Kai-yu Hsu's English translation (Hsu 1970, 2).

3. In most print versions of this poem, the parenthetical in the poem's title includes a typo of *Sagesse* spelled as "Sgesse."

4. In the 2001 edition, the editor has provided Chinese translations of the French phrases in footnotes. "Ma chère ennemie" is translated as 親愛的冤家, "Aime un peu" is 給我一點愛, and the footnote for the last line is 給我一點愛，對我來說已是太多了! (Dai 2001, 20). Some online versions of the poem do not include the French original but have already translated the French lines into the Chinese included in this note. Gregory Lee translates the title of "Huile xiner ba" to "Change Your mind!" (Lee 1989, 359).

Chapter 5

1. For more on Xu Xu and dreams, see Ouyang Zhisheng's MA thesis, "Wavering between 'Dreaming' and 'Crying': A New Way of Understanding Xu Xu's Novels" (Zai "meng" yu "ku" jian youyi: Xu Xu jiqi xiaoshuo de linglei jiedu 在"夢"與"哭"間游移—徐訏及其小說的另類解讀) (Changsha: Hunan Normal University, 2010), which analyzes Xu Xu's novels through the themes of dreaming and crying, both of which the author argues demonstrate a kind of "wavering."

Chapter 6

1. One notable exception is Elissa H. Park's 2013 dissertation, in which she discusses Pan Yuliang's work in the context of modern art discourse, calling Pan Yuliang a "conscious agent" who questioned and engaged with labels like "'mod-

ern/contemporary,' 'Chinese,' or 'woman' artist throughout her life in her artistic practice" (Park 2013, 3).

2. The word translates literally to the "banner robe" of ethnic Manchu clothing in the early Qing dynasty.

Conclusion

1. See for instance, "Mainland Chinese Painter Chang Yu, Poor His Whole Life and Loved Painting Nude women, Now His Work Auctioned at 1.28M," *Art Treasures International Art Center* 藝寶國際藝術中心, November 2, 2017, https://ebartshop.com/artnews/48.html

2. See, for example, Julia Andrews's "Art under Mao, 'Cao Guoqiang's Maskimov Collection,' and China's Twentieth Century": "Chinese activists found that European museums admired the novelty of Chinese ink paintings but had far less interest in their efforts in Western formats and mediums. Against this background, the Chinese art shows in Europe organized by Liu Haisu and Xu Beihong in 1934 and 1935 were exhibitions of *guohua*" (Yiu 2009, 57). On the term *guohua* 國畫, used to designate traditional ink paintings, Mayching Kao explains in her foreword that "paintings in the Chinese style and medium have been given the name *guohua* to distinguish them from Western and Western-style painting since the early years of this century. This term carries an additional meaning of 'national painting'; it is probably an abbreviation of 'painting of national essence' (*guocui hua*) under the influence of the Movement to Preserve National Essence (*baocun guocui yundong*) initiated at about the same time" (Kao and Cahill 1988, xxi).

3. English translation available in *World Literature Today* 83, no. 2 (March–April 2009): 54–56.

4. See, for instance, Brooke Allen in her book review for the *New York Times*: "I suspect that its gratification of French notions of superiority has had much to do with its best-seller status in that country" (Allen 2001).

5. As mentioned earlier in Chapter 3, Fu Lei was labeled a rightist and persecuted in the 1958 Anti-Rightist Campaign. Historical knowledge of his suicide at the beginning of the Cultural Revolution in 1966 makes the fictional doctor's remarks in Dai's novel that much more poignant for the narrator (and reader).

Bibliography

Allen, Brooke. 2001. "A Suitcase Education." *New York Times*, September 16. www .nytimes.com/2001/09/16/books/a-suitcase-education.html

Andrews, Julia F. (An Yalan 安雅蘭). 2001. "The debate on nude painting and the construction of modern Chinese art history" (Luotihua lunzheng ji xiandai Zhongguo meishushi de jiangou 裸體畫論爭及現代中國美術史的建構). In *Hapai huihua yanjiu wenji*. Shanghai: Shanghai shuhua, 117–50.

Andrews, Julia Frances, and Kuiyi Shen. 1998. *A Century in Crisis: Modernity in the Art of Twentieth-Century China*. New York: Guggenheim Museum.

Apter, Emily S. 2006. *The Translation Zone: A New Comparative Literature*. Princeton: Princeton University Press.

Barlow, Tani E. 2016. "Commercial Advertising Art in 1840s-1940s 'China.'" In *A Companion to Chinese Art*, edited by Martin J. Powers and Katherine R. Tsiang, 431–53. Chichester, UK: Wiley-Blackwell.

Barlow, Tani E. 2021. *In the Event of Woman*. Durham, NC: Duke University Press.

Barnhart, Richard M. 1983. *Peach Blossom Spring: Gardens and Flowers in Chinese Paintings*. New York: Metropolitan Museum of Art.

Baudelaire, Charles, and David Kelley. 1975. *Salon de 1846*. Oxford: Clarendon.

Bernards, Brian Christopher. 2015. *Writing the South Seas: Imagining the Nanyang in Chinese and Southeast Asian Postcolonial Literature*. Seattle: University of Washington Press.

Bevan, Paul. 2020. *"Intoxicating Shanghai"—an Urban Montage: Art and Literature in Pictorial Magazines during Shanghai's Jazz Age*. Leiden: Brill.

Bian, Zhilin. 1982. "The Development of China's 'New Poetry' and the Influence from the West." *Chinese Literature: Essays, Articles, Reviews (CLEAR)* 4 (1): 152–57. https://doi.org/10.2307/495616

Bien, Gloria. 2013. *Baudelaire in China: A Study in Literary Reception*. Newark: University of Delaware Press.

Burger, Cole. 2022. *Keyboard Skills for the Practical Musician*. New York: Routledge.

Bush, Susan. 1978. *The Chinese Literati on Painting: Su Shih (1037–1101) to Tung Ch'i-Ch'ang (1555–1636)*. Cambridge, MA: Harvard University Press, 1978.

Cahill, James Francis. 1960. *Chinese Painting*. Geneva: Skira.

Casanova, Pascale. 2007. *The World Republic of Letters*. Translated by M. B. DeBevoise. Cambridge, MA: Harvard University Press.

Centre Pompidou. 2003. *Alors, la Chine? Communiqué de presse*. Paris: Centre Pompidou. www.centrepompidou.fr/media/document/31/74/3174185e5d b26142e38d1d165071d2a0/normal.pdf

Chadourne, Marc. 1931. *Chine*. Paris: Librairie Plon.

Chan, Tak-hung Leo. 2004. *Twentieth-Century Chinese Translation Theory: Modes, Issues and Debates*. Amsterdam: J. Benjamins.

Chang, Eileen. 2005. *Written on Water*. Translated by Andrew F. Jones. New York: Columbia University Press.

Chang, Eileen. 2006. *Love in a Fallen City*. Translated by Karen S. Kingsbury. New York: New York Review Books Classics.

"Chang Yu: The Market Miracle That Was Lost from History" (常玉：历史的缺席市场的奇迹). 2017. *Sina* 新浪收藏, October 18, collection.sina.com.cn/cjrw/2017 -10-18/doc-ifymvuyt3884250.shtml

Chau, Angie. 2017. "Defining the Modern *Wenren* and the Role of the White Female Body in Modern Chinese Literature and Art." *Modern Chinese Literature and Culture* 29 (1): 1–54.

Chen Weiqi 陳維琪. 2018. "Pan Yuliang's Self-Portraits" (Pan Yuliang de zihuaxiang 潘玉良的自畫像). *Art Marketplace* (*Yishu shichang* 藝術市場), no. 4, 74–77.

Chen Xi 陳希. 2018. *The Sinicization of Western Symbolism* (*Xifang xiangzheng zhuyi de Zhongguo hua* 西方象征主義的中國化). Guangzhou: Zhongshan daxue chubanshe.

Chen Xuanbo 陳旋波. 2004. *Time and Light: Xu Xu and 20th Century Chinese Literary History* (*Shi yu guang: 20 Shiji Zhongguo wenxueshi geju zhong de Xu Xu* 時與光：20 世紀中國文學史格局中的徐訏). Nanchang: Baihuazhou wenyi chubanshe.

Chen Yanfeng. 1995. *Chang Yu: San Yu*. Taipei: Yishujia chubanshe.

Cheng Wendi 程文迪. 2000. "Li Jinfa, the Eccentric Poet" ('Shi Guai': Li Jinfa. '詩怪'：李金髮). *Shikan Poetry Journal*, March, 76.

Chirila, Ileana D. 2017. "Writing in a Cosmopolitan Age: Considerations of Ethnicity and Transculturalism in Sino-French Literature." *Contemporary French and Francophone Studies* 21 (1): 36–44.

Chou, Jay 周杰倫. 2022. "Greatest Works of Art" 最偉大的作品. *YouTube*, July 5. https://www.youtube.com/watch?v=1emA1EFsPMM

"The Chrysanthemum in Chinese Art." 1889. *Decorator and Furnisher* 15, no. 1 (October): 22.

Cinquini, Philippe. 2018. "Les artistes chinois à l'École des Beaux-Arts de Paris." *Histoire de l'Art* 82 (January).

Clarke, David J. 2000. *Modern Chinese Art*. Oxford: Oxford University Press.

Clunas, Craig. 1989. "Chinese Art and Chinese Artists in France (1924–1925)." *Arts Asiatiques* 44 (1): 100–106. https://doi.org/10.3406/arasi.1989.1262

Clunas, Craig. 2017. *Chinese Painting and Its Audiences*. Princeton: Princeton University Press.

Collier, Peter, and Robert Lethbridge. 1994. *Artistic Relations: Literature and the Visual Arts in Nineteenth-Century France*. New Haven: Yale University Press.

Croizier, Ralph. 1988. *Art and Revolution in Modern China: The Lingnan (Cantonese) School of Painting, 1906–1951*. Berkeley: University of California Press.

Croizier, Ralph. 2003. "Pan Yuliang." In *Biographical Dictionary of Chinese Women: The Twentieth Century 1912–2000*, vol. 2, edited by Lily Xiao Hong Lee and A. D. Stefanowska, 417–19. New York: M. E. Sharpe.

Da, Nan Z. 2018. *Intransitive Encounter: Sino-U.S. Literatures and the Limits of Exchange*. New York: Columbia University Press.

Dai Sijie. 2001. *Balzac and the Little Chinese Seamstress*. Translated by Ina Rilke. New York: Random House.

Dai Wangshu 戴望舒. 2001. *Dai Wangshu's Poems* (*Dai Wangshu shi* 戴望舒詩). Edited by Liang Ren 梁仁. Hangzhou: Zhejiang wenyi chubanshe.

Damrosch, David. 2003. *What Is World Literature?* Princeton: Princeton University Press.

Denton, Kirk A., ed. 1996. *Modern Chinese Literary Thought: Writings on Literature 1893–1945*. Stanford, CA: Stanford University Press.

Desroches, Jean-Paul, and Alessandra Chioetto, eds. 2004. *Sanyu: L'écriture du corps*. Paris: Skira.

Ding Ling. 1989. *I Myself Am a Woman: Selected Writings of Ding Ling*. Edited by Tani E. Barlow and Gary J. Bjorge. Boston: Beacon Press.

Dirlik, Arif. 2013. "Literary Identity/Cultural Identity: Being Chinese in the Contemporary World." MCLC Resource Center, September, u.osu.edu/mclc/book-reviews/literary-identity/

Dong Song 棟松, ed. 2013. *A Chronology of Pan Yuliang's Art* (*Pan Yuliang yishu nianpu* 潘玉良藝術年譜). Hefei: Anhui meishu chubanshe.

Du Dakai 杜大愷. 2012. "Chang Yu's Enlightenment to Modernity" (Chang Yu jiqi dui xiandaixing de qishi 常玉及其对现代性的启示), *Dongfang yishu* 5, no. 1 (March): 136–41.

Egan, Ronald C. 1983. "Poems on Paintings: Su Shih and Huang T'ing-chien." *Harvard Journal of Asiatic Studies* 43, no. 2 (December): 413–51.

English, James F. 2005. *The Economy of Prestige: Prizes, Awards, and the Circulation of Cultural Value*. Cambridge, MA: Harvard University Press.

Eoyang, Eugene Chen. 2005. *Two-Way Mirrors: Cross-Cultural Perspectives in Chinese-Western Comparative Literature*. Lanham, MD: Lexington Books.

Epstein, Jennifer Cody. 2008. *The Painter from Shanghai*. New York: W. W. Norton.

Fan Di'an 範迪安, ed. 2015. *The Collected Works of Pan Yuliang* (*Pan Yuliang quanji* 潘玉良全集). Hefei: Anhui meishu chubanshe.

Finnane, Antonia. 2008. *Changing Clothes in China: Fashion, History, Nation*. New York: Columbia University Press.

Fong, Wen C. 2003. "Why Chinese Painting Is History." *The Art Bulletin* 85, no. 2 (June): 258-280.

Fu Lei 傅雷. 1981. *Essays on Fu Lei's Translations* (*Fu Lei yi wenji* 傅雷譯文集). Hefei: Anhui renmin chubanshe.

Fu Lei 傅雷. 2000. *Fu Lei's Selected Essays* (*Fu Lei sanwen* 傅雷散文). Beijing: Beijing wenhua yishu chubanshe.

Fu Lei 傅雷. 2017. *20 Lectures on World Masterpieces of Art* (*Shijie meishu mingzuo ershi jiang* 世界美術名作二十講). Changsha: Hunan wenyi chubanshe.

Fu Lei 傅雷. 2018. *An Old Dream of My Hometown in June: Fu Lei's Best Poetry and Essays* (*Guxiang de liu yue jiu meng: Fu Lei shige sanwen jingdian* 故鄉的六月舊夢：傅雷詩歌散文經典). Taipei: Jilin chuban jituan gufen youxian gongsi.

Fu Lei 傅雷 and Guo Bing 國兵. 2001. *Fu Lei's Selected Writings* (*Fu Lei wenxuan* 傅雷文選). Haila'er: Neimeng gu wenhua chubanshe.

Gao, Xingjian. 1998. "L'esprit de liberté, ma France." *Le Monde*, August 19, www.le monde.fr/archives/article/1998/08/20/l-esprit-de-liberte-ma-france_36621 28_1819218.html

Gao, Xingjian. 2000. "The Case for Literature." NobelPrize.org, www.nobelprize .org/prizes/literature/2000/gao/25532-gao-xingjian-nobel-lecture-2000-2/

Genette, Gérard. 1997. *Palimpsests: Literature in the Second Degree*. Lincoln: University of Nebraska Press.

Goldblatt, Howard, ed. 1990. *Worlds Apart: Recent Chinese Writing and Its Audiences*. New York: M. E. Sharpe.

Goldhammer, Arthur. 2014. "A Few Thoughts on the Future of French Studies." *French Politics, Culture & Society* 32 (2): 15–20. https://doi.org/10.3167/fpcs.20 14.320203

Gu Yue 顧躍. 2009. *Avant-Garde Decadent: San Yu and the Study of Modern Chinese Art of Alternative Perspectives* (*Xianfeng tuifei: Chang Yu yu Zhongguo meishu xiandai xing yanjiu de linglei shijiao* 先鋒,頹廢:常玉與中國美術現代性研究的另類視角). Shijiazhuang: Hebei jiaoyu chubanshe.

Gunn, Edward M. 1980. *Unwelcome Muse: Chinese Literature in Shanghai and Peking, 1937–1945*. New York: Columbia University Press.

Gunn, Edward M. 1991. *Rewriting Chinese: Style and Innovation in Twentieth-Century Chinese Prose*. Stanford, CA: Stanford University Press.

Guo Jianying 郭建英. 2001. *Modern Shanghai: One Hundred Scenes from the Foreign Concessions in the 1930s* (*Modeng Shanghai: Sanshiniandai yangchang baijing* 摩登上海：三十年代洋場百景). Edited by Chen Zishan 陳子善. Guilin: Guangxi shifan daxue chubanshe.

Han Ming 汗明. 1934. "Haha, Women in Front of the Mirror" (Haha jingzi zhong de nüxing 哈哈鏡子中的女性). *Meishu shenghuo* 美術生活, no. 5 (August).

Hayot, Eric. 2003. *Chinese Dreams: Pound, Brecht, Tel Quel*. Ann Arbor: University of Michigan Press.

Hearn, Maxwell K., and Judith G. Smith, eds. 2001. *Chinese Art, Modern Expressions*. New York: Metropolitan Museum of Art.

Higgie, Jennifer. 2021. *The Mirror and the Palette, Rebellion, Revolution, and Resilience: Five Hundred Years of Women's Self-Portraits*. New York: Pegasus Books.

Hightower, James Robert. 1953. "Chinese Literature in the Context of World Literature." *Comparative Literature* 5 (2): 117–24, https://doi.org.10.2307/176 9184

Hong Qiu 洪球, ed. 1936. *Selected Essays on Modern Poetry* (Xiandai shige lunwen xuan 現代詩歌論文選), Vol. 2. Shanghai: Qizhi shuju.

Hsu, Kai-yu, trans. and ed. 1970. *Twentieth-Century Chinese Poetry: An Anthology*. Ithaca: Cornell University Press.

Hu, Mingyuan. 2017. *Fou Lei: An Insistence on Truth*. Leiden: Brill.

Hu Yixun 胡懿勋. 2013. "Solitary Chang Yu: Unusual Experience of Oil-Painting Masters and Outstanding Market" (Gudu Chang Yu: Youhua dashi de bufan de jingli yu bufan shichang 孤独常玉—油画大师的不凡经历与不凡市场). *Yishu shichang*, no. 25 (September 20): 108–11.

Huang, Nicole. 2005. *Women, War, Domesticity: Shanghai Literature and Popular Culture of the 1940s*. Leiden: Brill.

Hughes, Alex. 2020. *France/China: Intercultural Imaginings*. New York: Routledge.

ICONS: Masterpieces from across Time and Space. 2021. Hong Kong: Sotheby's Hong Kong Auction Catalogue.

Jenkins, Henry. 2008. *Convergence Culture: Where Old and New Media Collide*. New York: New York University Press.

Jin Qijing 金啓靜. 1928. "Reflections on Viewing Pan Yuliang's Painting Exhibit" (Canguan Pan Yuliang nüshi huazhan hou zhi ganxiang 參觀潘玉良女士畫展後之感想). *Shen Bao* (申報) (December 6): 12.

Jin Qijing 金啓靜. 1929. "Women and Art" (Nüxing yu meishu 女性與美術). *Ladies' Journal* (*Funü zazhi* 婦女雜誌) 15, no. 7 (July): 31–33.

Jin Shenghua 金聖華, ed. 1996. *Fu Lei and His World* (*Fu Lei yu ta de shijie* 傅雷與他的世界). Beijing: Shenghuo, dushu, xinzhi sanlian chubanshe.

Jin Ya 金雅, ed. 2009. *Cai Yuanpei Volume: Collected Works on Modern Chinese Aesthetics* (*Cai Yuanpei juan: Zhongguo xiandai meixue mingjia wencong* 蔡元培卷：中國現代美學名家文叢). Hangzhou: Zhejiang daxue chubanshe.

Joffroy, Pierre. 1946. "San-Yu: Peintre chinois de Montparnasse, ne peint ni en français ni en chinois." *Parisien libéré*, December 25.

Kamp, Justin. 2020. "Inside the Surging Market for Chinese-French Modernist Sanyu." *Artsy*, October 15, www.artsy.net/article/artsy-editorial-sanyu-chinese-french-modernist-market-sensation

Kao, Mayching, and James Cahill. 1988. *Twentieth-Century Chinese Painting*. Oxford: Oxford University Press.

Kilpatrick, Emily. 2015. *The Operas of Maurice Ravel*. Cambridge: Cambridge University Press.

Kilpatrick, Emily. 2020. "Ravel's 'Trois Poèmes de Stéphane Mallarmé': A Philosophy of Composition." *Music and Letters* 101, no. 3, 512–43.

Koo, Madame Wellington, and Isabella Taves. 1975. *No Feast Lasts Forever*. New York: New York Times Books.

Kuo, Jason, ed. 2007. *Visual Culture in Shanghai, 1850s-1930s*. Washington DC: New Academia Publishing.

Laing, Ellen Johnston. 2004. *Selling Happiness: Calendar Posters and Visual Culture in Early Twentieth-Century Shanghai*. Honolulu: University of Hawaii Press.

Lau, Joseph S. M., and Howard Goldblatt, eds. 2007. *The Columbia Anthology of Modern Chinese Literature*. 2nd ed. New York: Columbia University Press.

Lee, Gregory B. 1989. *Dai Wangshu: The Life and Poetry of a Chinese Modernist*. Hong Kong: Chinese University Press.

Lee, Gregory B. 1996. *Troubadours, Trumpeters, Troubled Makers: Lyricism, Nationalism, and Hybridity in China and Its Others*. Durham, NC: Duke University Press.

Lee, Leo Ou-fan. 1973. *Romantic Generation of Modern Chinese Writers*. Cambridge, MA: Harvard University Press.

Lee, Leo Ou-fan. 1999. *Shanghai Modern: the Flowering of a New Urban Culture in China, 1930–1945*. Cambridge, MA: Harvard University Press.

Lefebvre, Eric, ed. 2018. *Song of Spring: Pan Yu-lin in Paris* 春之歌：潘玉良在巴黎. Hong Kong: Asia Society Hong Kong Center.

Levine, Marilyn A. 1993. *The Found Generation: Chinese Communists in Europe during the Twenties*. Seattle: University of Washington Press.

Li, Shuangyi. 2022. *Travel, Translation and Transmedia Aesthetics: Franco-Chinese Literature and Visual Arts in a Global Age*. Singapore: Palgrave Macmillan.

Li Jinfa 李金髮. 1926. *Singing for Joy* (*Wei xingfu er ge* 為幸福而歌). Shanghai: Shangwu yin shuguan.

Li Jinfa 李金髮. 1986. *Light Rain: Collected Poems* (*Wei yu: Li Jinfa shiji* 微雨：李金髮詩集). Shanghai: Shanghai shudian.

Lin, Julia C. 1972. *Modern Chinese Poetry: An Introduction*. Seattle: University of Washington Press.

Li Yuyi 李寓一. 1929. Special issue on the "National Art Exhibition of the Ministry of Education" (Jiaoyubu quanguo meishu zhanlanhui teji hao 教育部全國美術展覽會特輯號). *Ladies' Journal* (*Funü zazhi* 婦女雜誌) 15, no. 7 (July): 1–4.

Liang Zongdai, trans. 1930. *Les poèmes de T'ao Ts'ien*. Paris: Éditions Lemarget.

Lin, Yutang. 1939. *My Country and My People*. New York: John Day.

Lin, Yutang. 1962. *The Pleasures of a Nonconformist*. London: Heinemann.

Liu, Chen. 2017. "Leonardo Unveiled by Chinese Writers: The Reception of Renaissance Art in Twentieth-Century China." *Art in Translation* 9 (3): 355–66. https://doi.org/10.1080/17561310.2017.1353267

Liu, Lydia H. 1995. *Translingual Practice: Literature, National Culture, and Translated Modernity—China, 1900–1937*. Stanford, CA: Stanford University Press.

Liu Haisu 劉海粟. 1925. "Human models" (Renti mote'er 人體模特兒). *Shishi xinbao* (October 10). Double Ten Supplement 4: 1.

Liu Xiaoling 劉小玲, ed. 2011. *Selected Works of Pan Yuliang* 潘玉良作品選. Shanxi: Shanxi chuban jituan.

Lloyd, Rosemary. 2002. *Baudelaire's World*. Ithaca: Cornell University Press.

Louie, Kam. 2009. *Theorising Chinese Masculinity: Society and Gender in China*. Cambridge: Cambridge University Press.

Lu, Hanchao. 1999. *Beyond the Neon Lights: Everyday Shanghai in the Early Twentieth Century*. Berkeley: University of California Press.

Ma, Lesley W. 2013. "Blossoming beyond the Pages: Female Painterly Modernities in *Liangyou*." In *Liangyou, Kaleidoscopic Modernity and the Shanghai Global Metropolis, 1926–1945*, edited by Paul Pickowicz, Kuiyi Shen, and Yingjin Zhang, 203–25. Leiden: Brill.

Mair, Victor H. 1994. *The Columbia Anthology of Traditional Chinese Literature*. New York: Columbia University Press.

Malmqvist, N. G. D. 1980. *Modern Chinese Poetry Collections 1900–1949*. Strasbourg: European Science Foundation.

Manfredi, Paul. 2014. *Modern Poetry in China: A Visual-Verbal Dynamic*. New York: Cambria Press.

McDougall, Bonnie S., and Kam Louie. 1999. *The Literature of China in the Twentieth Century*. New York: Columbia University Press.

Mi, Jiayan. 2004. *Self-Fashioning and Reflexive Modernity in Modern Chinese Poetry, 1919–1949*. Lewiston, NY: Mellen Press.

Morrison, Donald, and Antoine Compagnon. 2010. *The Death of French Culture*. Oxford: Polity.

"Ms. Pan Yuliang's Art Exhibit." 1928. *Shanghai Sketch* (*Shanghai manhua* 上海漫畫), no. 33 (December): 6.

Musée Cernuschi. 2011. "Artistes chinois à Paris, 1920–1958: De Lin Fengmian à Zou Wou-ki." Press release. Exhibit, September 9-December 31.

Ng, Sandy. 2015. "Gendered by Design: Qipao and Society, 1911–1949." *Costume* 49 (1): 55–74.

Ng, Sandy. 2019. "The Art of Pan Yuliang: Fashioning the Self in Modern China." *Women's Art Journal* (Spring/Summer): 21–30.

Nochlin, Linda. 1971. *Realism*. Middlesex, England: Penguin Books.

North, Michael. 2013. *Novelty: A History of the New*. Chicago: University of Chicago Press.

Pan Yuliang 潘玉良. 1936. "My Views on an Artistic Life" (Wode yishu shenghuo guan 我的藝術生活觀), *Contemporary Women* (*Dangdai funü* 當代婦女) (October): 177–79.

Pang Xunqin. 1931. *Such is Paris* (Ruci Bali 如此巴黎).

Pang Xunqin 龐薰琹. 1988. *This Is How It All Happened* (*Jiu shi zheyang zou guolai de* 就是這樣走過來的). Beijing: Shenghuo dushu xinzhi sanlian shudian.

Park, Elissa H. 2013. "Negotiating the Discourse of the Modern in Art: Pan Yuliang (1895-1977) and the Transnational Modern." Ph.D. dissertation. Ann Arbor: University of Michigan.

Peng, Xiaoyan. 2015. *Dandyism and Transcultural Modernity: The Dandy, the Flaneur, and the Translator in 1930s Shanghai, Tokyo, and Paris*. New York: Routledge.

Pickowicz, Paul, Kuiyi Shen, and Yingjin Zhang, eds. 2013. *Liangyou: Kaleidoscopic Modernity and the Shanghai Global Metropolis, 1926–1945*. Leiden: Brill.

Qi 啟. 1929. *Ladies' Journal* (*Funü zazhi* 婦女雜誌) 15 (7): 6.

Qian, Suoqiao. 2011. *Liberal Cosmopolitan: Lin Yutang and Middling Chinese Modernity*. Leiden: Brill.

Qian, Zhongshu. 2004. *Fortress Besieged*. Translated by Jeanne Kelly and Nathan K. Mao. New York: New Directions Press.

Qin, Ruili and Zhuo Lin. 2016. "Paris, Tokyo, Shanghai: Interaction and Communication of Chinese Modern Art." *Advances in Social Science, Education and Humanities Research*, Vol. 63, 369-374. Proceedings of the 2016 International Conference on Management, Arts and Humanities Science. Dordrecht: Atlantis Press.

Qiu Miaojin. 2014. *Last Words from Montmartre*. Translated by Ari Larissa Heinrich. New York: New York Review Books.

Ramakrishnan, J. R. 2021. "7 Literary Translators Whose Work You Should Read." *Electric Literature*, July 29, electricliterature.com/7-emerging-literary-translators-whose-work-you-should-read/

Rekdal, Paisley. 2000. "The Way We Live Now: 12-10-00: Questions for Gao Xingjian; Found in Translation." *New York Times*, December 10, www.nytimes.com/2000/12/10/magazine/the-way-we-live-now-12-10-00-questions-for-gao-xingjian-found-in-translation.html

Rivais, Rafaële, et al. 2007. "Pour une 'littérature-monde' en français." *Le Monde*, March 15,, www.lemonde.fr/livres/article/2007/03/15/des-ecrivains-plaident-pour-un-roman-en-francais-ouvert-sur-le-monde_883572_3260.html

Roberts, Claire. 2010. *Friendship in Art: Fou Lei and Huang Binhong*. Hong Kong: Hong Kong University Press.

Rosenmeier, Christopher. 2017. *On the Margins of Modernism: Xu Xu, Wumingshi and Popular Chinese Literature in the 1940s*. Edinburgh: Edinburgh University Press.

Saillens, Émile. 1925. *Toute la France: Sa terre, son peuple, ses travaux, les oeuvres de son génie*. Paris: Bibliothèque Larousse.

Sanyu (Chang Yu). 1945. "Opinions d'un peintre chinois sur Picasso." *Parisien libéré*, January 19.

Saussy, Haun. 2011. "China, World Literature, and the Shape of the Humanities." *Printculture*, MLA talk, January 10, www.printculture.com/index.php?itemid=2793

Schaefer, William. 2017. *Shadow Modernism: Photography, Writing, and Space in Shanghai, 1925–1937*. Durham, NC: Duke University Press.

Schwab, Michael, ed. 2018. *Transpositions*. Leuven: Leuven University Press.

Shao Xunmei 邵洵美. 2006. *Collected Works of Shao Xunmei* (*Xunmei wencun 邵洵美文存*). Edited by Chen Zishan 陳子善. Shenyang: Liaoning jiaoyu chubanshe.

Shen, Shuang. 2009. *Cosmopolitan Publics: Anglophone Print Culture in Semi-Colonial Shanghai*. New Brunswick, NJ: Rutgers University Press.

Shi Dawei 施大畏, ed. 2014. *Shanghai/Paris: Modern Art of China* (*Shanghai yu Bali zhijian—Zhongguo xian dangdai yishu jingpinji 上海與巴黎之間—中國現當代藝術精品集*). Shanghai: Shanghai renmin meishu chubanshe.

Shi Nan 石楠. 1983. *Soul of a Painter: Biography of Zhang Yuliang* (*Hua hun: Zhang Yuliang zhuan 畫魂：張玉良傳*). Beijing: Beijing renmin wenxue chubanshe.

Shi Nan 石楠. 2014. "Pan Yuliang, blending China and the West into one" (Pan Yuliang, rong zhongxi yu yiye 潘玉良，融中西與一冶). *Meishu jiaoyu yanjiu* (2): 1.

Shih, Shu-mei. 2001. *The Lure of the Modern: Writing Modernism in Semicolonial China, 1917–1937*. Berkeley: University of California Press.

Shih, Shu-mei, Chien-hsin Tsai, and Brian Bernards, eds. 2013. *Sinophone Studies: A Critical Reader*. New York: Columbia University Press.

Silvester, Rosalind, and Guillaume Thouroude, eds. 2012. *Traits chinois/lignes francophones*. Montreal: Presses de l'Université de Montréal.

Sotheby's Hong Kong. 2021. "ICONS: Masterpieces from across Time and Space." Auction exhibition catalogue. April 18. Hong Kong: Sotheby's.

Sotheby's Taiwan. 1995. *The Johan Franco Collection of Works by Sanyu*. Taipei: Sotheby's.

Stephens, Sonya, ed. 2017. *Translation and the Arts in Modern France*. Bloomington: Indiana University Press.

Su Xuelin 蘇雪林. 1938. "After Viewing Pan Yuliang's Exhibit" 看了潘玉良女士繪畫展覽會以後. *Qingdao ji* 青島集 (July): 203–13.

Sullivan, Michael. 1996. *Art and Artists of Twentieth Century China*. Berkeley: University of California Press.

Sze, Mai-mai, and Gai Wang. 1956. *The Tao of Painting; A Study of the Ritual Disposition of Chinese Painting with a Translation. The Chieh Tzu Yuan Chuan; or, Mustard Seed Garden Manual of Painting, 1679–1701*. Princeton: Princeton University Press.

Tao Yongbai 陶詠白 and Li Shi 李湜, eds. 1999. *Forgotten Histories: The History of Chinese Women's Painting* (*Shiluo de lishi—Zhongguo nüxing huihua shi* 失落的歷史—中國女性繪畫史). Changsha: Hunan meishu chubanshe.

Tawada Yōko. 2013. *Portrait of a Tongue*. Translated by Chantal Wright. Ottawa: University of Ottawa Press.

Tawada Yōko. 2020. "Lightning in a Bottle: A Case Study of Publishing Literary Translation." *YouTube*, August 4, www.youtube.com/watch?v=BlQYxc9NJok

Tcheng, Ki-Tong. 1884. *Les chinois peints par eux-memes*. Paris: Calmann Levy.

Teng, Emma Jin-hua. 2006. "The West as Kingdom of Women: Woman and Occidentalism in Wang Tao's Tales of Travel." In *Traditions of East Asian Travel*, by Joshua A. Fogel, 97–124. New York: Berghahn Books.

Teo, Phyllis. 2010a. "Maternal Ambivalence in Pan Yuliang's Paintings," *Yishu: Journal of Contemporary Chinese Art* 9, no. 3 (May/June): 34–47.

Teo, Phyllis. 2010b. "Modernism and Orientalism: The Ambiguous Nudes of Chinese Artist Pan Yuliang." *New Zealand Journal of Asian Studies* 12 (December 2): 65–80.

Teo, Phyllis. 2016. *Rewriting Modernism: Three Women Artists in Twentieth-Century China, Pan Yuliang, Nie Ou and Yin Xiuzhen*. Leiden: Leiden University Press.

Thien, Madeleine. 2018. "From Republican-Era Shanghai to Postwar Paris: Pan Yuliang's Bold Portraits." *Frieze*, no. 194 (March 12).

Thornber, Karen L. 2009. "French Discourse in Chinese, in Chinese Discourse in French—Paradoxes of Chinese Francophone Émigré Writing." *Contemporary French and Francophone Studies* 13(2): 223–32.

A Treatise on the Transposition of Music, with a New-Invented Circular Sliding Scale. 1790.

Tsu, Jing, and Dewei Wang. 2010. *Global Chinese Literature: Critical Essays*. Leiden: Brill.

Valéry, Paul. 1933. "Avant-propos." *Exposition de la peinture chinoise*. Exposition d'art chinois contemporain: Paris, Musée du Jeu de Paume, mai-juin 1933. Musée du Jeu de paume, Paris. Reprinted in "Quelques mots au sujet de l'exposition des peintres chinois." 2011. Dossier de presse. *Artistes chinois à Paris, 1920–1958: de Lin Fengmian à Zao Wou-ki.* Musée Cernuschi, 7.

Vartanian, Hrag. 2008. "From Prostitute to Post-Impressionist: China's Modern Art Ambassador." April 30. https://hragvartanian.com/2008/04/30/yuliang -modern-art-china/

Venuti, Lawrence, ed. 2004. *The Translation Studies Reader*. New York: Routledge.

Verlaine, Paul. 1973. *Sagesse*. Edited by Charles Chadwick. London: Athlone Press.

Villa, Angelica. 2021. "Christie's to Auction $11 M. Sanyu Still Life in Hong Kong." *ARTnews.com*, March 11, www.artnews.com/art-news/market/sanyu-still-life -christies-sale-1234586345/

Volland, Nicolai. 2014. "The Birth of a Profession: Translators and Translation in Modern China." In *Modern China and the West: Translation and Cultural Mediation*, edited by Xiaoyan Peng and Isabelle Rabut), 126–50. Leiden: Brill.

Volland, Nicolai. 2019. "In Search of the City of Light: Chinese Creative Communities and the Myth of Interwar Paris." *Modern Chinese Literature and Culture* 31 (1): 192–228, https://doi.org/10.2307/26895764

Walt, Melissa. 2018. "Rendezvous: Chinese Artists In Paris." Sothebys.com, September 7, www.sothebys.com/en/articles/rendezvous-chinese-artists-in-paris

Wang, David Der-Wei. 1992. *Fictional Realism in 20th Century China: Mao Dun, Lao She, Shen Congwen*. New York: Columbia University Press.

Wang, David Der-Wei. 2015. *The Lyrical in Epic Time: Modern Chinese Intellectuals and Artists through the 1949 Crisis*. New York: Columbia University Press.

Wang, David Der-Wei. 2017. *A New Literary History of Modern China*. Cambridge, MA: Belknap Press of Harvard University Press.

Wang Xutong 王旭統, ed. 1988. *China-Paris: Seven Chinese Painters Who Studied in France, 1918–1960* (中國—巴黎：早期旅法畫家回顧展). Taipei: Taipei Fine Arts Museum.

Wang Yixin 王一心. 1995. "Ba Ren and Xu Xu's Battle of Words" (Xu Xu yu Ba Ren de bimo guansi 徐訏與巴人的筆墨官司). *Shijie huawen wenxue luntan*, no. 1, 65–67.

Wangwright, Amanda. 2021. *The Golden Key: Modern Women Artists and Gender Negotiations in Republican China (1911–1949)*. Leiden: Brill.

Warnod, André. 1925. *Les berceaux de la jeune peinture: Montmartre, Montparnasse*. Paris: Albin Michel.

Wollaeger, Mark A., and Matt Eatough, eds. 2013. *The Oxford Handbook of Global Modernisms*. Oxford: Oxford University Press.

Wong, Rita. 2011. *Sanyu: Catalogue Raisonné: Oil Paintings*. Taipei: Li Ching Cultural and Educational Foundation.

Wong, Rita. 2014. *Sanyu: Catalogue Raisonné: Drawings and Watercolors*. Taipei: Li Ching Cultural and Educational Foundation.

Wong, Rita. 2017a. *Pan Yu Lin, Catalogue Raisonné: Prints*. Taipei: Li Ching Cultural and Educational Foundation.

Wong, Rita. 2017b. *Sanyu: Catalogue Raisonné: Prints*. Taipei: Li Ching Cultural and Educational Foundation.

Wu, Lawrence. 1990. "Kang Youwei and the Westernisation of Modern Chinese Art." *Orientations* 21, no. 3 (March): 46–53.

Wu, Shengqing. 2020. *Photo Poetics: Chinese Lyricism and Modern Media Culture*. New York: Columbia University Press.

Wu Yiqin 吳義勤. 2008. "Xu Xu's Legacy—in Honor of Xu Xu's 100th Birthday" (Xu Xu de yichan—wei Xu Xu danchen 100 zhounian er zuo 徐訏的遺產—為徐許誕辰100周年而作). *Wenxue pinglun* 6: 125–31.

Xavier, Subha. 2016. *The Migrant Text: Making and Marketing a Global French Literature*. Montreal: McGill-Queen's University Press.

Xie Lifa 謝里法. 1984. "Painting Soul from a Brothel: Pan Yuliang's Artistic Career" (Qinglou hua hun: Pan Yuliang de yishu shenya 青樓畫魂：潘玉良的藝術生涯). *Lion Art Journal* (*Xiongshi meishu* 雄獅美術), no. 157, 30–37.

Xingjian, Gao. 2000. "The Nobel Prize in Literature 2000 Gao Xingjian—Nobel Lecture." NobelPrize.org, www.nobelprize.org/prizes/literature/2000/gao/25532-gao-xingjian-nobel-lecture-2000-2/

Xu Xu 徐訏. 1940. *Sentiments from Abroad* (*Haiwai de linzhao* 海外的鱗爪). Shanghai: Yechuang shudian.

Xu Xu 徐訏. 1948. *Fragments from Abroad* (*Haiwai de qingdiao* 海外的情調). Shanghai: Yechuang shuwu.

Xu Xu. 2020. *Bird Talk and Other Stories: Modern Tales of a Chinese Romantic*. Translated and with commentary by Frederik H. Green. Albany, CA: Stone Bridge Press.

Xu Zhimo 徐志摩. 1927. *Fragments of Paris* (*Bali de linzhao* 巴黎的鱗爪). Shanghai: Xinyue shudian.

Xu Zhimo 徐志摩. 1983. *The Collected Works of Xu Zhimo* (*Xu Zhimo quanji* 徐志摩全集). Vol. 5. Taipei: Yangming shuju.

Xu Zhimo 徐志摩. 2007. *Xu Zhimo's Selected Classic Works* (*Xu Zhimo jingdian zuopin xuan* 徐志摩經典作品選). Beijing: Dangdai shijie chubanshe.

Yang Yunda 楊允達. 1986. *The Critical Biography of Li Jinfa* (*Li Jinfa pingzhuan* 李金髮評傳). Taipei: Youshi wenhua shiye gongsi.

Yao Daimei 姚玳玫. 2010. "Self-Defense: Pan Yuliang's Artwork" (守護自我：潘玉良與她的畫作), *Wenyi yanjiu* 文藝研究, no. 12, 129–37.

Yao Daimei 姚玳玫. 2011. "Draw Whom? Draw What? —Viewing the establishment of women's western-style painting in the Republican period from self-portraiture" 畫誰？畫什麼？—從自畫像看民國時期女性西畫的圖式確立) *Shi xue, meishu xue* 史學，美術學 (2011): 101–7.

Yao Yuxiang 姚漁湘, ed. 1932. *Anthology of Essays on Chinese Painting* (*Zhongguohua taolun ji* 中國畫討論集). Beiping: Lida shuju.

Yeh, Catherine Vance. 1997. "The Life-Style of Four Wenren in Late Qing Shanghai." *Harvard Journal of Asiatic Studies* 57 (2): 419–70. https://doi/10.2307/2719484

Yeh, Michelle, ed. 1992. *Anthology of Modern Chinese Poetry*. New Haven: Yale University Press.

Yiu, Josh. 2009. *Writing Modern Chinese Art: Historiographic Explorations*. Seattle: Seattle Art Museum.

Yu, Mia. 2017. "Pan Yuliang: A Journey of Silence." https://vimeo.com/277920517

Zhang Daofan 張道藩. 1937. "Introducing Pan Yuliang's exhibit"介紹潘玉良畫展. June 11, *Central Daily News* (*Zhongyang ribao*), sheet 2, 3.

Zhang Hongfei 張鴻飛. 1934. "The Convenience of Female Painters" (Nü huajia de bianli 女畫家的便利). *Meishu shenghuo* 美術生活, no. 5 (August).

Zhang, Longxi. 1998. "The Challenge of East-West Comparative Literature." In *China in a Polycentric World*, edited by Yingjin Zhang, 115–22. Stanford, CA: Stanford University Press.

Zhang, Yingjin, ed. 1999. *Cinema and Urban Culture in Shanghai, 1922–1943*. Stanford, CA: Stanford University Press.

Zhang, Yingjin. 2015. "Mapping Chinese Literature as World Literature." *CLCWeb: Comparative Literature and Culture* 17 (1), https://doi.org/10.7771/1481–4374.2714

Zhao Jiabi 趙家璧. 1981. *The Compendium of Modern Chinese Literature* (*Zhongguo xin wenxue daxi* 中國新文學大系). Shanghai: Shanghai wenyi chubanshe.

Zheng, Jane. 2007. "The Shanghai Fine Arts College: Art Education and Modern Women Artists in the 1920s and 1930s." *Modern Chinese Literature and Culture* 19, no. 1 (Spring): 192–235.

Zhou Liangpei 周良沛, ed. 1987. *Collected Poems of Li Jinfa* (*Li Jinfa shiji* 李金髮詩集). Chengdu: Sichuan wenyi chubanshe.

Index

1940, 156–59, *157*; *Self-Portrait*, 1945, 156, *158*, 159; *Self-Portrait in a Green Dress*, 154–56, *155*; *Self-Portrait with Fan*, 153, *154*, 156; *Solitary Beauty*, 147, *148*; *Solitude*, 144, *145*, 146–47. *See also* art education, Western, Pan Yuliang and

Pan Yuliang, critical reception of, 23, 138–39, 146–47, 148–51, 152–53, 161–63; early life and, 134, 135–36, 162, 174

Pan Yuliang, exhibitions by, 150, 168; in China, 138, 140, 144; in France, 141–42, 147, *148*, 153; strategy of, 151, 153, 160–61

Pan Yuliang and the nude, 134, 138, 141–42, 146–49, 160, 161; as progressive, 28, 147, 148; *Solitary Beauty*, 147, *148*; *Solitude*, 144, *145*, 146–47

Pan Yuliang and self-portraiture, 135, 142, 150–59, 162–63; as transposition, 28, 136–38, 151, 160–61, 174; *Self-Portrait*, 1940, 156–59, *157*; *Self-Portrait*, 1945, 156, *158*, 159; *Self-Portrait in a Green Dress*, 154–56, *155*; *Self-Portrait with Fan*, 153, *154*, 156

Pan Zanhua, 28, 132, 134, 136, 162

Paris, 6, 164–65, 169, 178; artistic freedom and, 8–9, 30, 46, 60, 170, 175–76; bohemianism and, 120, 126, 128, 165–66, 179; Chen Jitong in, 4–5; and Chinese identity, 4, 27, 30, 70, 125, 131; and Chinese modernism, 3–4, 12, 70, 71; Chinese political figures and, 4–5, 7, 14; classical Chinese literature and art in, 10, 12, 79, 114, 170, 184n2; climate/weather of, 94, 122, 123, 128; communicating experience of, 13, 22–23, 88–97, 116, 172; cultural capital conferred by, 14, 28; Dai Wangshu in, 105; dark side of, 128–30, 167, 169; disillusionment with, 15, 81, 128–30, 131, 166, 167, 169; École des Beaux-arts, 8, 12, 27, 34, 134; expectations of Chinese writers and artists in, 4, 6, 25, 33, 60, 166, 169; Fu Lei in, 26, 66, 70, 73–74, 79, 80–82, 172; as goal of foreign artists and writers, 8, 35, 78, 167, 169, 175–76; influence of Chinese visitors, 11, 120, 130, 168; influence on Chinese visitors, 11, 15, 70, 84, 166; Madame Wellington Koo in, 159; Latin Quarter of, 15, 78, 118; Li Jinfa and, 26, 83, 84, 88–97, 109, 179; Lin Fengmian in, 9; Liu

Haisu in, 51, 71, 78; Louvre museum in, 25, 63, 70, 78, 91, 100; and national history, 28, 30; Pang Xunqin in, 54, 72, 73, 74, 77–78; perception of Chinese in, 34–35, 37, 60, 125, 127, 170, 172; Wang Tao in, 4; Western artists and, 8, 51, 71; as Western cultural capital, 8, 35, 81, 96–97, 166; Xu Beihong in, 11, 34, 170; Xu Xu in, 26, 111, 112, 128–29, 174; in Xu Xu's writing, 27, 127, 128–31, 179 (*see also* "The Duel" (Xu); "Montparnasse Studio" (Xu)); Xu Zhimo in, 13, 15, 165, 166. *See also* Montparnasse

Paris, Chang Yu in, 25, 46–47, 50, 51, 55, 170; and connections with other Chinese, 54, 170; and lack of success, 29, 33–34, 35, 36, 60

Paris, Chinese descriptions of, 4, 81–82, 128–30, 165; French women and, 73–74, 88–89, 90–91, 96, 165; "Dejected at the Luxembourg Garden" (Fu), 81–82; "Luxembourg Garden" (Li), 88–91, 96, 97; "Paris Chitchat" (Xu), 128–30; "Paris Somniloquy" (Li), 91–97

Paris, cosmopolitanism and, 27, 35, 81, 138, 172; in Xu Xu's writing, 116, 120, 125–26, 127, 138

Paris, mythic nature of, 60, 70, 88, 164–65, 167, 175; contradiction of, 25, 129, 167; fostering artistic communion, 84, 88; national history and, 28, 30; as Western cultural capital, 8, 35, 81, 96–97, 166

Paris, Pan Yuliang in, 27–28, 29, 136, 138, 162; education in, 27, 134, 135, 140; exhibitions in, 141–42, 147, *148*, 153; identity and, 151–52, 160; return to, 27, 140, 160, 169

"Peach Blossom Spring" (Tao, Chang), 39, 43, *44*

philosophy, 65, 175; aesthetic, 22, 46, 47, 54, 63; Chang Yu and, 35, 45, 46, 61; in China, 9, 54, 55, 83; Fu Lei's, 71; Li Jinfa's, 83, 172; Maurice Ravel's, 23–24; poetic, 85, 149, 172; Xu Xu and, 26, 111, 112, 127

photography, 16, 48, 51, 121; portraits and, 132, *133*, 134, 144, 146, 153; self-portraiture and, 136, 149, 151, 156, 161

Picasso, Pablo, 8, 35, 53, 60, 171; Chang Yu on, 54–56